MW00572923

LIFE-GIVING WOUNDS

DR. DANIEL MEOLA and BETHANY MEOLA

Life-Giving Wounds

A Catholic Guide to Healing for Adult Children of Divorce or Separation

IGNATIUS PRESS SAN FRANCISCO

Cover art:
Sandro Botticelli, *Cristo Risorto* (c. 1480)
Detroit Institute of Arts

Cover design by Enrique J. Aguilar

ISBN 978-1-62164-540-5 (PB)
ISBN 978-1-64229-248-0 (eBook)
Library of Congress Catalogue Number 2023935059
Printed in the United States of America ♾

To all of the amazing adult children of divorce or separation whose lives we have been blessed to be a part of in various ways; you are extraordinary miracles of God's redeeming grace.

To one heroic "stander" whose witness to the fidelity of marriage and the joy of faith, despite great personal suffering, has greatly moved and inspired us.

And to our beautiful daughters, Zelie-Louise and Grace. You are the most precious gifts we could ever receive and our enduring motivation for all we do.

CONTENTS

FOREWORD

by Edward and Beth Sri

Wait, that's a thing? I (Beth) thought to myself in 2017 upon seeing a retreat flyer online. *There's a retreat now just for adult children of divorce?!*

Those of us with divorced or separated parents were often told "you're fine" and "you can be happy now because your parents are happy." We were expected to be resilient and strong, supportive and accepting of the new arrangement. And should we have felt anything to the contrary—fear, sorrow, anger, anxiety—we needed to "stuff" that down, keeping it hidden from those closest to us: our parents, who were now tasked with rebuilding their separate lives. Our family had split apart, and we had to just keep on keeping on. Truly, the anguish of the children of divorce was often a "suffering that was not allowed to be called suffering."[1]

I had recently committed to taking a deep dive into my own story as a child of divorce by reading all I could on the topic, seeking therapy and bringing it all to Jesus in prayer, the sacraments, and spiritual direction. It was heavy, arduous, soul-searching work, and while I read that there were millions out there who had similar childhood stories and experiences, there were few in my world who were willing even to discuss it.

[1] Leila Miller, ed., *Primal Loss: The Now-Adult Children of Divorce Speak* (Phoenix, Ariz.: LCB Publishing, 2017), back cover.

So, learning that there existed a Catholic retreat for adults who grew up in broken families was welcome news. I attended my first retreat run by Life-Giving Wounds in 2018 in Virginia, and my randomly (or providentially) assigned small-group leader was none other than founder Daniel Meola. All eight of us in the group struggled to find words for our pain, often attempting to share through sniffles and tears. But as that weekend went on, we also discovered the flipside: connecting with one another led to laughter and even joy. We were not alone in discovering the humor in our shared plight. Dan artfully led us to that place, holding space for the myriad emotions that arose in each of us, pressing in when he sensed there was more to our stories, and rejoicing at the unexpected goodness we found.

In this book you'll get to know Dan and his beautiful bride, Bethany—their own stories, trials, and triumphs as they've walked the road of life-giving wounds individually, together in their marriage, and alongside the hundreds they have helped in the ministry they founded.

In my (Edward's) experience teaching students in the college classroom and working with young adult missionaries in the Fellowship of Catholic University Students (FOCUS), I've seen the impact divorce has on young people. I had known from my studies that the deeper wounds of growing up in a broken home often rise to the surface for the first time when students emerge into adulthood, and especially when they enter into serious relationships of their own. I saw this firsthand. In their essays and in conversations, some college students made connections between their parents' divorce and their own fears and anxieties in life, their insecurities they experienced in their dating relationships, and their general doubts about whether they would ever find a lasting love. Some young professionals with divorced parents became aware of how averse they were to conflict, how afraid of commitment, and how eager to please others. Missionaries have shared how their parents' divorces even affected their view of God: *Is he trustworthy?*

Growing up without the committed love of their parents, many children of divorce had thought they just needed to be resilient, having never been given the chance to grieve and to seek the deeper healing God wanted for them. Thankfully, many are now finding support through counseling, spiritual direction, and the community of countless others who have experienced the wound of being a child of divorce—a community that Dan and Bethany Meola have fostered through the Life-Giving Wounds ministry and, no doubt, will continue to cultivate through their book of the same name. We pray that this book and this ministry will touch many more souls to help them know they are not alone and offer them a way forward through the healing power of Christ.

PREFACE

Disclaimer

We include throughout this book personal stories and quotes from adult children of divorce or separation. Where particular persons are mentioned by name, either their own or a pseudonym that they chose, they gave permission to use their words and stories as included here. We share other more general stories or representative examples of the experiences of adult children of divorce without identifying details to protect their anonymity. We are also grateful to the anonymous contributors to Leila Miller's edited collection of testimonies, *Primal Loss: The Now-Adult Children of Divorce Speak*,[1] several of whom we quote here.

Inclusion of quotes from, or references to, books and media sources throughout this book do not constitute approval of, or agreement with, the entirety of that particular source or everything produced by the parent company of the source.

Acknowledgments

This book has been a labor of love for several years, written in between the daily demands of running a young and

[1] Leila Miller, ed., *Primal Loss: The Now-Adult Children of Divorce Speak* (Phoenix, Ariz.: LCB Publishing, 2017).

growing national nonprofit apostolate and raising two young children: in early morning hours at Panera (Bethany) and late at night after the kids were asleep (Dan). There's no way these words would have seen the light of day without the help of many, some of whom we would like to thank here.

Several trusted advisors generously reviewed early drafts of this book, in whole (Dr. Andrew Lichtenwalner, Dr. Jill Verschaetse, Art Bennett, Father Dan Leary, Beth Sri, and Jessica Root) or in part (Father John Baptist Hoang, O.P., Father Christopher Singer, and Mary Rose Verret). We're also grateful to Michael Hernon, Dr. Mario Sacasa, Father Paul Sullins, Ph.D., and Dr. Andrew Sodergren for allowing us to include their insights and research on several topics and reviewing those sections for accuracy.

We are grateful to all of the Life-Giving Wounds volunteers around the country (over 150 at last count) who generously dedicate their time and efforts to helping the ministry grow and improve: especially our dedicated and hard-working board of directors (currently Art Bennett, Michael Hernon, Father John Baptist Hoang, O.P., Father Dan Leary, Dr. Andrew Lichtenwalner, Michael Manocchio, Jessica Root, Beth Sri, and Mary Rose Verret), our traveling retreat team (currently Father John Baptist Hoang, O.P., Matt Bigelow, Emily Carey, Michael Corsini, Jen Cox, Mary DePuglio, Hannah Dragonas, Sarah Hart, Father Jim McCormack, M.I.C., Lacy Prebula, Craig Soto, Teresa Swick, Dr. Jill Verschaetse, and Alex Wolfe), our national chaplain (Father Mario Majano), our blog editor (Sam Russell), our media and communications specialist (Katey Mooney), and all those who have served as speakers and small group leaders at Life-Giving Wounds retreats or support groups. A special thanks to Jen Cox and Alex Wolfe, who have dedicated hours upon hours to crafting and sharing the vision of Life-Giving Wounds and developing various new projects.

Thanks also to all who have spiritually guided us throughout the years, who have no doubt contributed to this book through forming us spiritually and intellectually, and through friendship—this includes the many holy priests and lay people from Erie, Pennsylvania, who shaped Dan's faith, especially Father Larry Richards, Father Steve Schreiber, Father Christopher Singer, Father Rich Toohey, and Greg and Stephanie Schlueter; all of the professors of the Pontifical John Paul II Institute for Studies on Marriage and Family, especially David S. Crawford, Nicholas Healy, Margaret Harper McCarthy, and David L. Schindler; holy priest friends in the Archdiocese of Washington, especially Father Scott Holmer, Father Dan Leary, Father Mario Majano, Father Jim McCormack, M.I.C., Father Ben Petty, and Monsignor K. Bartholomew Smith; and several other dear friends, especially Michael and Jessica Corsini, Sister Donata, O.L.M., Sister Gaudia, O.L.M., Sister Inga, O.L.M., Father Ambrose Little, O.P., George and Elizabeth Logusch, Father John Paul Mary Zeller, M.F.V.A., Steve and Caitlin Mariconti, Shaina Pia, Justin and Bernadette McClain, Mark and Becky Scheckelhoff, and many more we could not name individually here.

Bethany's parents and Dan's mom spent hours watching our children while we wrote, even over a writing getaway weekend that made a huge difference in the book's progress. We know that grandparent time was rewarding for everyone but also a great expenditure of energy for the grandparents, and we are grateful!

Thank you to our children, six-year-old Zelie-Louise and four-year-old Grace, for being yourselves, always bringing smiles to our faces, lifting our spirits, praying with us, and inspiring us to try to be the parents you deserve. We love you more.

Lastly, we are deeply grateful to the hundreds of adult children of divorce or separation we have had the privilege of meeting and accompanying through our Life-Giving Wounds ministry. That is the greatest joy of this work. To all of these men and women: your courage to face your wounds boldly with Christ and seek healing for them inspires us daily. We cherish your stories and honor your bravery. This book is something of a "love letter" to all adult children of divorce or separation who are seeking to overcome generational brokenness. The Lord sees you, meets you in your wounds, and loves you with an everlasting love. We hope this book continues to aid you in deepening that divine relationship.

INTRODUCTION

Five different houses
Four different spouses
Three different schools . . .
Imagine what it's like growing up loving life when you are six
But hating it when you are eight
Because of my parents.
My parents.
Parents . . .
To whom I should belong for that week
Monday Tuesday Dad
Wednesday Thursday Mom
Fridays Weekends we switch
Like the holidays we switch
As if our lives were a fair-trade in Monopoly
They've put me in jail, I want to be free
Only way to get out is if I pay the fee . . .

—Sofia Fernandez*

This poem, written by an adult child of divorce, begins to capture the rupture divorce or separation causes in the hearts of children. Through accompanying hundreds of adult children of divorce or separation in the Catholic apostolate we founded, Life-Giving Wounds, we have heard gut-wrenching stories of suffering, abandonment, and loss. We have also been inspired by the courage and

* Sofia Fernandez, "Family Tree," *Life-Giving Wounds* (blog), May 14, 2023, https://www.lifegivingwounds.org/blog/poem-family-tree.

insight of the men and women who recognize their brokenness and their need for recovery—people who commit to breaking the cycle of divorce and family dysfunction in their own lives with the help of Christ.

This book contains the collective wisdom that adult children of divorce or separation ("ACOD" for short) have imparted to us. So while we are the authors, this is a shared journey under the loving gaze of Christ, undertaken in community with these friends and fellow disciples, some of whom you will "meet" in these pages.

There is an urgent need today for healing family wounds because we are living in an unprecedented time of familial brokenness. Every single year, over a million children in the United States experience the divorce of their parents,[1] and one-quarter of all young adults in the U.S. are children of divorce.[2] Add to that the growing number of people whose parents never married but later separated,[3] and we reach a startling statistic: "less than half [of] the children in the United States today will grow up in a household with

There is an urgent need today for healing family wounds because we are living in an unprecedented time of familial brokenness.

[1] Paul Sullins, "The Tragedy of Divorce for Children," in *Torn Asunder: Children, the Myth of the Good Divorce, and the Recovery of Origins*, ed. Margaret Harper McCarthy (Grand Rapids, Mich.: Eerdmans, 2017), 19.

[2] Elizabeth Marquardt et al., "Does the Shape of Families Shape Faith? Challenging the Churches to Confront the Impact of Family Change," in *Torn Asunder*, 66.

[3] Juliana Menasche Horowitz, Nikki Graf, and Gretchen Livingston, "Marriage and Cohabitation in the U.S.," Pew Research Center, November 6, 2019, https://www.pewresearch.org/social-trends/2019/11/06/the-landscape-of-marriage-and-cohabitation-in-the-u-s/; Gretchen Livingston, "About One-Third of U.S. Children Are Living with an Unmarried Parent," Pew Research Center, April 27, 2018, https://www.pewresearch.org/short-reads/2018/04/27/about-one-third-of-u-s-children-are-living-with-an-unmarried-parent/.

continuously married parents."[4] And that doesn't account for the burgeoning phenomenon of "gray divorce," when parents call it quits after their children are grown.[5]

In view of this bleak landscape, this book seeks to meet a real need: the need for Christ-centered encouragement, advice, healing, evangelization, and accompaniment for the millions of men and women who come from broken homes. We focus on *adult* children of divorce, especially young adults, because research has shown that often it is not until adulthood that people realize how deeply their parents' divorce or separation has affected them with doubts, questions, and challenges.[6]

Even though millions of American adults are ACODs, their particular needs and concerns have been generally overlooked or even denied, with a few notable exceptions.[7] Very few nonprofits, ministries, or outreaches, let alone Catholic apostolates, dare to tend to these wounds. The men and women who experience the pain of their

[4] Melanie Wasserman, "The Disparate Effects of Family Structure," *Future of Children* 30, no. 1 (Spring 2020): 56. See also "Parenting in America," Pew Research Center, December 17, 2015, https://www.pewresearch.org/social-trends/2015/12/17/parenting-in-america. While our focus here is on those now-grown children who lost the unity of their parents through intentional parental separation, we are aware that other children, sadly, lose a parent to death, which of course entails deep sorrow and a pressing need for support.

[5] Renee Stepler, "Led by Baby Boomers, Divorce Rates Climb for America's 50+ Population," Pew Research Center, March 9, 2017, https://www.pewresearch.org/short-reads/2017/03/09/led-by-baby-boomers-divorce-rates-climb-for-americas-50-population. See also Bruce R. Fredenburg and Carol R. Hughes, *Home Will Never Be the Same Again: A Guide for Adult Children of Gray Divorce* (New York: Rowman and Littlefield, 2020).

[6] See Judith Wallerstein, Julia Lewis, and Sandra Blakeslee, *The Unexpected Legacy of Divorce: A 25 Year Landmark Study* (New York: Hyperion Books, 2000); Elizabeth Marquardt, *Between Two Worlds: The Inner Lives of Children of Divorce* (New York: Crown Publishers, 2005).

[7] For our curated, updated list of books, articles, and other resources directly addressing the needs of adult children of divorce, see "Adult Children of Divorce Resources," Life-Giving Wounds, accessed August 18, 2023, https://www.lifegivingwounds.org/adult-children-of-divorce-resources.

parents' split deserve compassionate attention and, better yet, the restorative balm of Christ the Healer. We hope this book awakens the hearts and consciences of Christian leaders and all people of good will to a richer understanding of the long-lasting impact of divorce and parental break-up on children. And we hope it contributes to a greater determination to dedicate new efforts, attention, and resources to the healing of adult children of divorce.

We also pray that this honest and open discussion of the wounds of adult children of divorce helps to transform the hearts of parents who have divorced or are contemplating divorce. We want to inspire them, where possible and safe to do so, to work toward mutual forgiveness and reconciliation.[8] We hope this book can help all divorced or separated parents better understand their children's possible hurts and needs, and can contribute to enriched and more honest conversations, opportunities for forgiveness and reconciliation, and deeper relationships. Our goal is not to point fingers at divorced or separated parents and declaim their faults, but to offer a pathway forward in healing for their children that culminates in a rich, joyful way of life with Christ. We pray that all divorced and separated parents, too, receive the graces and renewal that they need.

Our Backgrounds

Dan's parents separated when he was eleven and divorced when he was twenty-six, the year we got married. Bethany's parents separated twice during her childhood and young adult years, though they fortunately reconciled—a

[8] For an inspiring compilation of testimonies by couples who were at the brink of divorce, or had divorced, and later reconciled, see Leila Miller, ed., *"Impossible" Marriages Redeemed* (Phoenix: LCB Publishing, 2020).

great witness to perseverance in marriage. We have both been impacted by the fluctuations of our families.

We met at the Pontifical John Paul II Institute for Studies on Marriage and Family, in Washington, D.C., where we studied the Church's rich magisterium on love and the human person. We were both captivated by the beauty and power of the Church's teaching on marriage, especially its indissolubility and the security this brings to children raised within that union. By contrast, we also became more aware of what serious damage is inflicted—even on the *ontological* level, the core of a person's being—when the communion of spouses, meant to image God's faithful love to their children, is broken.[9]

After all the blessings we received at the JPII Institute, we felt called by the Holy Spirit to found Life-Giving Wounds, a Catholic apostolate dedicated to giving voice to the pain of adult children of divorce or separation and helping them find lasting healing in Christ. This book is one fruit of that work, drawing from our personal experiences and extensive research into the topic. It also communicates something of even greater value: what we have learned from years of accompanying hundreds of men and women from broken homes in the painful but necessary process of recognizing the depths of their wounds and advancing toward greater hope, peace, and healing.

Whom This Book Is For

This book is first and foremost for adult children of divorce or separation, those millions of men and women who

[9] For a robust but accessible treatment of the ontological impact of divorce on children, see Andrew Root, *The Children of Divorce: The Loss of Family as the Loss of Being* (Grand Rapids, Mich.: Baker Academic, 2010).

experience the pain and difficulties that follow when their parents split. This includes all those, of any age, who have lost—or never had—the love of their parents *together in the same home*, whether through prolonged marital separation, civil divorce (with or without also receiving a declaration of nullity), cohabitation dissolution, a breakup, and so on.[10] While in the book we often use the shorthand term "adult children of divorce" (or ACOD), we always have this broader audience in mind.

This book is also for all those who have a beloved ACOD in their lives—spouses, relatives, friends, children, and parents. Adult children of divorce need people who can "receive" their pain in a gentle and loving way, to help them heal. At the end of every other chapter, Bethany reflects on the way that spouses are impacted by an ACOD's broken family, and how they can facilitate healing.

We hope this book will reach Christian leaders who want to understand and better help men and women from broken homes. This includes priests and deacons, religious brothers and sisters, counselors, professional clinicians, youth ministers, young adult leaders, campus ministers, missionaries, marriage preparation and marriage ministry leaders, and more. Without a doubt, there are adult children of divorce among those whom these Christian leaders serve, and the first step in accompanying them is learning about their pain.

What This Book Is—and Isn't

This is not a typical "self-help" book, if what that means is relying *only* on one's self. Many of our community—

[10] Two related situations we do not address are (1) losing a parent, or both parents, to death and (2) being placed for adoption or into foster care. These challenging scenarios, while connected to the experiences of ACODs, are dissimilar enough to merit special attention.

including the authors—have already tried that and failed. We're made for communion and relationships with others, particularly with God. We cannot simply "do" healing on our own; we must receive it. We need face-to-face community and friendship, witnesses and mentors, and above all, life in Christ through the sacraments. Thus, this book points people to sources of healing *beyond* the confines of these pages.

We do not give a primarily psychological or sociological treatment of the trauma caused by parental divorce. Although we consider psychology very important, and we integrate psychological research into our writing, we approach everything from the perspective of the Catholic faith and from the lived experience of the hundreds of ACODs we have known.

We do not claim to give an exhaustive account of the wounds caused by parental divorce and how to heal from them. Our ministry is constantly growing and adapting to new or newly recognized needs and areas. It must be said, too, that there are many other grave harms that people experience in families beyond divorce or separation: the death of a parent or a sibling, psychological or physical abuse, addictions, mental illness, incarcerated parents, illness or injury, displacement, and homelessness. We touch on some of these topics throughout the book, but not extensively, since they are not in our area of expertise. Every one of us must bear some pain and suffering in this life, and we are all in need of Christ's healing, mercy, and love.

This book honors the pain of men and women from broken homes and offers a path of spiritual healing for them. In these pages, we focus on Christian redemptive suffering in the particular circumstances of parental divorce or separation. There are two different kinds of chapters: one kind illuminates a layer of the experience of ACODs ("The wound of ... "), while another discloses a new contour of the redemptive joy that can flow from these difficulties. For those who wish to go deeper either individually or with a group, the Life-Giving Wounds website offers suggested prayer practices, journal and discussion questions, and more to assist personal reflection and discussion with each chapter.

Advice to ACOD Readers

For those who have experienced the divorce or separation of their parents, this book may be difficult to read at certain points. The heavy topics and true stories of suffering may trigger strong emotional reactions. Anyone who experiences this should set the chapter down and come back to it at another time—or just skip it completely. The Lord is good and gentle and never wants to re-traumatize us as we seek healing. Go at your own pace in peace, knowing that the Lord can use many different means to give his grace. You need not immediately tackle everything to find profound healing.

We encourage you to go through this book slowly and prayerfully. It is not meant as a checklist. Healing is more than a pursuit of a goal; it's a walk of ever deeper intimacy with our Lord in response to our pain. While we describe *Life-Giving Wounds* as a *guide* for adult children of divorce, we don't intend it as a one-size-fits-all method. You might prefer to address themes in a different order, or perhaps skip over topics that seem less relevant. Discern with the Holy Spirit what is helpful to you and leave the rest aside.

Healing is more than a pursuit of a goal; it's a walk of ever deeper intimacy with our Lord in response to our pain.

As the adage goes, Jesus loves us just the way we are, but he loves us too much to let us stay that way. We hope that all who seek healing from broken homes will discover the abundant life our Lord promises, and know that even pain and wounds can—eventually—give *life*. The bedrock of this new life is God's Divine Mercy, especially through forgiveness, both received and offered. ACODs must resist the impulse—at times overwhelming—to pretend either that nothing is wrong or to dwell in bitterness. Instead, they must strive to let themselves be open to *love*, for God is love. At times, this process can be slow and difficult; all recovery takes work. But just as some-one healing from a back injury needs to stretch his ten-dons and muscles, so adult children of divorce must allow their souls, in all their complexity, to be stretched by Christ's mercy.

Good Friday is followed by Easter Sunday. This book is about going into your own Good Friday and finding your Easter Sunday—your own *life-giving wounds*.

I

The Wound of Silence

Why are you cast down, O my soul, and why are you disquieted within me?

—Psalm 42:5

Have you seen the sci-fi film *A Quiet Place*? The plot is simple: A family lives in a post-apocalyptic world ruled by murderous aliens with an extraordinary sense of hearing. If the humans make too loud a sound, the aliens will instantly learn their location and come to kill them. To survive, the family enters into an oppressive silence, one that engulfs the viewer. Watching it, you may find yourself wanting to shout just to find relief from the terrible quiet.

Has your life ever felt like *A Quiet Place*? Have you sensed that if you spoke up about something, bad things would happen? Dan's experience as an adult child of divorce has sometimes felt this way—a *wound of silence*. He felt that if he spoke about his pain, he would be rejected by his family, friends, significant other, society, and even his Church and God. So many ACODs have grown accustomed to silence regarding their suffering. Why? We will name some of the most common reasons.

Causes of the Wound of Silence

The Freeze

From the child's perspective, divorce can be traumatic.[1] In order to cope, children of divorce may shut out painful memories or deny that the difficult experiences affected them. They "freeze" the past, and it can take a long time to "thaw out" enough to feel ready to talk about it. Parents can likewise be traumatized by things that happened in the marriage or in the divorce, and may not be willing or able to discuss the situation with their children. In our ministry, it is not uncommon to meet older adults who, even decades later, feel like they are *only now* able to examine deeply their parents' divorce and the effects it had on them.

Survival Mode

The chaos of divorce and separation can put a family into survival mode. As parents rebuild their lives, often with little support, children, too, try to retain some semblance of sanity and calm. To do so, they often take on more responsibilities: more chores around the house, caring for their siblings, and even providing emotional or financial support for their parents. At a very early age, an ACOD

[1] The classic "adverse childhood experiences" (ACE) study done in 1998 by Vincent Felitti, M.D., and Kaiser Permanente includes parental divorce and separation in the trauma category for children and recognizes its deep, adverse impact on the people into adulthood. It is noteworthy that the *Catechism of the Catholic Church* (*CCC*) uses the language of "trauma," too: "Divorce is immoral also because it introduces disorder into the family and into society. This disorder brings grave harm to the deserted spouse, to children *traumatized* by the separation of their parents and often torn between them, and because of its contagious effect which makes it truly a plague on society" (no. 2385 [emphasis added]).

can end up, in one form or another, being a "parent" to his siblings or even to his parents. He may become his parent's go-to emotional confidant, replacing the missing spouse—an impossible task. This is called inversion parenting or "parentification,"[2] and in these situations, a child loses the opportunity simply to be a child around his parents. Operating in survival mode, there is little time or energy for the child's emotions and needs to be heard or responded to.

Fear of Disloyalty

Adult children of divorce may keep silent for fear of offending their parents. Children love their parents and fervently want to be loved by them. They may feel they are being disloyal by expressing their pain. Certain family cultures—as well as ethnic cultures—can compound this problem by considering it taboo to bring up "family issues," valuing "peace" above all else. Children of divorce may worry that if they share too much, one or both parents will become distant or even leave them. They might also have anxiety about alienating a sibling. They cannot bear any other losses, so they silence their feelings to preserve whatever love they can receive.

Further, children likely recognize the good that their parents *have* done, so they feel unjustified in questioning the divorce. They may think, "They did the best they could," caught between conflicting emotions of anger and love. Although compassion and respect for our parents are crucial, the common platitude about doing "the best they could" can be—as one clinical psychologist put it—a "thought-stopping cliché" that blocks the healing

[2] See, for example, Louise Early and Delia Cushway, "The Parentified Child," *Clinical Child Psychology and Psychiatry* 7, no. 2 (April 2002): 163–78.

process.[3] Besides, it simply cannot be true since we are all imperfect sinners. And sadly, we know that sometimes parents *do* intentionally inflict harm—in words and actions—upon children.

"Divorce Happy Talk"

ACODs commonly hear, in the aftermath of their parents' split, that it was "for the best." Sociologist Elizabeth Marquardt aptly calls phrases like this "divorce happy talk."[4] Here are some common refrains that we have heard:

- "Kids are happy when their parents are happy."
- "It's good for your parents to live their true, authentic lives instead of faking their happiness in a broken marriage."
- "Your second family is like a bonus family!"
- "A good divorce is better than an unhappy marriage."
- "Their love will grow for you now that they are apart and not fighting."

Consider the high-profile divorce between Jeff and MacKenzie Bezos, founders of Amazon and one of the richest couples in the world. After twenty-five years of marriage, the couple wrote about their split on Twitter. Their words were trumpeted around the Internet as a great example of a successful, happy divorce:

> As our family and close friends know, after a long period of loving exploration and trial separation, we have decided to divorce and continue our shared lives as friends. We

[3] Peter Malinoski, "The Sins of the Parents—Conveniently Denied," *Souls & Hearts* (blog), July 13, 2022, https://www.soulsandhearts.com/blog/the-sins-of-the-parents-conveniently-denied.

[4] Elizabeth Marquardt, *Between Two Worlds: The Inner Lives of Children of Divorce* (New York: Crown Publishers, 2005), 170–71.

> feel incredibly lucky to have found each other and deeply grateful for every one of the years we have been married to each other. If we had known we would separate after 25 years, we would do it all again. We've had such a great life together as a married couple, and we also see wonderful futures ahead, as parents, friends, partners in ventures and projects, and as individuals pursuing ventures and adventures. Though the labels might be different, we remain a family, and we remain cherished friends.[5]

From this statement, it seems like very little is lost—only "labels"—since they "remain a family" and are still "cherished friends." Indeed, according to them, much is *gained* by the divorce, with an expectation of "wonderful futures ahead." One wonders how their children feel about this wonderful future. (We have never met a child of divorce—forever forced to travel between two homes and the two worlds of his parents—who described his parents' breakup as just "changing labels.") More tragically, public statements like this are used by others to justify more "happy" divorces.

Some families, too, talk about the divorce as only a positive, or at least neutral, reality for the children. This can make the children feel out of place within their own family if they don't agree or feel differently. This may lead them to stuff their suffering down. Worse, they may force themselves to believe what many have told them: "It was for the best."

The Trickle-Down Theory

Society often shows a preference for the needs and concerns of divorcees over those of their children. An entire

[5] Jeff Bezos (@JeffBezos), "We want to make people aware of a development in our lives," Twitter, January 9, 2019, https://twitter.com/JeffBezos/status/1083004911380393985.

industry of websites and apps, media, divorce coaches, lawyers, social workers, and psychologists gives support to divorcees, but far fewer societal resources exist for the children. Within the Church, too, many Catholic dioceses and parishes have programs and retreats for divorcees, but little for the unique needs of the children of divorce—although we happily note that is beginning to change. We founded Life-Giving Wounds to address this need, and stress that the path of healing is *not the same* for children of divorce as it is for divorcees.

The widespread idea that happy parents make for happy children has contributed to this one-sided focus on support for parents. The argument goes something like this, as Judith Wallerstein and Sandra Blakeslee put it: "As a parent puts his or her life together in the post-divorce years, they say, the children will inevitably improve. Because an unhappy woman often has a hard time being a good mother, they argue, it follows that a happy woman will be a good mother."[6] However, as Wallerstein and Blakeslee point out:

> It is often true that an unhappy adult finds it hard to be a nurturing parent for unhappiness can deplete the adult's capacity to provide the care and understanding that children need. But it does not follow that a happy or happier adult will necessarily become a better parent. The "trickle down" theory is not relevant to parent-child relationships .... There is no reason to expect that the adult's greater happiness will lead to a greater sensitivity or greater concern for his or her children. To the contrary, circumstances that enrich an adult's life can easily make that adult less available to children.[7]

[6] Judith Wallerstein and Sandra Blakeslee, *Second Chances: Men, Women, and Children a Decade after Divorce: Who Wins, Who Loses, and Why* (New York: Ticknor and Fields, 1989), 10.

[7] Ibid., 11.

Even in Christian circles, it's not uncommon to find a hesitance to upset divorcees, and therefore a reluctance to give full voice to the children's perspective. Dan had this experience the very first time he shared publicly about the difficulties he was experiencing from his parents' separation. During a talk rehearsal in preparation for a high school retreat, Dan mentioned the suffering caused by his parents' split and how his faith helped him through it. One team member objected, "He shouldn't discuss his suffering about his parents' divorce. It will alienate the divorcees on the retreat." Others agreed, and Dan felt crushed. Providentially, a priest in charge spoke up and encouraged Dan to share. But the initial reaction betrays a common belief: the parent is more important.

Sadly, many ACODs do not experience the support of their church or religious community. According to Marquardt, two-thirds of young adult children of divorce in the United States report that *no one* from their church or synagogue reached out to them during their parents' divorce.[8] On our Life-Giving Wounds retreats, we ask participants about this, and most report the same thing: no one reached out. Some of these children eventually leave the pews of our churches, in part because of this neglect, an aspect of the wound that we'll examine further in a later chapter.

The Resiliency Theory

It is often said that children of divorce are "resilient." In other words, they may feel pain, but it's limited to a short period of time, after which they will be fine and go on to live successful lives. This may be partly true on some level; many *do* show a remarkable strength. However, this idea is used by some as justification for divorce, and it can

[8] Marquardt, *Between Two Worlds*, 155.

cause ACODs to minimize their struggles, thereby impeding real growth.

Divorce is a long, enduring grief and challenge for the children. One adult child of divorce put it this way:

> To say that kids are resilient is to dismiss what they are actually experiencing, which is the loss of all that is good, holy, true, and stable in their world .... While the parents may go on to find happiness, it is the children who cannot escape the situation and must relive it each and every holiday, each and every drop-off and pick-up, and even on their wedding day and the birth of their own children.[9]

In many ways, Dan is a poster child for resiliency: he earned a Ph.D., has a stable job, has been happily married for over a decade, is a loving father, and still has a relationship with both of his parents. What more proof could you need? But these outward indicators of success, while good in themselves, miss the inner struggles that, like so many children of divorce, Dan has had to face and continues to face. ACODs are never doomed to misery, but the doctrine of resiliency should not be utilized to silence the pain.

> **Divorce is a long, enduring grief and challenge for the children.**

The Sleeper Effect

Some minimize the pain of ACODs if the divorce happened long ago: "You're still mad about that? You're not

[9] Leila Miller, ed., *Primal Loss: The Now-Adult Children of Divorce Speak* (Phoenix: LCB Publishing, 2017), 162.

over it yet?" However, there is often a time lapse between when the divorce occurred and when a person feels ready to start processing it. This "sleeper effect" is well documented in the work of Wallerstein and Marquardt.[10] It is often not until young adulthood that a person feels able to dive into the impact of his parents' divorce, facilitated perhaps by greater space and independence from his parents, or triggered by the onset of a serious relationship or a failed one. In young adulthood, self-knowledge generally deepens, and a person will likely know more about his wounds as an adult than as a child, making the young adult years crucial for addressing them.

Gray Divorce

A growing phenomenon is "gray divorce," when parents break up after the children are adults.[11] Some think that the fact of adulthood—being "grown up"—means that the divorce will not hurt. However, as many children of gray divorce attest, the breaking of your family still causes serious damage in adulthood, and also brings new challenges in terms of caring for aging parents, dealing with newly complicated family dynamics, and so on.[12] Simply being grown doesn't mean that you don't desire to see the love of your parents together.

[10] See Marquardt, *Between Two Worlds*, 9–10; and Judith Wallerstein, Julia Lewis, and Sandra Blakeslee, *The Unexpected Legacy of Divorce: A 25 Year Landmark Study* (New York: Hyperion, 2000).

[11] Renee Stepler, "Led by Baby Boomers, Divorce Rates Climb for America's 50+ Population," Pew Research Center, March 9, 2017, https://www.pewresearch.org/short-reads/2017/03/09/led-by-baby-boomers-divorce-rates-climb-for-americas-50-population/.

[12] For more on gray divorce, see Carol Hughes and Bruce Fredenburg, *Home Will Never Be the Same Again: A Guide for Adult Children of Gray Divorce* (Lanham, Md.: Rowman and Littlefield, 2020).

The Ubiquity of Relational Brokenness

The sheer pervasiveness of divorce and family breakdown also contributes to the wound of silence. As we said in the introduction, fewer than half of all American children today will live with their continuously married parents throughout their entire childhood.[13] Given the ubiquity of relational brokenness in our society today, it can begin to seem normal. The children in these situations can get the impression, or be directly told, that their suffering is insignificant because *so many* people go through it and seem fine: "If they can get over it, then so can you." Society finds it hard to accept that many, many people may be suffering without the help they need. In this environment, some adult children of divorce internalize the message that their suffering does not count as suffering and therefore stay silent.

False Guilt and Shame

A phenomenon related to the wound of silence deserves special attention: the fact that it is common for ACODs—including Dan at times—to have a nagging feeling that their parents' divorce was somehow their fault. We need to label clearly this feeling as *false* guilt and *false* shame. To all ACODs, we state wholeheartedly: "Your parents' break-up *is not* your fault, but we know that feelings of shame or guilt about the divorce can contribute to not sharing about it with others."

In the most extreme case, some parents have literally told their children that they were a direct or indirect cause of the divorce. They may have said, for instance, "If you weren't such a difficult child, I would not have

[13] Melanie Wasserman, "The Disparate Effects of Family Structure," *Future of Children* 30, no. 1 (Spring 2020): 55–82.

fought so much with your mother." This is a form of scapegoating, instead of parents owning up to their own choices and behaviors.

Other ACODs may feel guilty because they think they could have or should have done more to prevent the split. This is especially true for those who were older when it happened. They may feel like they could have said more, counseled more, shared more resources, and so on. Some may regret that their silence of shock may have been interpreted as condoning the split. But many ACODs have gone to great lengths to help their parents, pleading with them to work it out and giving them resources, and yet their parents still divorced. Splitting up is *always* the parents' decision (or at least the decision of one of them), regardless of a child's action or inaction.

At times, one or both parents *involve* the child in the decision-making process of the divorce, asking the children whether they should divorce or stay married. Children who encourage the divorce may later feel complicit, ashamed, and at fault for the split. Parents might bring up these conversations later and argue that they were simply doing what the children wanted. But it is impossible for children to understand fully all the negative effects that will follow from a divorce or separation when they give their own perspective.

Other children may feel guilty because they expressed to their parents how much they hated to see them fight, maybe even asking them to divorce. But what is being expressed in this is a child's desire for peace, safety, and love, which is something holy and good. The Church teaches that the breakdown of conjugal living should always be considered a "last resort."[14] But it can be morally

[14]John Paul II, encyclical letter *Familiaris Consortio*, November 22, 1981, no. 83; Francis, apostolic exhortation *Amoris Laetitia*, March 19, 2016, no. 241.

legitimate for spouses to separate or even civilly divorce in certain cases, such as when one spouse is causing "grave mental or physical danger" to the other spouse or the children, or when civil divorce "remains the only possible way of ensuring certain legal rights, the care of children, or the protection of inheritance."[15] A child in a highly unstable family situation should therefore not feel ashamed or guilty about asking for the dysfunction to stop; this does not make him responsible for his parents' divorce. Children in tumultuous homes have two substantial painful experiences to grieve once the separation is complete: the toxic family behaviors that led to the split *and* the breakup itself.

Put another way, an ACOD can recognize (and even be grateful for) some legitimately good effects of his parents' separation or civil divorce—such as freedom from abuse or turmoil—while *at the same time* grieving the loss of an intact family. Any positive consequence that comes from parents separating doesn't change the fact that, deep down, what the child most fervently desires is for his parents to be healthy and virtuous enough to have a peaceful, safe, loving, and happy life together. So, to the question we're often asked, "Is the 'real' injury what happened before the divorce or the divorce itself?" we respond emphatically, "both."

> An ACOD can recognize some good effects of his parents' separation or civil divorce, while at the same time grieving the loss of an intact family.

Children of divorce may also feel guilt and shame about their response to the divorce "announcement," which

[15] *CCC*, no. 2383; see also Code of Canon Law, can. 1153; Francis, *Amoris Laetitia*, no. 241.

could have included silence, laughter, or angry outbursts. Or maybe they just kept on playing and ignored it. In retrospect, we ACODs may feel that we should have done something different at this critical moment, and if we had, maybe we could have prevented the divorce somehow. Here's an example: a young girl, upon hearing the news of the divorce from her father, yelled, "Fine, I hope you leave!" He walked out without saying a word. She ran to her bedroom sobbing, and for many years felt ashamed and guilty, thinking that her response somehow led to her parents' final decision to divorce or gave approval to it. However, she later realized that what the young "her" was doing was perfectly fine for a child, and even something positive. What she was really saying in that angry outburst was, "I don't like this at all, and I want you to fight for me and the family and not abandon us!"

Dan, too, carried guilt about his parents' divorce. His father often told him, "I did this *for you.*" So Dan thought that somehow he had given his father the impression that he wanted the divorce. He racked his brain for years trying to figure out why his father would have thought this. But he realized eventually that this was his father's own justification for his actions and not anything Dan actually said, wanted, or did.

Finally, ACODs often feel ashamed of the scandalous circumstances surrounding their parents' divorce—affairs, messy custody battles, or pre- and post-divorce fighting. This is compounded in the age of social media. The children may worry that someone will judge them or view them negatively. Others may put themselves under immense pressure to keep the scandal a secret. But children are entitled to disclose their family situation to whom they want, as long as it is done respectfully and for a good purpose, since it is part of their story and necessary for their healing. And other people's public disclosure of the divorce is beyond their control.

Declarations of Nullity

Another situation that can contribute uniquely to the wound of silence is when divorced parents receive a declaration of nullity—commonly called an annulment. Civil divorce is the legal dissolution of a civil marriage contract. But Catholics believe that no power on earth, not even civil authority, can undo the sacrament of Marriage, which God has established and proclaimed as indissoluble (Mk 10:9; Mt 19:3–9; Lk 16:18).[16] A declaration of nullity, issued by a Church tribunal, declares instead that a couple's previous relationship was not a valid marriage to begin with, due to some obstacle at the time of consent. Persons in this situation are considered by the Church to be unmarried, and thus are able to enter into a marital union.[17] But if the Church determines that the marriage in question is in fact valid, neither spouse is free to marry, even after a civil divorce.

The goal of the declaration of nullity process is to discover and reveal the truth about a particular couple's presumed marriage—which by this point has undergone a civil divorce—in order for all involved to have clarity

[16] See *CCC*, nos. 1650, 2382; Code of Canon Law, can. 1141.

[17] See *CCC*, no. 1629; Code of Canon Law, cans. 1095–1107. It's important to clarify that no divorced Catholic is obligated to undergo the declaration of nullity process. Many divorced Catholics continue to honor their marriage vows even after an unwanted civil divorce, which is a beautiful witness. Others may embark on the declaration of nullity process out of a desire to uncover the truth of their marital situation, or to enter into a new union in the Church with a clean conscience. Much discernment and prayer are needed in these matters.

about the situation. The Church does not (and cannot) "break apart" any valid sacramental marriage, but looks at what happened leading up to the wedding day and on the wedding day itself in order to determine whether or not a valid marriage actually took place.

Some children whose parents receive a declaration of nullity find that the process brings some healing and comfort. But for others, it raises questions about their identity and their relationships (which we will discuss in chapters 5 and 6). Fundamentally, children whose parents receive a declaration of nullity experience hurt similar to that of *any* child who has lost the love of his parents together. But some may feel an additional pressure to be silent about their pain because the declaration of nullity seems to suggest that this difficult "season" is now over. We must be careful not to treat a declaration of nullity as if it instantly or magically erases all hurt, especially that of the children, who have still experienced the breakdown of their original family.

Lack of Awareness of the Wound

Probably all of us know some ACODs who adamantly insist that they are unaffected by their parents' split. Maybe you are one of them. Sometimes stories like theirs are exploited as examples of how *all* ACODs should be: apparently unscathed and doing fine. Although we always rejoice to meet an adult child of divorce who has experienced deep healing, we would like to encourage each of you readers with divorced parents to ask yourself honestly: Were you given a chance to be affected? Were you given permission to grieve? Have you looked into the effects of divorce on children, and can you say that you never struggled in any of those ways? Have you seen growth in your life, thanks to kind support, to help heal the hurt that you did experience?

We have yet to meet an adult child of divorce who was truly unaffected by his family's breakdown although he might be uncomfortable with acknowledging his woundedness. As with an injury to our body, however, ignoring our interior injuries doesn't heal them; on the contrary, they can fester and poison us. We have seen time and time again how powerful it is when an adult child of divorce faces his pain for the first time. Although it's hard—excruciating, even—it leads to new freedom, peace, and connections with others who are journeying on the same path toward healing. When Dan first tried to look at his experiences by himself, it was a mess. He felt angry, frustrated, and lonely, and made some bad decisions out of his hurt. This made it seem like *not thinking* about the pain was the better route. But eventually the healing process changed his life and was worth all the effort and discomfort it entailed.

In the next chapter, we'll look at *life-giving grieving* as an initial holy response to all the wounds we have experienced.

2

Life-Giving Grieving

Blessed are those who mourn, for they shall be comforted.

—Matthew 5:4

"The wounds caused by our parents' divorce can feel like a phantom limb," says Life-Giving Wounds leader Beth Sri. What she means is, we don't even know something serious and necessary is missing from our lives and affecting our day-to-day existence because we have grown used to the silence, minimization, and normalization of our pain. Perhaps we ignore the "missing limb" because that's the only way we know how to function.

ACODs, you have lost something important. God wanted your parents' marriage to be a loving, lifelong bond. He wanted you to have a home within that loving communion. You have a right to grieve your losses no matter the circumstances of your family's breakdown. Jesus weeps with you.

The first step in healing from family wounds is to find the courage to break the silence of our suffering, face our pain, and grieve our losses. Like many children of divorce, grieving was far from Dan's mind after his parents separated. He wanted to be self-sufficient and strong. But deep

ACODs, you have lost something important. God wanted your parents' marriage to be a loving, lifelong bond.

down, he was simply scared that if he dug too deeply, felt his pain too keenly, the past would overwhelm him.

But we have to face these fears. To do so, we must know how the past affects us. The past is never simply the past, and the same can be said of the present and future. Through the God-given gifts of intellect, will, and memory (which includes emotions), we embody a unity of time in ourselves. The past *filters* how we live and see the present, for better or for worse. The present can *transform* the past's impact on our thoughts, imagination, and life, while contributing new ideas, memories, and choices that intermix with the past. And what we think about the future *shapes* our desires and actions in the present. In the human person, the three "times" are orchestrated into a single symphony. So why not make sure the past is helping rather than hindering us? It's never too late to confront the past and change how it affects the present. To do this, we first have to grieve.

The Central Wound

All children of divorce have *lost the love of their parents together* as a unified communion. This is true no matter how brief, fragile, or even nonexistent that love was; no matter how amicable or bitter the separation was; and no matter how much love and involvement each parent individually gave after the split. God designed marriage to be a lifelong, indissoluble union of persons, within which children would be welcomed and lovingly nurtured by their mother and father.[1] Christ made this perfectly clear to the Pharisees: "Have you not read that he who made them from the beginning made them male and female, and said, 'For this reason a man shall leave his father and mother and be joined to his wife, and the two shall become one'? ... What therefore God has joined together, let no man put asunder" (Mt 19:4–6). Putting marriage asunder injures the soul, and this wound must be named and mourned.

A child is the living embodiment and permanent expression of the one-flesh union of his mother and father, so the fracture of that union reaches to the core of his identity and being—even if all he ever knew was one parent or a stepfamily. Enduring married love is meant to provide a strong foundation for one's human development and give a model for all relationships to follow.[2] For the child, the breakdown of his parents' relationship is like a rock thrown into still water, with the effects rippling out in every direction. These ripples touch his very origin and identity, his pursuit of love and vocation, his emotional life, and more. Divorce is not just one event but waves of events. We need to acknowledge the many ripples and allow ourselves to grieve them.

[1] See John Paul II, encyclical letter *Familiaris Consortio*, November 22, 1981, no. 19; Francis, apostolic exhortation *Amoris Laetitia*, March 19, 2016, nos. 29, 63, 71, 73.

[2] While neither this book nor Life-Giving Wounds' ministry attend to the challenges caused when a child is placed for adoption or is removed from a natural parent's custody, we acknowledge (as adoptive parents ourselves) that those wounds, of losing a home and family life with one's first, biological parents, are real as well. While distinct in several important ways from the wounds experienced by children of divorce, they call out also for acknowledgement, understanding, and healing. In a similar vein would be the sorrow caused when a parent dies, especially when children are young, another loss not directly addressed by this book, but worthy of attention.

What Pixar and Jesus Teach Us about Grief

In some ways, the Pixar movie *Inside Out* beautifully expresses Christian grief. Eleven-year-old Riley and her parents move across the country for her father's new job. This move causes Riley great distress and disruption, but her mother asks her to be happy "for the family" because it is a stressful event for all of them. Out of love, Riley tries to be only joyful, but the internal tension she feels becomes insupportable, driving her to run away to her hometown, alone. Her parents are horrified and search frantically for her. When she finally returns home, Riley discovers that her parents truly love and embrace not only the "happy" her, but the "sad" her as well. This teaches all of them two important lessons. First, for there to be true peace, joy and sadness must coexist. In fact, in order to have profound happiness, you must at times *embrace* sadness. Second, for this sadness to lead to joy, it must be shared with others.

> Grief is an invitation to communion with God and with others who can "receive our wound."

Now turning to the Gospels and the words of Jesus: "Blessed are those who mourn, for they shall be comforted" (Mt 5:4). Here Christ connects blessedness (or in some translations, happiness) with mourning. Joy and grief not only coexist but are intrinsically related. This verse can be seen as a foreshadowing of the unbreakable relationship between the Cross and the Resurrection. And here Jesus emphasizes the communal nature of grieving. He speaks in the plural: "Blessed are *those* who mourn, for *they* shall be comforted." Christ is indicating that this blessedness, this happiness, comes through a *shared* experience of mourning and comfort. Grief is an invitation to communion with God *and* with others who can "receive our wound."

How is this transformative and communal work of life-giving grieving accomplished? What are ways in which we can grieve well? We will outline seven points.

Seven Marks of Christian Grieving

1. Love.

In Sacred Scripture, one of the most profound scenes of sorrow is when "Jesus wept" at his friend Lazarus' death (Jn 11:35). What is remarkable is that Jesus deeply mourned the death of Lazarus *even though* he knew he was going to raise him back to life! This shows us that we can mourn and take pain and wounds seriously even while believing core truths like the Resurrection and trusting that God can bring good out of suffering. Christ invites us in this passage not to "skip over" grieving. In fact, grief is an expression of love for who or what was lost. After Jesus wept, the people who were with Jesus immediately said, "See how he loved him!" (Jn 11:36).

By mourning the losses of our parents' love together, the unity of our family, a peaceful childhood, and other good and holy things, we are persevering in love for our parents, our family, and ourselves, as well as for marriage the way God intended it to be experienced. As a line from the Marvel television series *WandaVision* says, "What is grief but love persevering?"

2. Reveal to heal.

To grieve well, we must do the hard work of *specifically* naming our wounds, a process we can call "reveal in order to heal." The Scriptures—especially the book of Lamentations and the Psalms—are full of examples of voicing clearly delineated sorrows: "My tears have been my food day and night, while men say to me continually, 'Where is your God?' ... Why are you cast down, O my soul, and why are you disquieted within me? ... I say to God, my rock: 'Why have you forgotten me? Why do I go mourning because of the oppression of the enemy?'" (Ps 42:3, 5a, 9) Consider also the Gospel passage that relates how both Martha and Mary shared with Jesus their concrete regret that, had Jesus been there, their brother would not have died (Jn 11:21, 32).

Being *specific* about what we grieve helps us grow in self-awareness. It helps us understand the full extent and various layers of our injuries. We start to see where healing is most needed so we can present our wounds to the Divine Physician. This process of revealing takes time, especially if we need to overcome habits of silence and self-denial. Prayerful journaling can help us begin to untangle these feelings and experiences. If we ask, God will reveal our areas of hurt to us, and then we can weep with him. Christ never ran away from the sick or the suffering. Instead, he embraced them, even when society pushed them away. We also often need others to help us with this work of revealing—people who have known similar suffering and can show us a pathway forward through their own hard-earned insights.

3. Distinguish between the person and his acts.

At some point when we grieve, anger will likely arise at injustices we have experienced. Many ACODs—including Dan—feel caught between anger and love toward their parents and are unsure how to feel and express their pain while still loving their parents. In college, Dan learned the distinction between the person and his acts, which helped him see that when we grieve an offense done to us, our attention should be directed toward the *acts* committed, and not the *person* who committed them. We can fiercely detest and name as painful wounds conflicts, abuse, neglect, betrayals, abandonment, dysfunction, rejection, and the divorce or separation itself, but yet love our parents and respect their dignity as persons.

God says, "I hate divorce" (Mal 2:16), but Jesus shows great charity toward the Samaritan woman at the well who had multiple husbands (Jn 4:1–42). Jesus honors the woman as greater than her sinful actions, while calling out her sin and exhorting her to live differently now. It is possible to be angry that your parents are divorced while still loving your parents—no matter their faults and sins, they have inherent dignity.

4. Seek out those who can receive the wound.

To grieve well, we must find people who can receive the wound with love, understanding, and empathy. Grief is an invitation to communion, first with Jesus and then with others. Not everyone we share our suffering with will be able to receive it and honor it. Many ACODs have tried to express their suffering only to have it minimized, discounted, or flat-out rejected. This can happen because of the listener's own trauma, or his beliefs about divorce that prevent him from fully empathizing. Even Jesus had his pain minimized. When he wept at Lazarus' death, some questioned the authenticity of his grief: "Could not he who opened the eyes of the blind man have kept this man from dying?" (Jn 11:37).

Special graces come from talking with a supportive peer from a similar background, someone who is also trying to heal with the help of Christ. Burdens are always lighter when carried by two. Jesus allowed others to help bear his suffering—Simon of Cyrene helped carry his Cross (Mt 27:32). In our lives, our own "Simons" can mediate Christ's loving gaze and compassion to us. At last we have been heard, understood, and are no longer alone. Our "Simons" can help us find freedom from the pain's hold on us, and we can turn to them when different manifestations of the grief surface. This could happen in something as commonplace as a text message thread with close friends sharing about ongoing issues and asking for prayers. Spouses can also play an important role in receiving grief; Dan turns to Bethany when new hurts arise.

In addition to friends and peers, Catholic or Christian counselors, spiritual directors, and mentors can receive our wounds and provide reliable guidance and ongoing support in healing.[3] There should be no shame or stigma in asking for professional help.

5. Expand your heart and integrate the grief.

Some sorrows cannot be fully healed or "fixed" in this earthly life, if by "healing" we mean no longer experiencing any pain or negative effects caused by a difficult situation. The suffering caused by divorce or separation can be described as a *lifelong wound*. As Judith Wallerstein and Sandra Blakeslee say, "Divorce is deceptive. Legally it is a single event, but psychologically it is a chain—sometimes

[3] For advice on pursuing counseling and spiritual direction, see Cafea Fruor, "Seeking Therapy as an Adult Child of Divorce," *Life-Giving Wounds* (blog), July 9, 2020, https://www.lifegivingwounds.org/blog/seeking-therapy-as-an-adult-child-of-divorce; Graciela Rodriguez, "Are You Seeking Inner Peace? Spiritual Direction Can Help," *Life-Giving Wounds* (blog), April 20, 2021, https://www.lifegivingwounds.org/blog/spiritualdirection; Sister Kalin Holthaus, A.V.I., "A Religious Sister's Advice about Spiritual Direction for ACODs," *Life-Giving Wounds* (blog), August 12, 2021, https://www.lifegivingwounds.org/blog/a-religious-sisters-advice-about-spiritual-direction-for-acods.

a never-ending chain—of events, relocations, and radically shifting relationships strung through time, a process that forever changes the lives of the people involved."[4] Divorce (and ongoing separation) rears its head at numerous moments throughout life: at holidays and family get-togethers; during milestones like weddings, births of children, celebration of sacraments, and funerals; while raising children and taking care of aging parents; and so on. In addition, divorce introduces ongoing dysfunctional dynamics into relationships with family members. Thus, divorce or separation must be grieved not just at the moment it happens, but at *all* of the various difficult moments it causes into the future.

But this should not cause us to despair or become mired in self-pity. Alongside our grief, we can live a life of joy, peace, happiness, and love if we allow Christ to expand our hearts in response to the wounds.

Grief counselor Lois Tonkin says that people tend to think that grief naturally diminishes over time—the old adage "time heals all wounds." But what Tonkin found when working with clients who lost a loved one is that *we learn how to grow around grief* so it is better integrated into our life overall and has a relatively less prominent place within us.[5]

Drawing on Tonkin's insight, we can think of the goal of grieving over time as an ever-enlarging heart, becoming more and more like the Sacred Heart of Jesus. The grief over our parents' split remains part of our lives, but our hearts can expand to create ever more room for joy, peace,

[4] Judith Wallerstein and Sandra Blakeslee, *Second Chances: Men, Women, and Children a Decade after Divorce: Who Wins, Who Loses, and Why* (New York: Ticknor and Fields, 1989), xii.

[5] Lois Tonkin, "Growing around Grief—Another Way to Look at Grief and Recovery," *Bereavement Care* 15, no. 1 (1996): 10.

and love. We can integrate grief into these realities and vice versa. As Pope Francis says, quoting Saint Thomas Aquinas, "'joy' refers to an expansion of the heart," which through Christ's grace can take place even in the midst of great sorrow.[6] When we experience a fresh wave of grief, perhaps feeling the pain as intensely as before—the path is rarely linear—it has less of a hold on us and we can "ride the wave" of pain more serenely.

6. Cultivate hope and reject self-pity and the victim mentality.

Self-pity and a "victim mentality" are not Christian ways of grieving. What we mean by these terms is a self-indulgent, excessive focus on our own trials and a hypersensitivity to our lack that fixates on our perceived powerlessness to change the situation or improve our lives. Self-pity and a victim mentality say that "all is lost," "these bad things can never change," "I can never change," or "that's just the way I am." People with this mentality also compare their trials with those of others, thinking they have it uniquely worse than anyone else.

But Christian grieving rejects both self-pity and a victim mentality because it believes in the Lord's promise: "Blessed are those who mourn, for they *shall be* comforted" (Mt 5:4, emphasis added). We believe in the promise of God's comfort, a "being with" us that strengthens us (from the Latin, "*cum*-with," "*fortis*-strength or fortress"). Saint Paul writes:

> Blessed be the God and Father of our Lord Jesus Christ, the Father of mercies and God of all comfort, who comforts us in all our affliction, so that we may be able to comfort those who are in any affliction, with the comfort

[6] Francis, *Amoris Laetitia*, no. 126.

> with which we ourselves are comforted by God. For as we share abundantly in Christ's sufferings, so through Christ we share abundantly in comfort too. (2 Cor 1:3–5)

When we grieve, we must do so with hope in Christ that things *can* change for the better—that *I* can change for the better. Saint Paul exhorts the early Christian community not to "grieve as others do who have no hope" (1 Thess 4:13). The tension between grief and hope illuminates the paradoxical Christian concept of a "life-giving wound": we can acknowledge wholeheartedly the pain we have and carry with us, while also cultivating hope and trusting that good things can come from our wounds.

If grieving were on a continuum, on one side would be an extreme of silence and not sharing our true feelings, and on the other side would be self-pity and the victim mentality. In the middle—the virtuous mean—would be *grieving with hope*, vulnerably acknowledging our sadness while trusting that healing and joy is possible. We may not always get this right, and that's okay; grief doesn't have to be "done" perfectly. Silence may be our first response, and we may find ourselves feeling self-pity once our voice is heard. But we hope with the Lord's help to end up *grieving with hope.*

7. Move toward acceptance.

In his book *Interior Freedom*, Father Jacques Philippe says that the worst form of suffering is the suffering we reject.[7] Why? Because we add to the original pain either rebellion or resentment, which increases the tension and pain within us.[8] Father Philippe says that we must move

[7]Jacques Philippe, *Interior Freedom*, trans. Helena Scott (New York: Scepter, 2007), 46–47.

[8]Ibid., 29–31.

toward accepting or "choosing" the crosses that we did not give ourselves.[9]

Accepting our suffering does not mean condoning sin or "being okay with" the painful choices involved in our parents' separation or divorce, nor does it mean minimizing our pain. Acceptance means courageously acknowledging the depth of the grief yet still being willing to enter prayerfully and hopefully into this pain whenever it manifests itself. This is in contrast either to avoiding or to rejecting the reality of our wounds altogether, or maintaining an attitude of resentment toward them, an attitude incompatible with lasting peace. Through God's grace, prayerfully "choosing" or "consenting" to our wounds is the beginning of responding to them with virtue—especially the theological virtues of faith, hope, and love.[10] This is not easy work when we have been tremendously hurt, but it will help cultivate in us the interior freedom that Christ wants to give all of his disciples as part of his healing grace of salvation.

Grieving within the Father's Gaze

Tremendous peace can follow from the communion born of sharing grief together. Father Philippe calls this communal grief the "mediation of another's eyes," one who reflects back to us our grief and love *in* that grief.[11] How much greater still are the graces when we see this love reflected back to us in God the Father's eyes, when we allow his gaze to become our gaze upon ourselves and toward others.

[9] Ibid., 44–60, 29–31.
[10] Ibid., 31, 24–25, 44–60.
[11] Ibid., 35–37.

Let us grieve within God the Father's gaze. Simply getting our grief "off our chests" to God, or to another who sees us, understands us, and suffers with us, begins to release the negative hold of these wounds on our hearts and lives so that we can be more free to love. Grieving is not "doing nothing" or "wallowing in the pain." Far from it! Christian grief expresses love, specifically names the harm, continues to love the offender, leads to communion with others, expands our hearts, cultivates hope, and helps us authentically accept our suffering. Sounds pretty great, huh? No wonder our Lord declared, "Blessed are those who mourn, for they shall be comforted" (Mt 5:4).

A Non-ACOD Spouse's Perspective: Grieving Together

Bethany: When Dan and I were both graduate students at the John Paul II Institute, we drove with two classmates to a day-long outing in the Shenandoah Valley. During the drive back, we got to talking about our families. I distinctly remember Dan sharing that his parents were divorced and what effects that had on him. I was stunned and somewhat awed at how easily he could talk about something that was so inherently painful. I could tell how much Dan had already processed through these painful experiences, and I felt honored to receive this part of him.

We have learned over and over in our married life how much I can offer Dan by being a listening ear for him to share about past pains from his parents' divorce and current challenges their split causes him (and often causes us as a couple and family). I make no pretense to "fix" his hurt, but simply receive it, express my compassion, and offer my prayerful support. His grief has become something shared by us as a couple (we're both affected now), and my willingness to receive his wound has given him the stability to dive deeper into his healing.

I don't always receive his pain perfectly, but our commitment to grieve together has deepened our vulnerability, to the benefit of our communion. And we can also receive the joy of our own marriage and family more fully—and what a gift that is!

Dan's sharing about his wounds has also inspired me to confront my own hurts, share and grieve them with Dan, and find my healing too. Coming from an intact family, I sometimes forget that I too have wounds, and when Dan shares his hurt, it can open up a new horizon in my heart. The cycle of grief and healing has just become a part of our marriage. Through God's grace, it has led to a deeper, more profound joy in our love that we wouldn't have had without this shared suffering and healing together.

3

The Wound to Faith

My God, my God, why have you forsaken me?

—Matthew 27:46

"It seemed that God had left me."

"With the divorce, I didn't just lose the love of my parents together, but I also felt like I lost God as well."

These quotes, representative of participants in our Life-Giving Wounds ministry, reflect a deep wound in the hearts and souls of many ACODs. While this book presumes faith in God—and more specifically faith in Jesus Christ—as essential for healing, we know that many ACODs wrestle with questions of faith as the result of their parents' divorce.

Some adult children of divorce become more religious in the wake of their parents' split, turning to their faith and prayer for comfort. But others experience distance and doubt in their relationship with God and the Church, and still others lose their faith completely. Research into family breakdown and religious practice bears this out: those from broken homes are more likely to be religious "nones" (unaffiliated with any religious group) than those raised in intact homes (35 percent versus 23 percent).[1] ACODs are more likely than those from intact families to describe themselves as "spiritual but not religious."[2] Children of divorce who do identify with a religious affiliation are less active in their faith communities,[3] and only half as likely as those from intact homes to attend services regularly throughout childhood.[4] ACODs are also two to three times more likely to leave religious practice altogether than their peers with married parents.[5]

Every existential question and moment of suffering is also always a question addressed to God, about God and his will for us.

Clearly there is a pressing need to address family breakdown in evangelization efforts. We need most to address the potential injury to faith that divorce can cause because spiritual healing is the deepest level of healing we need. As Pope Benedict XVI said, "Often the deepest cause of suffering is the very absence of God."[6] Every existential question and moment of suffering is also always a question addressed to God, about God and his will for us, and has practical implications for how we approach healing.[7]

[1] Betsy Cooper et al., "Exodus: Why Americans are Leaving Religion and Why They are Unlikely to Come Back," Public Religion Research Institute, September 22, 2016, https://www.prri.org/research/prri-rns-poll-nones-atheist-leaving-religion/; Leora E. Lawton and Regina Bures, "Parental Divorce and the 'Switching' of Religious Identity," *Journal for the Scientific Study of Religion* 40, no. 1 (March 2001).

[2] Elizabeth Marquardt, *Between Two Worlds: The Inner Lives of Children of Divorce* (New York: Crown Publishers, 2005), 153.

[3] Cooper et al., "Exodus."

[4] Marquardt, *Between Two Worlds*, 154.

[5] Lawton and Bures, "Parental Divorce and the 'Switching' of Religious Identity," 106.

[6] Benedict XVI, encyclical letter *Deus Caritas Est*, December 25, 2005, no. 31.

[7] See John Paul II, apostolic letter *Salvifici Doloris*, February 11, 1984, no. 9.

In this chapter, we will outline some reasons why ACODs can experience a "wound to faith" and face obstacles to having a living, trusting relationship with God. In the next chapter, we will discuss the great gift of faith for healing and ways to discover, recover, and deepen faith.

"Unanswered Prayers" and Questions about Suffering

As children navigate the fallout of their parents' divorce or separation, they sometimes, like Dan, turn to God for help. Dan was raised Catholic and was eleven when his parents separated. This, as well as the fighting that preceded the separation, was the first real crisis in his life. He initially responded to the pain by praying *a lot*—four Rosaries and two Divine Mercy Chaplets many days—fervently hoping that his parents would get back together. This feverish prayer routine went on for years until a new crisis occurred that seemed to destroy any possibility of his parents' reconciliation. Crushed, Dan became disillusioned with his faith. God had not answered his prayers in the way he had hoped. He never stopped going to Mass, but interiorly he stopped fully believing and became distant from God, going through the motions.

We have heard similar stories of spiritual anguish from other ACODs. For many, the feeling that God is not answering their prayers can trigger past losses felt from parents' unkept promises. Elizabeth Marquardt recounts one such story from an ACOD:

> [Melissa] remembered, "I'd sit down and go, 'Okay, now how do I pray?' You'd usually start it as a letter. 'Dear God, how are you? I'm fine. Today was warm. I was

hoping that you could help me.'" She paused and laughed. "But then you kind of wonder about it because [he] never answer[s]. So that made me wonder, 'Well, I wrote to him. I didn't get a letter back. *That sounds like Dad*!'"[8]

Like others who face intense trials, many ACODs have profound and unsettled questions about God and suffering: Where is God in all of this mess? Why did he allow this horrible thing to happen? When the answers to these questions are not clear, the sufferer wonders whether suffering is meaningless and God is indifferent. he may feel abandoned by God. Marquardt reports that one-fifth of children of divorce agree, "When I think about bad things that have happened in my life I find it hard to believe in a God who cares."[9]

Difficulty with Familial Language

Throughout Scripture, familial language is used to describe God and the truths of the faith: God is "our Father" (Mt 6:6–15); God's love is tender like a mother's love (Is 66:13); and the relationship between Israel and God, as well as between Christ and the Church, is described in familial and nuptial language (Hos 1–3; Is 54:5–6; Eph 5:21–33; Mt 9:14–15).[10] The *Catechism of the Catholic Church* (hereafter "the Catechism") states that "the language of the faith thus

[8] Marquardt, *Between Two Worlds*, 143.

[9] Ibid., 140.

[10] See also *CCC*, no. 1617: "The entire Christian life bears the mark of the spousal love of Christ and the Church. Already Baptism, the entry into the People of God, is a nuptial mystery; it is so to speak the nuptial bath which precedes the wedding feast, the Eucharist. Christian marriage in its turn becomes an efficacious sign, the sacrament of the covenant of Christ and the Church. Since it signifies and communicates grace, marriage between baptized persons is a true sacrament of the New Covenant."

draws on the human experience of parents, who are in a way the first representatives of God for man."[11]

But what happens when the love of our parents, our "first representatives of God," didn't image God's faithful love? Or when our father or mother did not love us with a tender, steadfast love? Accepting and internalizing the familial language of the faith can be challenging for someone who has not experienced an intact loving family life. If my father has abandoned me, abused me, or ignored me, how can I call God *Father* and trust him? If my mother has abandoned me, abused me, or ignored me, how can I receive God's maternal, tender love? How can I trust Mother Church's love for me? These spiritual struggles lead some ACODs to find this familial language incomprehensible, or to jettison it for other descriptors. Research on children's psychological development reinforces these points, finding that children's images of God arise in part from their lived experiences of attachment with their parents.[12]

Stephanie, whose father left when she was two years old, describes the challenge for her of calling God "Father" in a poem entitled *Abba*:

> "Thank you, Father."
> Three words that make
> my heart leap with joy
> AND
> three words that make
> my heart tremble with fear.

[11] *CCC*, no. 239.

[12] Commission on Children at Risk, *Hardwired to Connect: The New Scientific Case for Authoritative Communities* (New York: Institute for American Values, 2003), 27–28; Chris Kiesling, "An Attachment Theory Approach to Narrating the Faith Journey of Children of Parental Divorce," *International Journal of Children's Spirituality* 16, no. 4 (2011): 303–13.

"Daddy, daddy."
Two words I long to say
AND
two words I have rarely uttered
when darkness crept in.[13]

And Father John Baptist, an adult child of divorce and Life-Giving Wounds leader, talks about his struggle with paternal language for God in this way: "When my father left the family during my late teens, I fell right back into infancy (from the Latin *infans*, which means literally 'one unable to speak'). I was unable to call my father 'Dad' because 'Dad' was no longer present. And that translated to my relationship with God: I did not call God 'Father' because it seemed that God had left me, too."[14]

Wrestling with Certain Scriptural Teachings

ACODs can also have unanswered questions or confusion about particular Catholic teachings and passages in Scripture, such as the fourth commandment to "honor your father and your mother" (Ex 20:12) and Jesus' teachings about marriage and divorce (e.g., Mk 10:2–12) and forgiveness (e.g., Mt 18:21–22). It's not so much that adult children of divorce reject these teachings; it's more that they are eager for faithful guidance and interpretation for how these passages are to be understood and lived in their circumstances of family breakdown. (We'll discuss

[13] Stephanie Gulya, "Abba," *Life-Giving Wounds* (blog), January 26, 2022, https://www.lifegivingwounds.org/blog/abba.

[14] John Baptist Hoang, O.P., "A Reflection on the Words 'Father' and 'Son' for Those Who Have Been Hurt,'" *Life-Giving Wounds* (blog), December 22, 2021, https://www.lifegivingwounds.org/blog/father-and-son.

an approach to the fourth commandment at length in chapter 14.)

In regard to Jesus' teaching on marriage and divorce, that "what therefore God has joined together, let not man put asunder" (Mk 10:9) and "whoever divorces his wife and marries another, commits adultery against her" (Mk 10:11), ACODs may wonder why the Church is not more vocal about marriage's indissolubility, or about the potential sin of divorce (if freely chosen and not for a serious exception as outlined in the Catechism and canon law), and the injunction against remarriage without a declaration of nullity. They may also wonder whether Jesus' description of marriage, "the two shall become one flesh" (Mk 10:8), is even real or attainable, given the model of a fractured marriage they received in their parents' marriage.

In regard to Scriptural passages about forgiveness, such as Jesus' exhortation to forgive others "seventy times seven" times (Mt 18:22), many ACODs desire more guidance about *how* to forgive those who have caused—and continue to cause—profound hurt, and the relationship between forgiveness and boundaries. They may have a visceral reaction against the very idea of forgiving those who have hurt them so deeply, regardless of the absolutely essential place of forgiveness in healing. (We'll discuss all this in chapters 11 and 12.)

Challenges in Church Communities

Some children of divorce had a close connection with their church community prior to the divorce but afterward are unable to attend services regularly due to custody arrangements or because of moving to a parent's new home. Happy memories of attending church as a family may become tainted with the pain of losing that togetherness. Or perhaps one or both parents stop practicing the faith altogether or become hostile to it.

Some ACODs didn't feel welcomed at their parish after their family crisis, or felt ashamed to be from a broken family. Marquardt tells of a child who made a great effort to show up to church services without his parents, but eventually stopped going because it was agonizing to see the other children with their parents while he sat alone.[15] Some ACODs turned to unhealthy and even sinful ways of coping (such as pornography, premarital sex, drugs, or drinking) and then felt unworthy to be part of a church community.

Unfortunately, many ACODs have felt that their church communities (or the Church as a whole) didn't attend to their needs as children of divorce. As we said earlier, two-thirds of young adults who were regularly attending a church or synagogue at the time of their parents' divorce said that *no one* from the clergy or congregation reached out to them.[16] If church members did broach the subject at all, they may have sugarcoated the issues or seemed unable to provide meaningful help or guidance. But most report silence or even an intentional avoidance of the topic because it was perceived as a "private" or "personal" issue.

Many ACODs have felt that their church communities (or the Church as a whole) didn't attend to their needs as children of divorce.

[15] Marquardt, *Between Two Worlds*, 146.
[16] Ibid., 155.

When Faith Seems Hypocritical

For the ACODs whose parents were churchgoing Christians and yet divorced anyway, the faith can be seen as ineffectual or, worse, hypocritical. Their parents' faith did not seem to make a difference in the decision to give up on the marriage (by one or both of them), presenting a spiritual dilemma. Why didn't their faith make more of a difference to their marriage? Why didn't their faith convince them to persevere in their marriage and to change sinful or unhealthy behaviors? Where was the church community to help them in their struggles?

Children from dysfunctional family backgrounds could also see the faith as hypocritical if the family was on their "best behavior" at church while life at home was filled with tension and animosity. Going to church later could trigger those unhappy memories of putting on a pious front while hiding their deep unhappiness about their family's dysfunction.

For those ACODs whose faith has been damaged by the behavior of their Christian parent(s) or community or both, it's not difficult to see why some wonder why they should bother with the faith at all. Consider the testimony of an adult child of divorce who shares the damage her parents' divorce did to her faith and her siblings' faith:

> I was 13 when my dad said he was leaving, and it was a huge shock, as we never thought that would happen to our family, especially after eight kids and over 25 years together .... My family was involved in the Church and we all attended mass weekly .... We kept going to church with our mom, but the divorce really changed how we saw God and life .... My faith, and that of most of my siblings, wavered tremendously.

> My siblings and I all went through pagan, secular, hardly-believing-in-anything periods. In those years, we were hopeless, often aimless, [and] depressed.[17]

This person goes on to share that she eventually returned to the Catholic faith, thanks in large part to her mother's heroic witness of faith, but other children of divorce never return. In fact, although there are divorced mothers and fathers who are praiseworthy witnesses to their faith in the midst of severe trials, ACODs are more likely than those from intact homes to "doubt the sincerity of our parents' religious beliefs."[18]

If a parent has an affair with someone from the church community or with another Christian, this understandably causes great scandal and embarrassment for the offended spouse and children. One or both parents may be encouraged by people in their church communities to divorce in circumstances that do not morally necessitate it. Fellow Christians who encourage the divorce—or the divorcing parents themselves—may twist Scripture or Church teachings to justify the divorce. For ACODs who *want* to stay committed to their faith, these situations of hypocrisy or false teaching cause more suffering.

Distrust of Institutions and the Impact of Scandals

In our experience, adult children of divorce or separation are more likely to distrust authorities and institutions as a whole because the most important authority figures in their lives, their parents, have let them down. Because of

[17] Leila Miller, ed., *Primal Loss: The Now-Adult Children of Divorce Speak* (Phoenix: LCB Publishing, 2017), 17–18.

[18] Marquardt, *Between Two Worlds*, 156.

this, institutional scandals can affect them deeply. Such scandals seem to prove their worldview that institutions and authorities should *never* be trusted.

The scandals that have plagued the Catholic Church in recent decades, particularly the child sexual abuse crisis, have understandably caused great sadness, anger beyond words, anxiety, and distrust for many people. For some ACODs, these travesties hit in a unique way because they evoke losses related to their parents' divorce. One adult child of divorce we know, who was abused by a family member, struggled to come back to the Church because the scandals reminded her about the abuse she endured.

In the next chapter, we'll look at ways that adult children of divorce can recover or deepen their faith lives, and how the faith itself is a tremendous source of healing.

4

Life-Giving Faith

Your faith has made you well; go in peace.

—Mark 5:34

Faith and Healing

The connection between faith and healing is abundantly clear in the Gospels, for example in the healings of the hemorrhaging woman (Mk 5:25–34), the blind man Bartimaeus (Mk 10:46–52), the paralytic (Mk 2:1–12), and more. Faith heals us by purifying and renewing our understanding of God as a good Father with a good plan for our lives, by helping us find meaning in suffering, and by showing us the truth both about God and about ourselves. Faith is also an ever-deepening, loving union with God that counters the lack of love we have experienced as ACODs.

Faith has played a tremendous role in Dan's healing. In high school, six years after his parents' separation, he went on a retreat at the behest of his mom. Here his image of God was transformed. Dan realized that his younger self's image of God was "off." It was a view of God that said, "If you do this, then I'll believe in you." For instance, if he prayed enough, he could earn God's love and favor. It was a view of God that didn't enjoy God's presence for its own sake, but only for the benefits God gives, like answering prayers in the way Dan wanted.

On that pivotal retreat, Dan learned that Christ doesn't always take away our suffering but *always* fills it with his presence and love. That revelation changed Dan's view of God from Santa Claus to Emmanuel—God *with us*. He discovered that the God of the Universe grieved with him over his parents' divorce. He learned that meaning could be found in the suffering, transforming it into something beyond sheer pain. He saw that the response to his prayers all along was Christ's loving presence, which is the deepest answer to all the longings of our hearts, and that Christ through this presence in Dan's suffering was purifying and strengthening his desires for what was good and holy (especially in marriage and family life). He heard Christ say clearly for the first time: "Be *with* me. I am enough for your heart's longing."

Looking back, Dan realizes he would not have found the wholeness he has today, have a joyful marriage with Bethany, or co-founded a nonprofit that helps other ACODs heal, if God hadn't broken through his angry exterior to change his outlook on faith and suffering. Faith can indeed move mountains—and sometimes those mountains are our hardened hearts. As then-Cardinal Ratzinger said, "The truth of Jesus' word cannot be tested in terms of theory. It is like a technical proposition: it is shown to be correct only by testing. The truth of what God says here involves the whole person, the experiment of life. It can only become clear for me if I truly give myself up to the will of God, so far as he has made it known to me."[1]

[1]Joseph Cardinal Ratzinger, *God and the World: A Conversation with Peter Seewald*, trans. Henry Taylor (San Francisco: Ignatius Press, 2002), 46.

Let the Children of Divorce Come to Me

We have depicted the heroic act of faith by children of divorce in a piece of sacred art by Michael Corsini commissioned for Life-Giving Wounds, entitled *Let the Children of Divorce Come to Me.* In the painting, the resurrected Christ walks on water toward a child of divorce, a reference to Christ walking on the sea in the midst of a storm to meet his terrified disciples in their boat (Mt 14:22–33). Jesus is willing to risk the storm's danger; he first moves toward us.

The child in the artwork makes an act of faith by taking a tentative step forward to meet Christ. To those who struggle with faith because of the unrelenting waves of suffering, Jesus lovingly says what he said to his trembling disciples in the boat: "Take heart, it is I; have no fear" (Mt 14:27). Let us be bold like Peter and cry out, "Lord, save me" (Mt 14:30). Christ will always stretch out his nail-pierced, resurrected hand to lift us up. He has shown again and again that he is true to his promise: "I am with you always, to the close of the age" (Mt 28:20).

The New Vision of Faith

The "darkness" of suffering can impede our relationship with the Lord; we feel alone in our difficulties. In faith our eyes *adjust* to the darkness to see that actually Christ has been with us the whole time. Scripture often connects faith with the act of seeing, such as in this passage from the Gospel of John: "Then the other disciple, who reached the tomb first, also went in, and he saw and believed" (Jn 20:8).[2] Faith looks at our lives and our suffering *differently*

[2] See also John 11:40, 11:45, 12:44–45.

Michael Corsini, *Let the Children of Divorce Come to Me*, 2021, oil on canvas. Copyright © Life-Giving Wounds.

and, through this new sight, approaches our suffering differently, with greater peace.

On our retreats, we encourage participants (if they feel ready to do so) to recall an instance of family brokenness and ask God to show them where he was in that moment or what truth he is now speaking to them about this experience. One participant recalled a memory of her parents fighting, and herself as a child slumped against the wall. In prayer, she came to see both Jesus and Mary standing above her protectively, shielding her with their presence.

Another ACOD had the painful experience of her dad abandoning the family on Christmas day. She struggled with this for years, asking the Lord why, out of all days, would Christmas be the time to experience such pain? Through prayer, she came to realize that the Lord—the infant Christ—was with her in a special way *because* it was Christmas. His Incarnation filled that painful experience with his presence and love in a new way.

> The Lord fills our suffering with his presence, incorporating past events and memories into a greater life-story that is good—the story of Christ's enduring love for us.

Faith cannot instantly "fix" or completely undo the past hurts of our lives, including our family's breakdown. But faith can help us trust that the Lord *is* in control, as sovereign, *and* is immanently present with us in our suffering. He fills our suffering with his presence, incorporating past events and memories into a greater life-story that is *good*—the story of Christ's enduring love for us. Faith gives us a new outlook on life that helps us navigate the effects of past suffering in a different, transformed way. This kind of healing takes time, so if you find yourself in the dark place of suffering, trust in the *slow* work of God who helps our eyes adjust to the darkness, to see his love in the experiences of our lives.

Reclaiming the Familial Language of God

As we saw in the previous chapter, some ACODs struggle with accepting and integrating within themselves the familial language of Scripture and Church teaching because of their difficult family backgrounds. In light of this, we need to reexamine and renew our understanding of God as a good and faithful Father who is *transcendent* but also *immanent*.

God transcends any earthly reality that is compared to him, including familial concepts such as "Father." He cannot be simply equated to our parents or to any human reality, nor can he be reduced to or altered by the examples of family, love, marriage, and parenthood that we have experienced. Having a father who has abandoned us does not and cannot change who God is as Father. Having a mother who was uninterested in us does not and cannot change the tenderness of God the Father's love for us, depicted in Scripture with maternal imagery, nor does it change Mary's love for us as our Mother. Experiencing parental divorce does not and cannot change Christ's loving union with the Church, depicted as a faithful marital union (Eph 5:21–33).

At the same time, God in his immanence is "closer to me than I am to myself," as Saint Augustine wrote. In the Incarnation, God (the Divine Son, the Second Person of the Trinity) becomes fully man and enters human reality as a child in a family. God not only describes himself in familial language, but he *lived* family life fully in the heart of the Holy Family.

With this in mind, central to understanding properly our faith's familial language for God is that the revered, familial titles for God revealed in Scripture, such as "Father," *analogously express something true and essential about God's nature*, within an ever-greater dissimilarity to and transcendence of created reality.[3] Jesus revealed God as Father in a new and profound way: "he is eternally Father in relation to his only Son, who is eternally Son in relation to his Father."[4] In other words, it is no coincidence that Scripture and Church teaching consistently use familial language when describing God and truths of the faith. Human fatherhood and motherhood receive their ultimate meaning from God's Fatherhood (see Eph 3:14–15) but also, in an imperfect but real way, reveal something true and meaningful about who God is as Father. Thus it would be a mistake to jettison or avoid these terms.[5]

Marriage and parenting, like all human relationships, will never perfectly image God's love, but their deepest God-given purpose is to reveal as fully as possible the lasting love of God for his people. Family breakdown hurts so profoundly in part because of the noble calling of fatherhood and motherhood to image God's faithful love, and the sadness when that calling is not lived out.

Instead of avoiding familial terms about God because they bring up pain experienced in our earthly families, ACODs can reflect on the *gift* that this divine familial language and reality is. Encountering God as our Father,[6]

[3] For more on this theological topic, see the treatment of this theme by the Fourth Lateran Council, as found for example in Jacques Dupuis, ed., *The Christian Faith: Doctrinal Documents of the Catholic Church*, 7th ed. (New York: Alba House, 2001), 153.

[4] *Catechism of the Catholic Church* (CCC), no. 240.

[5] See ibid., no. 239.

[6] This includes the analogous understanding mentioned above and described well in the Catechism: "[God] transcends human fatherhood and motherhood, although he is their origin and standard." Ibid., no. 239.

Mary (as well as the Church) as our Mother,[7] and Christ in union with the Church as a marital and familial reality can help *purify* our notions of marriage, family, and parenthood. It can help rediscover the true source of these earthly relationships, and can deepen our faith in God. The *mirror* of these images of God's love may be broken in our families, but the *reality* that it was called to reflect remains forever.

We who are baptized are given a *new family* and become beloved children of God. We see this beautifully in the Our Father prayer and in Nicodemus' desire to be "born again" (Jn 3:1–21). It is here, dwelling in the familial love of Christ and the Church, that we can heal and recover not just our understanding of God, but also of ourselves.

Rediscovering God's Reliable Love as a Good Father

Faith entails the risk of trusting another: "What God asks of us is, as it were, an advance of confidence. He says to us: I know, you don't understand me yet. But trust me anyway, believe that I am good, and dare to live by this trust."[8] ACODs can struggle mightily with trust because trust has been broken by one or both parents. But faith and trust in God is not blind; it is based on something solid and certain: his love for us, which he definitively revealed to us in Christ.

God loves us first by creating us, and then by revealing his love further in Christ. He is not a disinterested or neglectful parent but a loving Father who seeks us before

[7] See ibid., nos. 963–75, 2030, 2040.

[8] Joseph Cardinal Ratzinger, *Co-Workers of the Truth: Meditations for Every Day of the Year*, trans. Sister Mary Frances McCarthy, S.N.D., and Reverend Lothar Krauth (San Francisco: Ignatius Press, 1992), 64.

we even turn to him. Pope Francis says that God's love is trustworthy because he has kept his promises in Christ:

> The history of Jesus is the complete manifestation of God's reliability. If Israel continued to recall God's great acts of love, which formed the core of its confession of faith and broadened its gaze in faith, the life of Jesus now appears as the locus of God's definitive intervention, the supreme manifestation of his love for us.... *Christian faith is thus faith in a perfect love, in its decisive power, in its ability to transform the world and to unfold its history.* "We know and believe the love God has for us" (1 Jn 4:16).[9]

We can have faith in Christ and lean on him for security because he has loved us reliably, with a perfect love. Our faith is not in our flawed self, parents, family, relationships, or church community, but instead in Jesus' perfect love shown definitively in the Cross and the Resurrection. His perfect love counters and is greater than all sins, scandals, and wounds.

Discovering (or rediscovering) God's trustworthiness can bring deep healing to adult children of divorce, as we see in Stephanie's story. Her father's abandonment of his family when she was two years old was the first of many experiences of abandonment and unreliableness by him. She says that her earliest childhood memory is of herself as a little girl "sitting on the loveseat in our living room, looking out the window ... waiting ... watching ... hoping he shows up ... but utterly expectant of the coming disappointment."[10]

This cycle of anticipation and disappointment has continued throughout her life: "On my birthday this year, my

[9] Francis, encyclical letter *Lumen Fidei*, June 29, 2013, no. 15 (emphasis added).

[10] Stephanie Gulya, "The God Who Shows Up," *Life-Giving Wounds* (blog), June 1, 2021, https://www.lifegivingwounds.org/blog/the-god-who-shows-up.

father failed to show up again or to do more than text me. I am tempted to yet again make excuses for his behavior ... I *know* deep down in my soul there has to be a better way." Despite the many little "deaths" of abandonment over the years, Stephanie continued heroically to strive for some type of relationship with her father. Caught in the tension of either making excuses for her dad or drowning in the pain, she found a third way infused by faith:

> There it is: a ray of light, a shard of hope ... the wound and the healing, side by side, held together on the Cross by Christ. For the first time in my life, by the grace of God, I don't want to run from this tension. I thought this journey was ripping my heart apart, but instead it has been stretching so it can be filled with Love and Mercy itself. Now we come full circle. I sit. And wait. How long? I don't know. This time, I don't wait with the burden of disappointment on my shoulders. I wait for the God who shows up.

Through faith, Stephanie discovered a different kind of fatherhood in God than what was present in her earthly example of fatherhood: God is a Father *who shows up*, whose love is reliable. Her faith gives her a new, freer way of living with her pain so it has less of a hold on her heart. She can rest in the peace of God, who doesn't disappoint her. Even though the wounds remain, faith is beginning to heal her heart.

Father John Baptist, too, experienced a significant deepening of his faith in God the Father following his parents' divorce. We heard part of his story in the previous chapter, how for a time after his earthly father left, he felt unable to call God "Father." But later, he writes: "Several months after my parents separated, at the Christmas Midnight Mass, the priest ended his homily: 'God loves you.'

And in prayer, I heard God the Father speak to me: 'I love you.' These were not only *sacred* words spoken to me; they were *sanctifying* words."[11]

As sanctifying words, they transformed not just what he thought about God the Father, but what he thought about himself. He was God's beloved son, and knowing this truth transformed his entire way of acting and being. He discovered the healing gift of faith and went on to reflect that this also was a recovery of his identity:

> As children of divorce, we have experienced a sense of abandonment from our parents. We have experienced a feeling of not being "at home" because the home that we grew up in became a house-divided or a house-emptied. But the language we learn by faith is the language that only God, Our Father, can teach us. They are the *sacred* words that Our Savior, Jesus Christ, taught us. And they are the *sanctifying* words that are written on our hearts by the Holy Spirit in baptism—that sacred and holy day when God spoke and said to us: "You are my beloved son." This is not merely human speech; this is *divine* speech. It is the sacred language of divine love.

Finding a Home in the Church, the "Family of Families"

Pope Francis exhorts church communities to become "a family of families."[12] Many in our parish communities, including children of divorce, lack a solid, reliable family to turn to. ACODs are eager for reliable guides and

[11] John Baptist Hoang, O.P., "A Reflection on the Words 'Father' and 'Son' for Those Who Have Been Hurt,'" *Life-Giving Wounds* (blog), December 22, 2021, https://www.lifegivingwounds.org/blog/father-and-son.

[12] Francis, apostolic exhortation *Amoris Laetitia*, March 19, 2016, no. 87.

mentors for the life of faith and discipleship. Priests and religious brothers and sisters in particular can provide a witness of spiritual fatherhood or spiritual motherhood for those without fathers or mothers in their lives. Heather wrote about the effect a priest's solicitous care had on her: "All of these acts of love by a spiritual father were like a consistent witness to God's love for his children .... It's not the kind of love I witnessed from a father growing up. It has been extremely healing."[13]

Faithful mentors (clergy and lay) can also give adult children of divorce practical guidance in the spiritual life, which is often important since many from broken or dysfunctional homes did not have reliable guidance about prayer or matters of the faith. The witness of a vibrant relationship with God can inspire someone struggling to trust God fully, or someone who has previously sensed hypocrisy or lukewarmness in other believers.

The Communion of the Saints

Our Christian community is not just with those on earth, but with the Church Triumphant, our family in Heaven. Jennifer shared the importance of the saints for a major breakthrough in her healing journey. For her, they became her "spiritual parents":

> God gave me two beautiful spiritual parents: Saint Teresa of Avila and Saint John of the Cross. I turned to them in my abandonment and ... I learned about God's love for me from their exhortations on contemplative prayer and

[13] Heather Strickland, "Mass Suspensions and Abandonment: The Gift of Spiritual Fatherhood," *Life-Giving Wounds* (blog), May 15, 2020, https://www.lifegivingwounds.org/blog/mass-suspensions-and-abandonment-the-gift-of-spiritual-fatherhood.

> supernatural marriage. Saint Teresa taught me, "prayer and comfortable living are incompatible," and Saint John taught me, "Where there is no love, put love, and you will draw out love." Instead of seeking to dispose of the cross as a child of divorce and seeking comfort, I followed their holiness and put the love of Christ where there was no love, no more marriage between my parents, and found an even greater love, one that healed and restored me.[14]

Others discover in Saint Joseph, as Heather puts it, "a father who stayed."[15] And there are many saints (including perhaps some lesser-known men and women) who lived holy lives in the midst of family dysfunction; they include Saint Felix of Valois, Saint Eugene de Mazenod, and Saint Martin de Porres, among others.

The Eucharist: Sacrament of Unity

For a disciple, communion with Christ begins in baptism and is increased by all the sacraments, but especially the Eucharist, by which "the unity of believers, who form one body in Christ, is both represented and brought about."[16] Dan experienced the reality of the Eucharist as the sacrament of unity in a special way at World Youth Day in Toronto (2002). Here, Eucharistic adoration and Sunday Mass took place in a gigantic airfield. A million young pilgrims from all over the world gathered together

[14] Hidden Daughter of Carmel (pseudonym), "My Parents' Divorce Left Me an Orphan, but God Became My Refuge," *Life-Giving Wounds* (blog), July 16, 2020, https://www.lifegivingwounds.org/blog/my-parents-divorce-left-me-an-orphan-but-god-became-my-refuge.

[15] Heather Strickland, "St. Joseph: A Father Who Stayed," *Life-Giving Wounds* (blog), March 16, 2021, https://www.lifegivingwounds.org/blog/st-joseph-a-father-who-stayed.

[16] *CCC*, no. 960; Second Vatican Council, Dogmatic Constitution on the Church *Lumen Gentium*, November 21, 1964, no. 3.

to celebrate joyfully. It was a world gathered together in prayer and peace, a world *united* by something greater than man—Jesus Christ. Here was the unity that Dan was seeking, a unity that could heal the effects of the disunity he felt in his family. In that gigantic airfield, Dan experienced the Church as the sacrament of unity, a truth experienced again and again at Mass and Eucharistic adoration. And he experienced the Church as a family who cares for him, a family founded upon the Holy Family. Christ offers the same invitation to each person: "Come, be healed by rediscovering through faith the Church as *your* family."

Christ offers the same invitation to each person: "Come, be healed by rediscovering through faith the Church as your family."

A Non-ACOD Spouse's Perspective: Growing in Faith Together

BETHANY: One of the biggest blessings of our marriage is sharing the faith together and helping each other grow closer to God. It was eye-opening for me to learn about the ways in which having a broken family could affect someone's relationship with God; what a sad consequence! In view of that, it's remarkable to me what a strong faith Dan has, a faith that's been tested in the fire and proven worthy. We're both conscious of the treasure of our faith, our marriage's lasting foundation. As one of our mentors said to us, "The best gift of yourself you have to give to your future spouse is 'God in you' by sharing your faith in prayer and all of the other ways that faith can permeate family life." Something I can offer to Dan as the "non-ACOD" spouse is to learn from all that he's learned on his faith journey through some difficult moments, such as the feeling of having his prayers for his family's unity go unanswered. Having wrestled with that serious topic, Dan has so much hard-won insight to offer our children and me when this difficulty with prayer occurs in our own faith lives. His faith has truly been tested and purified, and this is a great gift to our faith life together. It makes me a more faith-filled spouse. Likewise, I know Dan has taken time to learn from my faith through my own struggles and prayer life.

We have discovered how important it is to grow *together* in the faith and we try to avoid having completely separate faith lives. My faith journey and way of praying may be different from Dan's, and that's okay. We try to work through awkwardness and encourage each other, especially when we face suffering, whether it comes from the woundedness in our families or something else. There have been plenty of times when Dan has picked me up in the faith, and vice versa. Lastly, I'm grateful for Dan's desire to witness God's faithful love to our children, especially since he didn't witness an image of unity growing up. While we don't do that perfectly, it's a great joy to share with our children about the love of God and how important he is in our marriage and in our lives.

5

The Wound of a Broken Identity

O Lord, *you have searched me and known me!*

—Psalm 139:1

In the biographical crime movie *Catch Me If You Can*, Leonardo DiCaprio plays the part of real-life con artist Frank Abagnale Jr., whom we first meet as a happy kid living with his father Frank Sr. and his mother Paula. There is clearly love present in this marriage, and we hear an oft-told story about how the couple met and fell in love. However, due to his father's financial difficulties and his mother's affair, Frank Jr.'s parents decide to divorce when he is a teenager. His parents tell Frank Jr. about their decision in a scene that movingly depicts the real difficulties that children of divorce face in relation to their identity:

Divorce Lawyer, *to Frank Jr.* Many times, these decisions are left up to the court, but that can be very expensive, Frank, for people fighting over their children.

Paula. Nobody's fighting. Look at me, Frank, nobody's fighting.

Frank Jr. looks toward his father and mouths quietly, "What's going on? What's going on?" His father looks imploringly at him, not saying anything.

PAULA. Do you understand what we are saying to you, Frank?

Frank Jr. shakes his head no.

PAULA. Your father and I are getting a divorce.

FRANK SR. Nothing's going to change. We're still going to see each other.

PAULA. Stop it, Frank, please don't interrupt.

DIVORCE LAWYER, *showing Frank Jr. the divorce papers.* Frank, you don't have to read all of this stuff, as most of this is for your parents, boring adult business, but this paragraph right here, this is important because it states who you are going to live with after the divorce, whose custody you will be in.

PAULA. And there is a blank space right here.

DIVORCE LAWYER. Now, I want you to go into the kitchen and sit at the table and put a name down; and you can take as long as you want, but when you come back into this room, I want to see a name on that line.

Frank Jr. freezes and starts shaking. We see, foreshadowed, him running away from the situation right after this encounter.

FRANK SR. Frank, just write down a name and this will all be over. It's going to be okay.

FRANK JR. Dad, what name?

DIVORCE LAWYER. Your mother or your father. Put the name there. It is as simple as that and don't look so scared as it is not a test. There is no wrong answer.

Frank Jr. refuses to answer, but abruptly gets up, dashes out of the house, and runs away to catch a train.

It is worth noting that the director of *Catch Me If You Can*, Steven Spielberg, is an adult child of divorce, which perhaps helps to explain the authenticity of the child's perspective throughout the film.[1] Frank Jr. is given an

[1] Spielberg's 2022 film *The Fabelmans* is his semi-autobiographical depiction of his own parents' divorce.

impossible dilemma, from which he flees. Choosing to live with either parent *is* a wrong answer; there is no right answer, and the tension he feels is palpable.

This scene shows a fundamental dilemma that every child of divorce faces: the wound to his identity. The child, as the visible embodiment of his parents' union, always negotiates his identity in relation to his mother and father and their union, no matter how brief or flawed. While the parents can often move on from the past union to a new life with new partners, the child can never extricate himself from his origin. His parents' contribution to who he is is indelibly written into his appearance, his mannerisms—into his very DNA. To be sure, the child's identity transcends his parents and their union, but it is shaped by this relationship in fundamental ways.

The wound to identity is often missed by those commenting on the effects of parental divorce on children, as it is not easily quantified. Andrew Root, a theologian and adult child of divorce, argues that as a society we tend to see the main challenges for children of divorce as either a "problem of thinking correctly (e.g., 'the divorce was not your fault')" or a problem of "maintaining social solidarity (what social theorists have called 'social capital'),"[2] for example, the need for well-enforced child support laws. While acknowledging the value of these goals, Root highlights what he calls the "ontological" depth of the wound.[3] That is, for children of divorce, a significant source of suffering comes from the question, "Who am I?" that may anguish their inner lives and provoke questions even at the level of their existence and their being-in-the-world—to use the philosopher Martin Heidegger's concept—since the wound involves the

[2] Andrew Root, *The Children of Divorce: The Loss of Family as the Loss of Being* (Grand Rapids, Mich.: Baker Academic, 2010), xix.

[3] Ibid., xviii–xix.

split of the very people who helped to bring them into the world.

The wound of a broken identity is at times invisible but at other times visible in sadness, lack of self-worth, insecurity, and so on. It's essential to understand the wound to identity and find healing here, by recovering our truest identity as children of God, before moving on to other topics such as love, emotions, virtue, boundaries, and forgiveness.

Who Am I? What's My Place in the World?

The child, as the visible embodiment of his parents' union, faces a unique crisis vis-à-vis parental divorce or separation. His parents' union has been severed, but he is still intimately connected to both of them forever. As a result, his parents' break-up raises questions about his identity, like "Who am I now?" and "To whom do I belong?" Or more specifically, "Who am I, as the fruit of this union, when the union not only no longer exists but was rejected by one or both parents?" Existential and ontological questions like these can lead to a deep sense of insecurity regarding identity and place in the family and the world.

This is why comments by one or both parents such as "I never should have married your father" or "I never loved your mother" can be devastating to a child. The child thinks to himself, "What does that mean for me? I never would have been born if you never married." He can see those comments as implying, "I wish you were never born," even though his parents likely neither intended nor envisioned such a meaning.

Or children of divorce may question their worth, wondering, "Why was I not worth the effort and sacrifice to stay together and work on the marriage?" This feeling of rejection can be exacerbated if one or both parents enter new unions, perhaps with new children, and the original children feel superseded.

Torn between Two Parents and Multiple Worlds

For ACODs, the wound of a broken identity can be described in part as being split between their two parents. As sociologist Elizabeth Marquardt says, children of divorce feel torn "between two worlds."[4] Instead of the parents forging one common world for the child to live in, the child must travel between two worlds, two homes with different rules, moral codes, religious views, family dynamics, secrets, traditions, and opinions. In other cases, the child is raised in one home with his custodial parent and wonders about the inaccessible life in the other home of the absent or noncustodial parent.

ACODs may also have to navigate between their parents' divergent feelings about and readings of the divorce or separation—a disorienting experience. Parents may give different reasons for why the divorce happened, have conflicting versions of the divorce timeline, intentionally withhold key details, overshare, or lie about events. One parent may speak glowingly about the positive benefits of the divorce, while the other never wanted the divorce and is miserable. Some parents try to insist that the child accept their version of events and perceive it as an act of disloyalty to accept any other version.

Further, children of divorce may have to navigate or travel between their parents' ongoing dysfunctions and arguments with each other, which do not always end with the divorce. Parents may continue to be bitter, resentful,

[4] See Elizabeth Marquardt, *Between Two Worlds: The Inner Lives of Children of Divorce* (New York: Crown Publishers, 2005).

and blame the other spouse through angry, defensive diatribes to the child whenever something related to the divorce comes up. This animosity can occasionally go so far as one parent threatening to withhold love or access if the child chooses to have a relationship with the other parent. The pressure on a child asked to "choose sides" between two people with whom he will always be connected is excruciating.

Legal custody processes can further exacerbate the child's feeling of being torn between two parents. As in *Catch Me If You Can*, some children are asked for input about which parent they want to live with, while others are just told what will happen. In the most heartbreaking cases, neither parent wants custody of the child, so they let the court decide. Custody arrangements themselves vary widely, from splitting time precisely down the middle (half the week here, half the week there), to work week and weekend arrangements, school year and summer arrangements, or holidays and "ordinary time" (so to speak). Arrangements can be negotiated and changed multiple times as the children grow and their parents' lives change. Adding to the complexity, various siblings can have various custody arrangements, further dividing the family. Remarriages or subsequent divorces lead to more changes and transitions. In truth, many children of divorce have to navigate not just *two* worlds but *several* worlds.

Many children of divorce have to navigate not just two worlds but several worlds.

In the midst of this familial complexity, the child finds himself responsible for reconciling his parents' different worlds into one identity, a task that can lead him to feel overwhelmed and dis-integrated. As Andrew Root puts it, "When there are two family worlds, the child is asked to do the impossible. To find his being in two opposed worlds, he is asked to be two people."[5]

Emotional Homelessness

All of these transitions and losses can lead to a sense of emotional homelessness, the feeling that children of divorce have of not quite fitting into either their father's or mother's new worlds. They don't feel at home in either because neither is the united home of their origin. One ACOD describes it this way: "I felt like I was like the toy Magna-Tiles. I wasn't essential to either home or life. Just like a Magna-Tile, I clipped in at one home and then clipped out and moved to the other home. Each one went on, whether I was there or not."[6] ACODs can feel uprooted, overlooked, forgotten, and alone, even when at home. According to Marquardt's study, children of divorce were three times more likely to agree with the statement, "I was lonely a lot as a child."[7]

The feeling of emotional homelessness is amplified when it coincides with literally losing one's childhood home or losing access to one's belongings during frequent transitions. A house and material goods are not mere "backdrops," especially for children, but instead (ideally) represent security, joy, happiness, memories, family, and love. Christians with a sacramental worldview can well

[5] Root, *Children of Divorce*, 85.

[6] She shared this analogy in a presentation at a Life-Giving Wounds virtual support group meeting.

[7] Marquardt, *Between Two Worlds*, 139. See also a similar conclusion about the correlation between being a child of divorce and loneliness in Xiaoyu Lan, "Disengaged and Highly Harsh? Perceived Parenting Profiles, Narcissism, and Loneliness among Adolescents from Divorced Families," *Personality and Individual Differences*, no. 171 (March 2021).

understand that material things can communicate invisible meaning, such that the visible "stuff" in a home is invested with invisible meaning, having become signs of love and stability. So, moving away from a childhood home (without both parents), or losing treasured childhood belongings in the chaos of transitions, is a major emotional loss. Several ACODs have shared with us the feeling of relief they felt when they moved to college and finally had all their essential belongings in one place. For Dan, it was tremendously healing to move into our first home together after we got married, *one* unified home that we shared.

Abandonment

Divorce or separation is often experienced by children as abandonment. This could mean literal abandonment, when one parent leaves entirely. In these situations, 80 percent of children lose frequent contact with the noncustodial parent (usually the father).[8] Many ACODs recall the exact moment a parent left the family and that memory is hard to think about even decades later.

Even when both parents maintain a relationship with the child, he can still feel a sense of abandonment, even at a very young age. One divorced parent told us that after her husband left, her child, who was three years old at the time, said, "Daddy gone. Daddy no love me." Even in a best-case scenario, when a child of divorce has two loving, compassionate, and involved parents, the time spent with one parent is now a reminder of the absence of the other parent.

The post-divorce sensation of abandonment and loss, as an existential fact for the child, is one of the tragic legacies of divorce that might not be talked about frequently, or

[8] Frank Furstenberg, "The Life Course of Children of Divorce: Marital Disruption and Parental Contact," *American Sociological Review* 48, no. 5 (1983).

even noticed, but inwardly affects practically every experience of the child. Dan remembers feeling this acutely in the years that followed his parents' separation, and he still feels it occasionally even decades later. When he's with his mother, he misses his father, and when he's with his father, he misses his mother. In such moments, perhaps at an otherwise festive occasion, he finds himself thinking, "I really just want to have time with both of my parents, here. I'm sad that I am forced, again and again, to choose between them and have half as much time as I would like with both of them." The loss of time together and lack of shared experiences can feel especially acute at holidays or at events that used to be attended by both. An ACOD might recall happy memories of both mom and dad together, but now the occasion has been transformed by the lack of one parent. In addition, an ACOD may feel alone in his sadness because he's often the only one feeling the other parent's absence as a loss. Even if both parents do occasionally share a rare experience together with their children after divorce, this exceptional circumstance is not the same as prior to the divorce because the child is aware of the division that still exists between his parents.

The Loss of Childhood, Play, and Rest

In the aftermath of their parents' divorce, many ACODs had to grow up quickly and become what Marquardt calls "little adults."[9] Parents in crisis often turn to their children for emotional and practical support. The child may look after many of the emotional and material needs of the parent, rather than receiving guidance and support

[9] Marquardt, *Between Two Worlds*, 33–54.

himself. Parents and other adults may have encouraged these behaviors by complimenting the children on how mature, self-reliant, and resourceful they were, without seeing their inner discomfort at taking on roles that should have been handled by their parents. In psychological literature, this phenomenon has been described as "inversion parenting" or "parentification."[10]

The responsibilities inherent in "inversion parenting" can increase children's anxiety and create false guilt; they may feel like the well-being of the whole family depends *completely* on them, and if they fail, the family will disintegrate even further. Several ACODs have told us that they felt they couldn't cry as children because they had to be strong in front of their parents, but admitted that they cried by themselves.

Many ACODs also remember losing times of play or even losing the *ability* to play because they were so focused on being caretakers for others. This is lamentable because there is an inherent goodness to play. It reinforces to a child that he is loved simply because of who he is, not because of anything he does. In play, parents can delight in simply *being with* their children. Play often involves a sense of wonder, with children being allowed to express their unique personalities. For many people, some of the fondest memories of childhood are playing with their families. But often an adult child of divorce remembers a clear "before" and "after" a particular crisis, separation, or divorce, when he no longer had time to play or just be a kid with his parents.

Later in adulthood, it can be difficult for ACODs to rest and have leisure, to *just be*. It may be a struggle to take

[10] See, for example, Louise Earley and Delia Cushway, "The Parentified Child," *Clinical Child Psychology and Psychiatry* 7, no. 2 (April 2002): 163–78.

off adequate time from work simply to delight in family and friends. Some may fill their time with distractions, and their hearts and minds may feel restless all the time. This inability to rest and to play can affect the ability to receive joy. For Christians, this struggle to have rest and leisure should be a reminder of why God set aside the sabbath (the Lord's Day) for rest, as a *commandment.*[11]

Fierce Independence

Taking on too much parental-like responsibility, being in survival mode during family crises, and not being able to rely on our parents or siblings often lead ACODs to be very independent. We may pride ourselves on this independence, and the ability to care for others is laudable. But these scenarios can also create a fierce and unhealthy independence, an inability or unwillingness to depend on another person for help, love, affirmation, and working through our feelings. As a result, we don't seek out help, healing, relationships, or love as much as we need to. This attitude of doing everything for ourselves bypasses the virtue of reciprocity in friendship and love by eliminating the need we all have to be receptive to another who loves and cares for us. Fierce independence may manifest as self-sacrifice, taking care of everyone except ourselves. Or it may lead to "looking out for number one," being controlling toward others, and being willing to cut people completely from our lives who upset us or impede our goals in any way.

Fierce independence may also include seeing reliance on God as a weakness. After all, where was God when I needed

[11] For more on the sabbath and the commandment to rest, see Sonja Corbitt, *Just Rest: Receiving God's Renewing Presence in the Deserts of Your Life* (Notre Dame, Ind.: Ave Maria Press, 2021).

help? We would rather ignore the reality of God, reduce God to a moral ideal, or do God's work for him rather than trust and be dependent on him. Fierce independence sets us up for inevitable failure because we cannot possibly do everything on our own; we are fundamentally relational beings who need others and God. This failure can then cause guilt and shame for not being strong enough to do everything on our own. We can slip into self-condemning thoughts such as "I am worthless, useless, or irrevocably damaged." An appropriate love for self begins to evaporate, leading in turn to low self-esteem, sadness, or worse, despite insisting that we have it all together.

Fierce independence is the denial of a healthy dependence upon others, while enmeshed dependence means becoming so invested in relationships that one loses a healthy sense of self.

Enmeshed Dependence

If fierce independence is the denial of a healthy dependence upon others, then its opposite would be *enmeshed dependence*, which means becoming so invested in relationships that one loses a healthy sense of self, detachment, and independence from others. Enmeshed dependence is different from a healthy dependence *within* independence, and different from mutually reciprocal friendship that necessitates a whole and healthy self to give and to receive love.

Enmeshed dependence sometimes manifests as codependence, which can take different forms and can result from many causes. Originally, codependence referred to people whose lives were affected negatively by someone who experienced drug or sexual addictions, alcoholism, or compulsive disorders, but in recent years the term has been broadened to apply to other unhealthy relationships.[12] Codependency in this broader sense can be described as an excessive psychological or emotional reliance on someone to the point that the sufferer does not have a clear sense of self outside of this relationship and therefore obsesses over controlling the other's behavior. This other person becomes "everything" even to the point of usurping God's place.

There are several reasons why ACODs can find themselves in relationships of enmeshed dependence. First, as we have mentioned, in the aftermath of divorce, parents need to rebuild their lives from the ground up and are often in survival mode, which may result in leaning too much on a child for support. Many children naturally want to help by taking care of their parents and siblings, but they can become *excessively* concerned for them and feel responsible for the needs and moods of their parents and siblings. The child may become obsessed with how the parent and siblings feel and will do anything to keep the peace.

Another reason that enmeshed dependency can occur is that when the child is reeling from the divorce, he's uncertain about whether his legitimate needs will be met. He might think, "If my mother or father can divorce and leave the family, then any good thing can be taken away from me as well." Unfortunately, whether it be due to a parent's own wounds, mental illness, emotional immaturity, or another cause, some divorced parents lack an ability to affirm, care for, and love their children. Children then seek in earnest whatever little affirmation or love they

[12] See Melody Beattie, *Codependent No More: How to Stop Controlling Others and Start Caring for Yourself* (Center City, Minn.: Hazleden, 1992), 31–37. This book includes a checklist for self-evaluation of codependency tendencies, which can be helpful for self-awareness.

can receive from such a parent. They become enmeshed with the parent and seek to please him in the hopes of being noticed, affirmed, and loved.

Slowly, their sense of worth, purpose, and feelings become *dependent* on how well they can please their parent(s). When they cannot achieve a good mood or outcome, just like the fiercely independent child, they too can fall into self-condemning thoughts, low self-esteem, or depression. Their very selves and well-being are lost in the process, despite appearing as if they have it all together. As in the case of fierce independence, enmeshed dependence impedes the mutuality of love that is necessary for healthy relationships.

Enmeshed individuals can become worn out, tired, isolated, and angry. While it is noble for these self-sacrificial persons to assist their families in times of crisis—and maybe it was truly needed for a time—it becomes a problem when they excessively focus on their parents' or siblings' needs and moods to the point that they derive their identity from the reactions of these others. This eliminates the healthy independence and detachment that is necessary for living a truly reciprocal relationship, in which we freely give and receive from another who loves and cares for us.

Destructive Labels

After the divorce, ACODs may feel negatively labeled. Parents sometimes label their children as being like or unlike the ex-spouse, which can cause a fear of rejection: "My mom divorced my dad, so if I'm compared to him, what does mom think of me?" Many children of divorce recall trying to "tone down" being like one parent around the other parent out of fear of disapproval. Some agonize about looking like the other parent and fear that these physical features will be an unwelcome reminder of what one parent doesn't like in the other parent.

Other ACODs have shared with us how they felt labeled by church members, friends, classmates, relatives, and others, as *less than* those who came from loving, intact homes. One ACOD told Dan that he felt he needed to pretend to everyone that he was from a "normal" family, so he never talked about his parents' divorce. Another was worried that people would judge him based on his parents' divorce and mistakes. This prevented him from acknowledging his hurt and how it impacted his life and identity.

In a bid for their parents' love and affirmation, siblings may label each other, too. This especially occurs if there is a deficit in love and affirmation from parents following the divorce. The labels siblings give each other may include some of the commonly agreed-upon labels or roles that members of dysfunctional families take on: hero, scapegoat, lost child, mascot, caretaker, enabler, golden child, and so on.[13] Other labels could include the favorite child, unfavored child, or the troublemaker. Sadly, these labels and this competition for the parents' love potentially create rivalry or distance between siblings.

Fundamentally, labeling a person is wrong because it takes one aspect of that individual and makes it his entire identity. He then feels trapped in a false, one-sided, limited identity. We are always more than our wounds, and more than a label that's assigned to us.

[13] For two extended treatments of the various roles that children in dysfunctional families can take on, see Lindsay C. Gibson, *Adult Children of Emotionally Immature Parents: How to Heal from Distant, Rejecting, or Self-Involved Parents* (Oakland: New Harbinger Publications, 2015); Sharon Wegscheider-Cruse, *Another Chance: Hope and Health for the Alcoholic Family* (Palo Alto, Calif.: Science and Behavior Books, 1989).

The Mixed Label of "Victim"

One label that should to be addressed directly is the label of "victim." Sometimes ACODs feel uncomfortable when it is mentioned that they were true *victims* of their parents' divorce or separation. "Victim" here acknowledges that they were objectively hurt by their parents' decisions. But some ACODs have been labeled as victims in an inaccurate sense. Someone may say in response to an expression of pain, "Stop playing the victim." "Victim" in this case implies that a person is manipulative, ungrateful, stuck in the past, or wrong for thinking he was wounded. (Gaslighting can be at work here as well, a manipulative attempt at making a person question his perception of reality.) This sense of "victim" is harmful because it shames a fellow human being and reduces him to a stereotype.

Another faulty use of "victim" is to see ACODs as *only* damaged. We are *always* more than our wounds. As Saint John Paul II said, "We are not the sum of our weaknesses and failures; we are the sum of the Father's love for us and our real capacity to become the image of his Son."[14] Our fundamental identity is not "children of divorce" but "children of God." *All* people are wounded in some ways, first by original sin that leaves the mark of concupiscence (an "inclination to sin"[15]) and then by whatever sins and trials we have endured. A one-sided attribution of "damaged" prevents serious discussion of the hurt experienced ("victim" in an accurate sense) because it questions whether it is good to acknowledge the pain and find healing. We *are* wounded, but we are also so much more.

[14] John Paul II, Homily at the Seventeenth World Youth Day, Toronto, July 28, 2002.

[15] *Catechism of the Catholic Church* (CCC), nos. 1264, 1426.

Identity and the Special Situation of Declarations of Nullity

The situation of declarations of nullity can have a unique impact on the identity of the children involved. As we said in chapter 1, the goal of the declaration of nullity process is for the Church to discover and reveal the truth about a particular couple's presumed marriage, in order for all involved to have clarity about the situation. For some people whose parents both civilly divorced and then went through the declaration of nullity process, it can be a relief to know the objectively true status of their parents' marriage, especially if one or both of them have entered new unions.

But for some of us whose parents received a declaration of nullity (i.e., their presumed marriage was not in fact a valid marriage), this can raise deep questions about our identity and lived experiences as children in the family. Alex, whose parents received a declaration of nullity, describes the situation in this way:

> For children in these situations (like me), it's difficult enough to have to deal with our parents getting divorced. To then be told that our parents' marriage was invalid in the first place? This can often be confusing and even more devastating than the civil divorce .... We might ask ourselves: Who am I, now that my parents' marriage has been declared invalid? Am I a mistake in some way? And what should I think about all of the memories and experiences we had growing up when my parents were presumed to be married? Were they real?[16]

Having a marriage determined not to be valid does *not* make children of the union "illegitimate," nor does it hold

[16] Alexander Wolfe, "Eternal Father, Strong to Save: A Reflection on Annulments," *Life-Giving Wounds* (blog), August 19, 2021, https://www.lifegivingwounds.org/blog/eternal-father-strong-to-save-a-reflection-on-annulments.

any real relevance in terms of their belonging to the Church, their access to the sacraments, or anything to do with their lives as Christians. It could potentially apply in certain legal scenarios, but that lies beyond the Church's purview. Also, the Code of Canon Law is clear that "the children conceived or born of a valid or putative marriage are legitimate."[17] *Putative* means presumed to have been valid, which is the case for every marriage being examined by the tribunal.

The deeper question, though, is, "What does it mean for me, for my identity, that my parents' marriage never existed?" As Alex noted, having one's parents' marriage declared null can make family memories and experiences seem "fake." Were we even a "real" family? As an additional layer to the wound, in certain scenarios, such as when a child was conceived out of wedlock, the child can later gain the realization that his coming-into-being was actually a reason why his parents' marriage was determined to have been invalid (due to lack of genuine freedom at the time of the wedding). This is, understandably, a significant, unique burden to bear about one's existence and identity, and we'll address this in the next chapter.

[17] Code of Canon Law, no. 1137.

6

Life-Giving Identity in Christ

This is my beloved Son, with whom I am well pleased.

—Matthew 3:17

Divorce and separation raise deep ontological and existential questions around identity for the children involved. Realizing the value of addressing these issues from a mental health perspective, we believe there is another powerful source of healing: our faith in Christ. Our task is to go *beyond* the broken origins of our parents' relationship to rediscover and reclaim our deeper, truest identity as God's created and beloved son or daughter, capable of great love.

First and foremost, we must root deeply into our hearts the firm conviction that God says to each and every one of us: "*It is good that you exist.*" No human being is an accident or a mistake. Each and every person is willed into existence by God through the mediation of his parents. Saint John Paul II says: "Man's coming into being does not conform to the laws of biology alone, but also, and directly, to God's creative will .... *God "willed" man from the very beginning, and God "wills" him in every act of conception and every human birth.*"[1] This is true no matter the

[1] John Paul II, Letter to Families, February 2, 1994, no. 9 (emphasis in original).

circumstances of a person's conception. Some pregnancies are described as "unplanned," "unwanted," "untimely," or even a "mistake." We know more than one adult child of divorce who has been burdened by the belief that their inopportune conception either influenced their parents' decision to marry, a decision they later regretted, or led to marital difficulties that contributed to the eventual divorce. Children in these situations can feel like their entrance into the world was a dilemma, a problem, and even the *cause* of their parents' later split; what a heavy burden to bear! As we said in chapter 1, this is *false guilt* because no child is ever responsible for his parents' relationship difficulties or decision to divorce.

From God's perspective, while parents' reception of a new child can vary widely, from unfiltered joy to fear to rejection, *no child* is a "mistake" or an accident. A child is *always* a gift, and parents' attitude toward their children ought to be a profound sense of being *entrusted* with a new human person that God willed into existence.

It is good that you exist. No matter our flaws or what others say about us, *we are good and we are loved.* Our worth transcends our abilities, accomplishments, and utility to others. This is an essential truth for those ACODs who struggle to believe in their inherent worth as *good.* It is also an important truth for those who have difficulty living an identity beyond the "role" they play in their family or the "labels" they were given by their family or others.

In the Creation narrative, God creates man and woman on the sixth day and says that "it was very good" (Gen 1:31). There is a sense here of God *rejoicing* in every person's creation by declaring it *very* good, putting an "exclamation point" on it, so to speak. Man, created in the image of God, is "the only creature on earth that God has willed for its own sake."[2] God created man not to serve a utilitarian purpose but simply *to be*, to share in God's life. He created man out of love and for love. It can be healing to reflect on examples of "affirming another's goodness" in order to internalize how God sees us. We see affirmations of goodness when a new couple simply enjoys being in each other's presence; when a long-married couple has no need for words to feel connected; when a new parent gazes at his sleeping newborn, delighting in her tiny fingers and furrowed brow; when your friend listens wholeheartedly to your story, with no further agenda beyond the sharing of hearts.

No matter what good (or not so good) things we have done, God tells each and every one of us: "*It is good that you exist!*" This is the voice that matters the most, the voice of truth we need to listen to in order to counter all of the identity lies spoken from the outside and inside.

Becoming God's Children in Baptism

We find the source for an even deeper sense of identity in a transformative event shared by all Christians: our baptism. In baptism, God the Father claims each one of us as his beloved son or daughter. Through baptism, all sins that keep us from communion with God are forgiven and we become adopted members of God's family, configured to Christ and welcomed into the communion of the Church.

We can reflect on Jesus' baptism as a touchstone for our own identity. The Catechism says that at Jesus' baptism, God the Father proclaimed "his entire delight in his Son."[3]

[2] *Catechism of the Catholic Church* (CCC), no. 356. See also Second Vatican Council, Pastoral Constitution on the Church in the Modern World *Gaudium et Spes*, December 7, 1965, no. 24.

[3] CCC, no. 535.

Remember, Jesus' baptism takes place *before* he begins his public ministry. So the Father's delight is not in any of Jesus' miracles, astute homilies, or accomplishments, but simply in who Jesus is, as his Son.

At our baptism, too, God the Father expresses his delight in us, and we receive a new identity as sons and daughters of God. To each one of us, the Father says, "This is my beloved son [or daughter], with whom I am well pleased" (Mt 3:17). *This* is the only "label" that counts, the truest and deepest identity we have. In baptism, we are given a new relationship with God. No longer is he only our Creator; he is now our Father.[4] We read in Scripture, "See what love the Father has given us, that we should be called children of God; and so we are" (1 Jn 3:1).[5]

Raised from the waters of baptism, we are now *children of God*. This phrase is so familiar that there is a danger of losing its true depth. But if we reflect for a moment, we can see how startlingly dramatic it is: children *of God*? How can that be? We are fleshly creatures, born of a human mother and father. For the Creator of the universe to claim us as his own, as his children ... what higher honor could be imagined?

We never stop being our parents' children; that is part of our identity forever, in both good and challenging ways. But it is neither our only identity nor our deepest one. Our parents are not our creators; they mediated life to us. Man is "not the master of the sources of life, but rather the minister of the design established by the Creator."[6] In the reflections of Saint John Paul II on the "genealogy of the person," we see that everyone traces his

[4] See ibid., no. 1243.

[5] See also Rom 8:14–17 and Gal 4:4–7, among other passages.

[6] Paul VI, encyclical letter *Humanae Vitae*, July 25, 1968, no. 13.

origins back to God's Fatherhood, the source and model of all human parenthood.[7]

Our response to our parents' "yes" to life should be one of profound gratitude, even in painful situations when we know, or suspect, that that "yes" was given begrudgingly or as an afterthought. But our gratitude to our Creator should exceed even our gratitude to our parents, since it was God who willed us into existence. In our baptism, God claims us as his own children, giving us a place in his perfect, forever family. As the Psalmist says, "For my father and my mother have forsaken me, but the LORD will take me up" (Ps 27:10).

For ACODs, our baptismal identity is an important truth to reflect upon, especially when we're tempted to believe lies about our identity. Rebecca shared with us that her primary struggle in life has been the question of identity that arose from her parents' divorce:

> When my parents split, it was as though a beautiful puzzle with its many intricate pieces broke apart, and then me, a part of that puzzle, consciously or subconsciously tried to find a new puzzle to fit into. This constant internal scanning—looking for new people to belong to and find my identity in—brings an unnecessary layer of pressure and anxiety into any relationship that is just starting to grow and bloom, whether that be a new friendship or new dating relationship .... This anxiety made me feel crazy.[8]

Rebecca cried out to Jesus for consolation, healing, and peace. She writes:

[7]John Paul II, Letter to Families, no. 9.

[8]Rebecca Smith (pseudonym), "Identity in Christ: Finding My Worth After My Parents' Divorce," *Life-Giving Wounds* (blog), May 26, 2020, https://www.lifegivingwounds.org/blog/identity-in-christ-finding-my-worth-after-my-parents-divorce.

> Our good Jesus said to me in prayer, in a moment I won't ever forget: "*Find your worth only in Me, for you are the daughter of a King.*" This beautiful consolation from our Father was the key that unlocked *everything* for me. Of course we all say that we belong to God, that we are his children ... but do we really, truly believe it? Daughter of a King. Son of a King. This identity is a real, physical, substantial, living, present identity! My worth, my identity, begins, continues, and ends, in Jesus.

Rebecca was beginning to discover in a deeper way her baptismal identity, and to accept this reality in her heart. She goes on to share: "Finding my identity in Jesus is not always easy .... But Jesus is constantly reminding me of the primacy of my relationship with Him .... If I start my day off saying, 'My main identity is in Jesus, and I first and foremost belong to Him,' my attitude shifts and the things my parents do or say do not have the same negative influence on my peace as they did before."

ACODs can be tempted to believe that they are fundamentally broken, but God says to this lie: "You are much more my beloved than broken."

Children of a Perfect and Everlasting Marriage

In our baptism, too, we are incorporated into the Church and brought into a perfect and everlasting marriage, that of Christ and the Church.[9] As the Catechism says, "Baptism,

[9] The image of the Church as the Bride of Christ is an ancient image with Scriptural foundations and various layers of meaning and application. In one sense, we can see ourselves as children of the union of Christ and the Church, with the Church as our Mother. In another sense, we ourselves, as the Church, are called to live ever more as the faithful Bride, reflecting Christ's faithful love for us (and reflecting the faithful response of Mary and the saints). When seen from the perspective of the Church on earth, the Church as Bride is also in the process of becoming ever more sanctified and

the entry into the People of God, is a nuptial mystery; it is so to speak the nuptial bath which precedes the wedding feast, the Eucharist."[10] We see this mystery further illuminated in Saint Paul's extended meditation on marriage in Ephesians 5, part of which reads: "Husbands, love your wives, as Christ loved the Church and gave himself up for her, that he might sanctify her, *having cleansed her by the washing of water with the word*, that he might present the Church to himself in splendor" (Eph 5:25–27, emphasis added). Baptism welcomes us into a Love that will never fail: Christ's faithful, superabundant love for his bride, the Church. In baptism, we are given the dignity of being children of a perfect and everlasting marriage. No matter what kind of flawed image of marriage (or lack of image entirely) we saw in our parents' marriage, as part of God's family we receive a perfect image of marital love: Christ's never-ending love for the Church.

In baptism, we are given the dignity of being children of a perfect and everlasting marriage.

This truth deeply impacted one adult child of divorce we have accompanied. "I'm the girl without a mom," Teresa would often tell herself because her parents divorced when she was four and her mom eventually abandoned the family. This damaged identity led to feelings of abandonment by God, suicide attempts, promiscuity in her teens, entering a toxic marriage at twenty-five that ended with her husband's death from drug overdose—and three abortions.

faithful, with her perfection being realized fully in the eschaton (after this world has passed away). In any case, viewing ourselves as children of this perfect and everlasting marriage between Christ and the Church is one, though not the only, way of looking at the image of the Church as the Bride of Christ and applying it to ourselves.

[10] *CCC*, no. 1617.

Teresa made it out of this harrowing darkness by choosing to receive help for her many wounds in her early thirties. She eventually entered a healthy marriage, converted to the Catholic faith, and found security in her identity as a woman immersed in Christ's love. Teresa says:

> When I pray in adoration, the first thing that Jesus puts on my heart is "Perfect love casts out fear" (1 Jn 4:18). Jesus already loves perfectly. We cannot ask for anything more than God himself to love us perfectly. When you look at the Divine Mercy painting, the rays that come from his heart are straight coming down to us. There are no breaks, no cracks, no broken rays. Just straight clean rays. God is pouring his love out to us without pause. It is us, when returning the rays of love back to Jesus, our rays are broken, cracked, and nicked. Those are our wounds from our parents' divorce, and if you are like me, also from the choices I have made because of my woundedness. Those nicks, cracks, and brokenness in my love for God is where Jesus wants me to let him in, as only He can make my rays straight again .... In return [for Jesus' perfect love], I will become the person Jesus calls me to be. Someone who knows she is loved and will no longer live a life of fear, but a life as a beloved daughter of God. Perfectly made, perfectly loved.[11]

Teresa now uses her past wounds and healing journey to be Christ's rays of light for others as a leader in our ministry.

Beloved by Mary, Our Mother

At the foot of the Cross, Jesus gave Mary as Mother to the Church by entrusting her to "the disciple whom

[11] Teresa (pseudonym), "Child of Fear to a Child of God," *Life-Giving Wounds* (blog), September 14, 2022, https://www.lifegivingwounds.org/blog/child-of-fear-to-a-child-of-god.

he loved": "When Jesus saw his mother, and the disciple whom he loved standing near, he said to his mother, 'Woman, behold your son!' Then he said to the disciple, 'Behold, your mother!'" (Jn 19:26–27). *Behold, your mother.* Those words are spoken by Jesus to us as well. In Mary, we have a mother who is ever-ready to receive, console, guide, and encourage us. We can seek protection under her mantle in our times of crisis, and we can entrust the burdens of our heart to her.

Mary's maternal care is a blessing to all Christians, but perhaps in particular to those whose mothers did not provide reliable maternal care. While it is less common for mothers to abandon the family entirely, or not to be the custodial parent, it does happen. And wives are more often the ones who commence divorce proceedings,[12] creating circumstances in which children may feel abandoned or betrayed by their mothers, or blame their mothers for breaking up the family (justly or not). Mothers going through the crisis of divorce, too, may find it more difficult to give their children the time and emotionally attentive care they desire (and that most mothers desire to give), perhaps in part because of newly strained financial circumstances following the divorce for many single mothers.[13]

Many adult children of divorce find special comfort in Mary's title as *Our Lady of Sorrows*, as does Daniel, writing about an image of Mary under this title: "Her eyes, puffy from her tears, revealed an immense sorrow, mourning,

[12] See, e.g., "Women More Likely Than Men to Initiative Divorces, But Not Non-Marital Breakups," American Sociological Association, August 22, 2015, https://www.asanet.org/women-more-likely-men-initiate-divorces-not-non-marital-breakups.

[13] Newly single mothers and their children are five times more likely to live in poverty than families in married households, according to 2021 U.S. Census data on income and poverty. "Table S1703," U.S. Census Bureau, accessed August 21, 2023, https://data.census.gov/table?q=Poverty&tid=ACSST1Y2021.S1703.

loneliness, and a kind of tiredness from experiencing such pain. In her eyes I saw the pains I had experienced over and over since my parents separated 16 years ago. I saw my own hurt, tears, loneliness, and tiredness." Drawing near to Our Lady of Sorrows helped Daniel not to feel alone in his own sorrow, and courageously address his wounds: "When I saw that Our Lady was welcoming me to mourn with her, to join my sufferings to hers and the Lord's, how could I refuse? As she beckoned ever so gently as the perfect mother that she is, and as I would return to her holding the body of our Lord, my fears of those wounds began to dissipate."[14]

An Identity That Can Never Be Lost

Our baptismal identity is *indelible*, meaning that it can never be removed or lost; baptism can only be celebrated once.[15] Even when we sin, our deepest identity endures.[16] When we are the "lost sheep," God pursues us vigorously (see Lk 15:4) and never gives up on finding us.

What a comfort this permanence of baptismal identity can be to ACODs who wonder about their place in their families or in the world! While they will literally always be their parents' children, practically and emotionally they can sometimes wonder, "Am I even their child anymore?" Or more to the point, "Do they even consider me their child anymore?" But these are not questions we need to ask of God: "Can a woman forget her sucking child, that she should have no compassion on the son of her womb? Even these may forget, yet I will not forget

[14] Daniel A. (pseudonym), "The Compassion and Promise of Our Lady of Sorrows," *Life-Giving Wounds* (blog), November 4, 2021, https://www.lifegivingwounds.org/blog/the-compassion-and-promise-of-our-lady-of-sorrows.

[15] *CCC*, no. 1271.

[16] Ibid.

you" (Is 49:15). Even though sometimes in our earthly families we may feel that we have to earn our place as a valued member of the family, this is never the case with the family of God. Through our baptism, we are claimed by God the Father forever.

Rediscovering a New Childhood

As we said in the previous chapter, one challenge faced by many ACODs, vis-à-vis their identity, comes from having to grow up too quickly, becoming "little adults," and missing out on parts of their childhood like play, rest, and being trustfully dependent on others. Jesus calls *all* of us to "become like children" (Mt 18:3), no matter our age: not childish, but *childlike*. Doing so can help us both heal from whatever loss of childhood we experienced and also live out fully our *new* childhood as children of God. It can also help heal the ways that our childhood, through the continuity of time preserved in our memories and bodies, continues to impact us into adulthood.[17]

At the heart of our identity is being loved "just because" by God, and being loved "just because" is what children do best. As Jesus said, "Unless you turn and become like children, you will never enter the kingdom of heaven" (Mt 18:3). Two practices in particular can help us accept

[17] For those who have experienced trauma, memories of the traumatic event(s) can feel as if they are occurring in the present—even if the trauma happened a long time ago. Because of our neurology, these events are not only recorded in our memories but in our very bodies, a point explored in depth in Bessel van der Kolk, *The Body Keeps the Score: Brain, Mind, and Body in the Healing of Trauma* (New York: Penguin, 2014). Therefore, when we pray for emotional healing, we should also pray for bodily and spiritual healing. They all go together.

and live in this new childhood: frequently recalling our baptismal identity and living what could be termed "the virtues of childhood."

Recalling our Baptismal Identity

Choose and use a short "identity phrase."

Come up with a short, meaningful phrase that reminds you of your baptismal identity. It could be as simple as "Beloved" (recalling Jesus' baptism). Or it could be a phrase like "I'm a child of God," "I'm a beloved son or daughter," "I'm a child of a perfect and everlasting marriage," "I'm more than my wounds," "It is good that I exist," and so forth. Speak this truth aloud or internally every day, but especially in instances when lies or fears about your identity surface. You could write out this word or phrase and put it somewhere to recall it often: on the bathroom mirror, a water bottle, a lock screen on your phone, and so on.

Reverently pray the Sign of the Cross.

Every Catholic prayer begins with these words: "In the name of the Father, and of the Son, and of the Holy Spirit, Amen." This oft-repeated prayer can become rote, but it is a powerhouse of grace! At our baptism, the cross is traced on our foreheads by our parents and godparents, a sign that marks "with the imprint of Christ the one who is going to belong to him."[18] This sign *claimed us for Christ* and communicated our belonging to him.

When we pray the Sign of the Cross, we reaffirm this belonging. We are saying again, with our gestures and words, that we know to whom we belong. We reaffirm our place within the communion of the Holy Trinity,

[18] *CCC*, no. 1235.

that never-ending expression of love that is the communion of the Three Divine Persons. Take the time to say the Sign of the Cross prayerfully and with focus; this gives numerous chances throughout the day to remember our deepest identity. This "remembering" is made even more vivid when we bless ourselves with holy water at the same time, either when entering a holy space or at home, recalling our baptism.

Celebrate your baptismal anniversary.

Everyone's birthday deserves to be celebrated, but everyone's birthday *as a child of God* deserves to be celebrated, too! If you don't know your baptismal anniversary (because often "family records" can become lost or overlooked when families are in crisis), you could call the parish where you were baptized. Or if that isn't successful, simply choose a day, perhaps a saint's feast day that is important to you; the Lord knows!

Parents, it's never too late to start this tradition with your children as a beautiful way of affirming *their* deepest identity. In our family, we celebrate our children's baptismal anniversaries by getting out their baptism boxes (with cards and mementos), lighting their baptism candle, and having a sweet treat. Even if you don't have any of the visible "signs" of your baptism anymore, you can still celebrate through prayer, and indulge in a celebratory treat. This would be a perfect day to spend time reflecting on how beloved you are by the Father!

Practicing the Virtues of Childhood

Cultivate trustful dependence and receptivity.

Children, especially very little children, are completely at home with being dependent on others; babies are dependent on their parents for practically every need. And even as they grow, children in a stable, loving home know instinctively that they can turn to their parents for their material and emotional needs. Cultivating greater trustful dependence and receptivity in our lives helps us rediscover our childhood. Trusting dependence means being bold in intercessory prayer, asking God for our needs and truly believing that he will meet them. Receptivity can be practiced in prayer by receiving God's words in Scripture, meditating upon them, and carefully discerning what he is saying to us and calling us to do in a particular situation or circumstance. In relationships, trustful dependence and receptivity can be developed by giving others the opportunity to care for us, even in small ways, and not immediately stepping in to meet every need of ourselves and others. It can feel vulnerable to be dependent on others, but it also provides opportunities for growth in intimacy and mutual care.

Practice joy and gratitude.

One of the first phrases children learn is "thank you," and they are often quick to express wonder and awe, even at seemingly simple things. Children don't tire of hearing the same song or joke again and again, but have a wellspring of joy for the things that delight them. In the spiritual life, joy and gratitude can be practiced by praising God for things he's done, by singing a hymn or song, or by writing a poem or letter of gratitude to God. In our relationships, we can cultivate joy and gratitude by proactively delighting in happy moments, by *trusting* the joy (and not immediately resorting to cynicism), and by expressing our gratitude, whether out loud or in our hearts. It can also be truly healing for adult children of divorce to discover (or rediscover) a hobby, an activity in which they find joy for its own sake, and delight in that time of pleasure.

Take time for rest and Eucharistic adoration.

Childlikeness is also found in resting, releasing our hold on having to *do* in order to prove ourselves to others or to God. Work was created for rest and not rest for work.[19] In a healthy environment, children are not workaholics but love to play; they are content with *being*, knowing they are loved "just because." We are beloved sons and daughters of God and creating time for rest and contemplation helps us remember this identity. We can do this by following God's commandment to keep the sabbath holy (Ex 20:8) and setting aside intentional times of worship and prayer on Sunday as the apex of all rest, as well as spending time with family and friends doing non-"labor" activities.[20] Rest affirms that your identity is more than your accomplishments and work and that your work doesn't all depend upon you.

Rest affirms that your identity is more than your accomplishments and work and that your work doesn't all depend upon you.

One spiritual practice that can help "re-set" our hearts and remind us of the importance of rest is regular Eucharistic adoration. During adoration, we can *just be* with Jesus. There are numerous guides for a Holy Hour that

[19] See Josef Pieper, *Leisure, the Basis of Culture*, trans. Alexander Dru (San Francisco: Ignatius Press, 2009).

[20] See *CCC*, nos. 2168–2195. Cardinal Ratzinger points out that God created the Sabbath to order all creation, including work, toward rest, which finds its fullest realization in the worship of God. See Joseph Cardinal Ratzinger, *In the Beginning*, trans. Boniface Ramsey, O.P. (Grand Rapids, Mich.: Eerdmans, 1995), 27–32.

can help those who appreciate a guided prayer routine, but adoration is also a beautiful opportunity to reclaim your inner childhood identity, time to *just be*. It can be a time to simply rest in our Lord's presence, basking in his love for us as we are. Jesus in the Blessed Sacrament is there waiting for us, seeking to love us and be with us. We can sit with him, even in silence, just feeling his love. Perhaps we can speak to him as "Abba, Daddy," and share our hearts with him as we would with a loving Father.

Responding to the Special Situation of Declarations of Nullity

ACODs whose parents received a declaration of nullity may have particular questions about their identity, since their parents' marriage not only ended civilly but was also declared by a Church tribunal never to have existed. Children in this situation need to internalize the truth that no matter what happened in their parents' relationship and presumed marriage, their existence is *good*. Alex, whose parents received a declaration of nullity, gives this encouragement to others: "You are not 'illegitimate,' a mistake, or flawed; you were lovingly conceived in the heart of the eternal Father, who can never be 'nullified' and who made you in *absolute freedom*!"[21]

Further, for children in this situation, even though a *valid marriage* did not objectively exist between their parents, genuine family love and togetherness could have still been *true* in their home. The lack of a valid marriage does not negate

[21] Alexander Wolfe, "Eternal Father, Strong to Save: A Reflection on Annulments," *Life-Giving Wounds* (blog), August 19, 2021, https://www.lifegivingwounds.org/blog/eternal-father-strong-to-save-a-reflection-on-annulments (emphasis in original).

every aspect of their shared life together. Canon lawyer Father Christopher Singer puts it this way: "A declaration of nullity does not in any way negate the genuine love, devotion, and friendship that the man and the woman had for each other and their children. It's just that, for sometimes complex human reasons, that love did not reach the level of becoming sacramental and indissoluble."[22]

A Non-ACOD Spouse's Perspective: Helping Your Beloved Rediscover His or Her Identity

BETHANY: I'm grateful that Dan did a great deal of healing work before we met, especially through the timely help of caring priests and other mentors. I say this because issues related to identity can quickly become challenges for relationships. If someone feels constrained by certain roles from his childhood, it can be hard to discover the *real* person beneath those survival-focused roles. Understandably, Dan (like me, to an extent) still has moments where his identity feels shaky, or a new difficulty with his family causes him to lose his firm grip on his identity as God's beloved son. For us, the key touchstone has been prayer: continual remembering of our fundamental identities through our relationship with our loving Father. Encouraging each other to pray, and praying together as spouses, helps us continually accept and maintain strong baptismal identities, which in turn allows our love and intimacy to be stronger as well.

[22] Ibid. In the case of putative or presumed marriages in the Church between a baptized Catholic and an unbaptized person, a declaration of nullity would mean that the presumed marriage was never a valid, natural marriage.

I try to affirm Dan beyond what he "does" for our family or others, too. I affirm who he *is* in his good virtues, like patience and kindness, and how much I enjoy his company (he has a *great* sense of humor). We set aside times where we can just *be* together. Sundays are as free of work as possible, to have extra time for prayer and leisure. This carries over into our family life, too. We love to "waste time" with our children, as Pope Francis is fond of saying.[23] It may seem like a small thing, playing with our children, but we know that many adult children of divorce simply did not have this childhood joy, so we don't take it for granted. In making time for play and leisure with our family, we help cement our identities beyond our function or utility.

[23] See, for example, Pope Francis, Meeting with Recently Confirmed Young People during Pastoral Visit to Milan, March 25, 2017.

7

The Wound of a Damaged Vision of Marriage and Unhealthy Self-Protection

What therefore God has joined together, let no man put asunder.

—Matthew 19:6

My parents divorced when I was very young, and as I grew into my teenage years, I never developed much interest in marriage or even dating. As a matter of fact, my life plan included becoming a single mother. I loved the idea of being a mom, but I couldn't picture myself married. I didn't dream about my wedding or my perfect husband ....

My mom has been married multiple times, and she told me that when she walked out of the church after her first wedding, she knew immediately that she had made a mistake. This thought haunted all of my dating relationships. I was 100 percent committed to never getting divorced, but I fully expected that when I got married, I would be very unhappy. I would suck it up and live with it. I thought that everyone who was married was going through life this way. After all, I hadn't met anyone who was in a happy marriage, as far as I could tell.[1]

[1]Joanna A. (pseudonym), "Healing a Mountain of Relationship Fears," *Life-Giving Wounds* (blog), September 25, 2019, https://www.lifegivingwounds.org/blog/stories-of-healing-a-mountain-of-marriage-fears.

Joanna's story here illustrates well the damage widespread family breakdown can do to ACODs in their own pursuit of love and marriage, including deep-seated anxiety and fear about relationships and dramatically altered "visions" of love, marriage, and family. For many, the *possibility* of a joyful marriage seems hopelessly out of reach. Is it any wonder that the marriage rate has fallen dramatically in recent decades, and that only 30 percent of young adults are married today, the lowest percentage ever recorded in the United States?[2]

Children of divorce and separation can have difficulties with starting and maintaining their own happy, healthy relationships. One adult child of divorce quoted by Elizabeth Marquardt put it this way: "If the most important relationship in your life, which of course is the one with your parents, is irretrievably broken at a young age, and one of the defining components of your life is that that core relationship was not there, you have to have fundamental trust issues."[3] These trust issues include the ways in which a person can keep himself partially closed off to others in an unhealthy way—a dynamic we call "unhealthy self-protection."

In this chapter, we will discuss the impact divorce or separation has on a child's vision of marriage and family and the self-protective behaviors often learned in the "school" of a broken family. In the next chapter, we'll

[2] "America's Families and Living Arrangements Tables: 2018," U.S. Census Bureau, accessed August 21, 2023, https://www.census.gov/data/tables/2018/demo/families/cps-2018.html. Judith Wallerstein's longitudinal study of children of divorce found that "forty percent of the men and women in this divorce study have never married, a figure that exceeds the national average for adults in this age group raised in intact families." Quoted in Judith Wallerstein, Julia Lewis, and Sandra Blakeslee, *The Unexpected Legacy of Divorce: A 25 Year Landmark Study* (New York: Hyperion, 2000), 289.

[3] Elizabeth Marquardt, *Between Two Worlds: The Inner Lives of Children of Divorce* (New York: Crown Publishers, 2005), 148–49.

reflect on how ACODs can recover the Church's beautiful vision of marriage and the family and heal from unhealthy self-protective tendencies in order to have greater confidence and success in their relationships.

Missing Out on the Roadmap of Love

Adult children of divorce or separation, by definition, did not see their parents live married love until "death do us part." They were not blessed with a living tableau of lifelong married love within which they could find stability and on which they could base ideas for their own future relationships. As one adult child of divorce put it, "Sometimes I feel like I don't know 'how to be married.' "[4] Their families educated them about relationships implicitly and perhaps explicitly, as all families do, but the lessons taught may have been more about love's fickleness and the pain relationships cause, rather than lessons about forgiveness, love as a total self-gift, self-sacrifice, perseverance in suffering, and the joy of love.

Think of children from families with loving, married parents as receiving a roadmap about love that, while not perfect, at least gives generally reliable directions toward the desired destination. In contrast, adult children of divorce are given a roadmap with whole sections missing, scribbled out, or wrong, leading them to dead ends. "There are times when I have struggled for lack of a blueprint," says one now-married adult child of divorce. "I just never saw my mom and dad do life together, day to day."[5]

[4] Leila Miller, ed., *Primal Loss: The Now-Adult Children of Divorce Speak* (Phoenix: LCB Publishing, 2017), 108.

[5] Ibid., 126.

Or ACODs may distrust the map entirely and think that the destination of stable married love isn't a real "place" but a fantasy or outdated ideal. With perseverance, God's grace, and timely guidance, many of them will avoid the false paths that brought their parents pain and suffering. And thanks to God's grace, the gaps in their received maps can become ways of growing closer to God and of avoiding false paths. But many others will struggle mightily with love because of missing out on that "map."

Fundamentally, divorce communicates the message that marriage is temporary and love is conditional. Instead of saying "for my whole life, in good times and bad," divorce says, "just for now." It says that promises and vows are not trustworthy.[6] These lessons are often internalized in the child's heart. Affairs—if they are part of the marital breakdown—give an anti-witness to the fidelity of marriage. And for couples that never got married and later split up, there was never even an acceptance of the totality and commitment that marriage entails.

Divorce communicates the message that marriage is temporary and love is conditional.

Research confirms the deleterious effect that divorce has on children's future marriages: "Marriages involving a partner from a divorced family were *four times* more likely to end in divorce than marriages in which neither partner

[6] There are situations, of course, where a spouse is unjustly abandoned against his or her will, or where separation and even civil divorce are necessary for the safety of the spouses or the children (as we discussed in the first chapter). In such circumstances, spouses who remain faithful to their marriage vows, even while living apart, give a tremendous witness to marital fidelity, one that is often hidden and sacrificial. This can be a deeply meaningful example for their children, despite the perduring brokenness of the family situation.

was a child of divorce."[7] And "when both husband and wife come from divorced families, the odds of divorce are at least *200 percent higher*."[8]

Children of divorce are also less likely to marry at all: they are 47 percent more likely to be currently cohabiting versus their peers from intact homes, and 61 percent more likely to favor cohabitation as a preliminary step to marriage.[9] In one study, a young man said that with cohabitation, you can "get to know the person and their habits before you get married. So that way, you won't have to get divorced."[10] But cohabitating generally does *not* help prevent divorce in future marriages: one study found that "those who cohabit before marriage are about 25 percent more likely to divorce than couples who married without cohabiting."[11]

These statistics are *not* destiny for any child of divorce; there is *always* hope for breaking generational dysfunction. But they are sober reminders that there *are* wounds in need of healing in order for ACODs to have their best chance at happy, lasting marriages.

[7] Paul Sullins, "The Tragedy of Divorce for Children," in *Torn Asunder: Children, the Myth of the Good Divorce, and the Recovery of Origins*, ed. Margaret Harper McCarthy (Grand Rapids, Mich.: Eerdmans, 2017), 34 (emphasis added). See also Nicholas H. Wolfinger, "More Evidence for Trends in the Intergenerational Transmission of Divorce," *Demography* 48.2 (2011).

[8] Richard Fitzgibbons, "Children of Divorce: Conflicts and Healing," in *Torn Asunder*, 54 (emphasis added). See also Nicholas Wolfinger, *Understanding the Divorce Cycle: The Children of Divorce in Their Own Marriages* (New York: Cambridge University Press, 2005).

[9] W. Bradford Wilcox, "The Evolution of Divorce," *National Affairs*, no. 1 (Fall 2009); see also Brienna Perelli-Harris et al., "The Rise in Cohabitation and Divorce: Is There a Link?," *Population and Development Review* 43, no. 2 (2017).

[10] Wilcox, "The Evolution of Divorce."

[11] Sullins, "The Tragedy of Divorce," 37. See also Anita Jose et al., "Does Premarital Cohabitation Predict Subsequent Marital Stability and Marital Quality? A Meta-Analysis," *Journal of Marriage and Family* 72, no. 1 (2010).

Unhealthy Self-Protection: The "School" of Divorce

Parents are their children's first educators in the "school" of life: how to be human and how to relate to others and to God.[12] While all families bestow both more desirable and less desirable legacies on children, some unique negative "lessons" are taught in a family where the parents' relationship did not last. We examine these here in order to understand better the specific effects family breakdown has on children's future relationships. In what ways does it become more difficult to live out our vocation to love and be loved? We group the "lessons" taught in a broken home under the general heading of "unhealthy self-protection." But first, an illustrative story to set the stage:

When we were in the process of adopting our oldest daughter, we attended a conference for foster and adoptive parents. The focus was on how best to parent "kids from hard places": children who had lost their biological parents at a young age, who had grown up in orphanages, who had experienced abuse and neglect, et cetera. Understandably, children who have faced serious trauma will exhibit behaviors that are challenging to caregivers. For example, a child may steal and hoard food, even in a home where there's plenty to eat.

One point that stuck with us, and which is relevant for understanding the behavior of *anyone* who has triumphed over past trauma and dysfunction, is that children "from hard places" should first have their ability to survive *recognized and honored*. A child steals food because he

[12] See *Catechism of the Catholic Church* (*CCC*), no. 1657; Pontifical Council for Justice and Peace, *Compendium of the Social Doctrine of the Church* (Washington, D.C.: United States Conference of Catholic Bishops, 2004), no. 212.

is desperately hungry, and it's almost impossible for him just to "flip a switch" and stop stockpiling food after he's out of a food-poor environment. (In this case, as in all cases of trauma, the effects can reach into the child's biology and brain circuitry as well.[13]) Yes, parents want their child to stop hoarding food; that's the goal. But the key is to see the frustrating behavior not as *bad*, or as a character flaw, and especially not as something intentionally meant to annoy the parents. First, parents should see the child as tremendously brave, a survivor. Secondly, parents should help the child see that his survival techniques are no longer needed because he is safe now in a healthy situation.

Adult children of divorce, too, have been through a crisis and have faced dangers—sometimes material ones like poverty and unsafe environments[14]—or the just-as-real emotional and relational dangers that occur within a disintegrated family: instability, abandonment, dismissal of emotions, and more. It is only natural that in a situation rife with such dangers, a child would try to protect himself. He would turn to what we could call "self-protective behaviors," like keeping potentially unsafe or untrustworthy people at arm's length or, in contrast, making friends quickly to hedge against pervasive loneliness (and breaking with these friends just as quickly, before *they* leave). We first affirm and *honor* the ways in which children of divorce have tried to survive, keep their identities

[13] See Bessel van der Kolk, *The Body Keeps the Score: Brain, Mind, and Body in the Healing of Trauma* (New York: Penguin Books, 2014).

[14] "Divorce strongly increases the risk of poverty for both mothers and children." Sullins, "The Tragedy of Divorce," 22. And, "One of the most dangerous places for a child in America to find himself in is a home that includes an unrelated male boyfriend." W. Bradford Wilcox, "Suffer the Little Children: Cohabitation and the Abuse of America's Children," *Public Discourse*, April 22, 2011, https://www.thepublicdiscourse.com/2011/04/3181/.

intact, and just *get through* the family chaos. Yes, children *are* resilient, sometimes amazingly so. But having to *be resilient*, having to find ways to cope with family turmoil, can leave lasting injuries that deserve attention.

Once grown and no longer in the same unsafe, insecure environment, the ACOD's self-protective behaviors may no longer help him but instead may hinder the development of lasting relationships. These behaviors become maladaptive, making it difficult to foster true intimacy. Self-protection becomes "unhealthy" when in *good* relationships behaviors, thoughts, or expectations impede *the mutual giving and receiving of love* that is necessary for these relationships to flourish. Unhealthy self-protection can take many different forms, which we will now outline.

Distrusting Joy

When you have witnessed the breakdown of your parents' marriage, it is hard to trust that any relationship can last. One survey found that 80 percent of ACODs fear that their own marriages may end in divorce, 72 percent believe that their parents' divorce affected their ability to sustain close relationships, and 52 percent said that they lack self-confidence in love relationships.[15]

For ACODs whose parents' low-conflict marriages ended, the family's split may have come as a tremendous shock to the children, who may not have known that anything was amiss (despite the parents being keenly aware of their relational difficulties). Children in high-conflict homes probably saw one or both parents erupt into anger and animosity out of nowhere or over seeming trivialities. In these homes, an otherwise happy day

[15] M. Gary Neuman, *The Long Way Home: The Powerful 4-Step Plan for Adult Children of Divorce* (New Jersey: Wiley, 2013), 14.

could unexpectedly explode into heated arguments. Having something good and stable implode without warning, and perhaps without clear reasons *why*, teaches the heart that any good thing can be taken away without notice—a recipe for increased anxiety not only in relationships but in life in general.

We can describe the resultant self-protective behavior as *distrusting joy*. Even when things are going well, they could suddenly change; the sunniest day could end in a surprise thunderstorm. To guard themselves and their hearts from being let down, many ACODs (often unknowingly) distrust the good and constantly analyze the environment for what could go wrong—waiting for the other shoe to drop all the time. It can feel impossible to *enjoy* a relationship when they are feeling anxious, scanning for every sign of impending doom. This propensity also makes it scarier to enter a relationship altogether.

Cynicism

Cynicism is a sad effect of the Fall; tempted by the serpent to question God's words, Adam and Eve doubted the goodness of God and his Fatherhood. A cynical approach to love and relationships is another self-protective behavior that ACODs may adopt. At its root, cynicism is protective because by not daring to believe that love could be *real* and relationships could *last*, the cynic avoids the risk and devastation of heartbreak; of course, he also cannot experience the joy of openhearted, trusting love. Cynicism takes many forms: it may look like keeping expectations for relationships very low; zeroing in on the challenging parts of a relationship, while deeming positive, life-giving aspects as rare or flukes; or abandoning a good relationship out of fear of eventual rejection.

Cynicism can also look like pondering "exit strategies," the cut-and-run plan for when a relationship (inevitably) goes south. A friend shared with us that when she and her husband argued, she would start calculating how much money she would need for her and the children to leave, where they would go, what to pack, and so forth. She felt genuinely shocked when she became aware of this automatically activated interior exit strategy. Another child of divorce said, "For the first few years of my marriage, I was very on-guard and prepared for my husband to leave. In fact, I expected it . . . . It wasn't that I wanted him to leave, but in my mind it wasn't even a question of *if* it would happen, but *when*."[16]

Someone approaching relationships cynically would, as you might expect, be less likely to commit to a long-term relationship or marriage to begin with. Once married, he may struggle to trust fully the other's love, impeding deeper intimacy and joy. Believing that relationships do not last, he feels it's safer not to try. He keeps expectations low and reserves parts of his heart and self from the other.

Romanticism

Romanticism or idealism is the "flipside" of cynicism. This self-protective mindset zealously refuses to engage with the hard parts of relationships that predictably bring some discomfort. For example, out of a desperate attempt to achieve stability, a person may focus only on the positive aspects of a relationship, ignoring glaring issues that must be addressed. The *right* relationship is seen as the "out," the fairytale ending—and the other person a savior who will fix all of the problems inherited from the family of origin. The *right* relationship will be conflict-free, virtually

[16] Miller, *Primal Loss*, 116.

effortless, and bring happiness without necessitating self-sacrifice, suffering, and perseverance. Someone with a romanticism mindset might relationship-hop, leaving a relationship when it becomes difficult, to start another that might finally be "the one," and so on. Of course, not even the best relationships are easy all the time. Good relationships and lasting marriages can help heal hurting hearts, but it is too much to expect another person—including your spouse—to solve *all* your problems. If you have an overly romantic approach, you may feel crushed, and eventually cynical, when relationships fail to be perfect or conflicts arise. Enmeshed dependence can occur due to your desire to do anything to keep the relationship going, even if your own needs are sidelined.

Romanticism can also lead to unhealthy lies about yourself ("I am not capable of love") or the other individual ("I've married the wrong person"). Shaina wrote about her struggles with romanticism: "The wounds of divorce tell me that anything less than a perfect marriage spells disaster. It means 'I have failed,' 'I didn't discern well,' [or] 'I must have married the wrong man.'"[17] What Shaina came to realize is that "the less than perfect marriage does not equal disaster" and that even good marriages take work, too.

Settling for Sub-Par Relationships

Some ACODs can be tempted to settle for relationships that are not the right fit for them or for someone who is not a good match for them. This partly comes from only

[17] Shaina Pia, "The Less than Perfect Marriage Does Not Equal Disaster: Godly Expectations for Love," *Life-Giving Wounds* (blog), September 2, 2019, https://www.lifegivingwounds.org/blog/stories-of-healing-the-less-than-perfect-marriage-does-not-equal-disaster.

seeing examples of grown-ups who exhibited unhealthy behaviors or made poor relationship choices, and partly from unhealthy self-protection. The deep-seated fear of losing another person or experiencing another relationship rupture is a strong motivator to stay with someone—anyone.

Researcher Judith Wallerstein shares the story of a young woman from a divorced home who lived miserably with a man for years despite the fact that he had no job, ambitions, or education. After finally moving on and happily marrying someone else, she tells Wallerstein that much of her rationale for staying with a man so obviously unprepared for a serious relationship was, "At least I know he won't betray me. At least I'm safe from that."[18]

Some ACODs, too, can struggle with a sense of unworthiness, thinking, "What *fully healthy* person would love someone with baggage like mine?" People in such relationships run the risk of not recognizing abusive behavior and staying in harmful, even dangerous situations (a complex subject worthy of extended treatment by experts).[19]

Repeating Unhealthy Patterns and Roles

Many adults find themselves repeating their parents' good and bad behaviors, mannerisms, and "quirks." But for ACODs, this can give rise to the fear that they will end up "just like their parents" and not succeed in their relationships either. It can feel nearly impossible to forge a new and different path from that observed in childhood.

ACODs may also notice that they play unhealthy "roles" in romantic relationships similar to those they played in their

[18] Wallerstein et al., *Unexpected Legacy of Divorce*, 29.

[19] For a robust Catholic response to domestic violence, see the resources of *Catholics for Family Peace*.

family growing up: the hero, the scapegoat, the lost child, the mascot, the caretaker/enabler, the golden child, and the clown, to name a few. During family chaos, ACODs may have needed these roles to help protect themselves and care for family members, but they are generally inappropriate in good, healthy relationships. We can see that there are good characteristics to some of these roles. For example, a peacemaker prioritizes peace in relationships. But this good could be taken to an extreme: the peacemaker could pursue peace at all costs, at the expense of his own legitimate needs or to the neglect of confronting conflict in a healthy way as a couple. A role held too tightly can also become an unhealthy foundation for his identity.

Someone who has grown accustomed to living an unhealthy or rigid role can tend to enter into relationships where those roles are reenacted. It is a comfortable—or at least familiar—type of relationship, offering a sense of safety in knowing what lines to say and what behaviors to perform. This dynamic can help explain why some people end up dating or marrying people who repeat some of their parents' serious flaws.

The Fear of Abandonment

Some unhealthy self-protective behaviors are directly related to the experience of abandonment in childhood. For ACODs, losing someone through the break-up of a relationship or the ending of a friendship may feel terrifying because it triggers the childhood memories of abandonment and reinforces the belief that they're unloved or unlovable.

It's not uncommon for ACODs to deal with the fear of abandonment in relationships by always being the first to leave. Sandy describes it this way:

> To overcome my fears of being left, I was always the first to leave a relationship; I hurt many people along the way. Leaving first was a form of self-preservation that was necessary in childhood (staying unattached) but became unhealthy behavior in my adult relationships. For many children of divorce, being the first to leave gives a sense of power or control that we felt was lacking at the time of the divorce or even into adulthood, for example having to accept new family dynamics, interact with people we would rather not, and accommodate our schedules to fit the needs of the various family members that are now a part of our world.[20]

The fear of abandonment may also result in possessiveness and jealousy. Again, Sandy shares her struggle: "I've also started to notice over the years how possessive I am of my friends and family members. If they start to get too attached to someone else, I feel threatened. It's hard for me to 'share' my friends and family members with others, even other people within my own family. I get jealous and fearful that I will lose them, their love, their loyalty, or my special relationship with them."[21]

Pursuing Sex and Other Pleasures in an Unhealthy, Sinful Way

Compared to peers from intact homes, children of divorce (especially females) are more likely to become sexually active at a younger age, have more sexual partners, and are more likely to have an early, untimely pregnancy or contract a sexually transmitted disease.[22] Why is this?

[20] Sandra Howlett, "How Fear of Abandonment Can Affect Your Relationships," *Life-Giving Wounds* (blog), May 15, 2021, https://www.lifegivingwounds.org/blog/abandonment.

[21] Ibid.

[22] See Vicki Thorn, "The Biological Effects of Divorce on Children," in *Torn Asunder*, 49. See also Ed Spruijt and Vincent Duindam, "Problem Behavior of Boys and Young Men after Parental Divorce in the Netherlands," *Journal*

One reason is that in the aftermath of their parents' split, children of divorce are more likely to seek affirmation, love, and affection anywhere they can get it, including in sex and physical intimacy. Others repeat a pattern of people-pleasing and do not want to disappoint their partner, regardless of their own values and feelings. And others fall into cynicism, believing that love will not last, so why not get the most "enjoyment" out of relationships?

Some ACODs have shared vulnerably that they have sought out sex, pornography, or masturbation as ways to numb the painful feelings caused by their family's brokenness. These behaviors become survival mechanisms to try to deal with the almost unbearable tensions in their family, and sometimes lead to addictions or compulsively acting on these sexual urges.[23] Other addictive-type behaviors can also serve as unhealthy coping techniques: workaholism, substance or alcohol abuse, overeating, eating disorders, overspending, and addictions to video games or other entertainment. With all of these, ACODs in some way seek to avoid the painful feelings caused by a broken home.

Unhealthy "Testing" of Relationships

Insecurity about relationships, and a deep-seated desire to feel safe in them, can manifest through "testing" relationships in unhealthy ways. Discernment is a healthy

of Divorce and Remarriage 34, nos. 3–4 (2005); R. F. Anda et al., "Adverse Childhood Experiences and Risk of Paternity in Teen Pregnancy," *Obstetrics and Gynecology* 100, no. 1 (2002): 37–45.

[23] See, e.g., John McLain, "Overcoming Pornography Addiction as an ACOD: Part 1," *Life-Giving Wounds* (blog), April 24, 2022, https://www.lifegivingwounds.org/blog/overcoming-pornography-addiction-as-an-acod-part-1; John McLain, "Overcoming Pornography Addiction as an ACOD: Part 2," *Life-Giving Wounds* (blog), May 8, 2022, https://www.lifegivingwounds.org/blog/overcoming-pornography-addiction-as-an-acod-part-two-pathways-to-healing.

way to test a relationship, and we'll talk about that in the next chapter. On the other hand, one unhealthy way of testing a relationship is cohabitation, considered by many as a "test run" to marriage: if we can handle this for a few months, a year, et cetera, then we are marriage material after all. As mentioned above, those of us from broken homes are more likely to cohabitate when compared with our peers from intact homes. But cohabitation is associated with greater marital instability and a greater chance of divorce.[24] It is also an unreliable way to discern a relationship because we become too emotionally, physically, and financially dependent, such that it is hard to break off a bad relationship or to acknowledge and address serious problems.

Beyond cohabitation, ACODs may find themselves "testing" a relationship—perhaps unconsciously—through instigating fights or doing obnoxious things to try to answer the question, "Does this person *really* love me? What if I'm not so pleasant? Will he leave me?" One child of divorce described it in this way: "Since the beginning of my own marriage, I have been 'testing' its permanency .... I have been playing 'I'll leave you before you leave me' ... for most of my life."[25] This causes unnecessary difficulties for an otherwise good relationship; it may even sabotage it as, understandably, the other party may not appreciate being continually "tested" in this way. It can thus end up as a self-fulfilling prophecy: if the relationship ends, the child of divorce considers it "proof" that it was doomed to fail from the beginning.

[24] Sullins, "The Tragedy of Divorce," 37. See also Jose et al., "Does Premarital Cohabitation Predict Subsequent Marital Stability and Marital Quality?"

[25] Miller, *Primal Loss*, 109.

Difficulty with Conflict

Adult children of divorce learned a variety of "lessons" about conflict in their "school of the home." Tragically, some grew up with frequent conflict, or even violence in their homes. They never saw disagreements handled with patience and love. They never saw forgiveness and reconciliation up close. Other ACODs never saw conflict handled well because they never saw conflict at all. In low-conflict marriages, the children may have been unaware of their parents' disagreements altogether and never saw problems worked out before the marriage ended.

Because of this, many ACODs enter relationships and marriage with fewer practical skills at handling conflict than their peers from loving, intact homes. This puts their marriages more at risk of breakdown. On the whole, children of divorce report higher levels of conflict in their marriages and are less likely to communicate constructively.[26] Judith Wallerstein notes:

> Because children of divorce don't know how to negotiate conflict well, many reach for the worst solutions when trouble strikes. For example, some will sit on their feelings, not mentioning complaints or differences until their suppressed anger blows sky-high. Others burst into tears and are immobilized or retreat into themselves or into the next room and close the door. But the most common tendency is to run away at the first serious disagreement.... This is because from the perspective of the child of divorce any argument can be the first step in an inevitable chain of conflict that will destroy the marriage. It's easier to run away.[27]

[26] Fitzgibbons, "Children of Divorce," 54. See also Pamela Webster et al., "Effects of Childhood Family Background on Adult Marital Quality and Perceived Stability," *American Journal of Sociology* 101, no. 2 (1995): 404–32.

[27] Wallerstein et al., *Unexpected Legacy of Divorce*, 56.

To ACODs, dealing with conflict can feel like navigating a minefield. Beyond learning skills to "do" conflict well, children of divorce also need to address and overcome potentially paralyzing anxiety about engaging in conflict at all.

Art, who grew up in a high-conflict home, tells a story about having dinner at his then-girlfriend's house.[28] At some point during the dinner, her father complained to her mother that there was too much garlic on the pizza. This comment made Art immediately feel anxious: "I'd seen this movie before and it's not going to go well!" But to his astonishment, his girlfriend's mother said calmly, "You're right. I did promise to tone down the garlic, especially when we have a guest over for dinner," and the meal continued on peacefully. "In my mind, it was a miracle," Art writes. After getting married (to this girlfriend), he had to "re-engineer" his way of responding to honest comments and disclosures, and to learn how to disagree and "do" conflict in a peaceful, happily married home, which he had never witnessed personally.

Fear of Getting Married and Having Children

Finally, many ACODs harbor lingering fears about marrying at all and about having children. "Marriage seems impossible," said one adult child of divorce. "I desire it, but I fear it."[29] The memories of their parents' divorce can remain vivid even years later. The extremely strong desire not to repeat those mistakes, and *definitely* not to

[28] Art Bennett, "My Dinner with Bill & Teje: On Re-learning Conflict and Communication as an ACOD," *Life-Giving Wounds* (blog), May 29, 2022, https://www.lifegivingwounds.org/blog/my-dinner-with-bill-teje-on-re-learning-conflict-and-communication-as-an-acod.

[29] Miller, *Primal Loss*, 110.

subject any child to the trauma of a broken home, can make adult children of divorce "freeze," unable to move forward with discernment or action concerning the life-altering decisions of marriage and childrearing.

Many ACODs harbor lingering fears about marrying at all and about having children. "Marriage seems impossible," said one adult child of divorce.

We have spoken with several ACODs who have dated someone for several years in a good relationship, but who feel virtually unable to take the next step and propose. Or some couples will put off having children for years, finding it difficult to trust that their marriage will last, or fearing that they may be bad parents or not prevent the kinds of wounds they experienced in their family.

In her longitudinal study of children of divorce, Judith Wallerstein found that two-thirds of her research subjects "have decided not to have children." She notes that "childbirth is down everywhere, but children of divorce who choose not to have children specifically cite divorce as the main reason."[30] She says ACODs can question their ability to parent well, saying things like, "How can I be a parent? Look at the upbringing I had," or "My life is too insecure to think about having a kid."[31] They also fear that children would not deepen their marital unity but bring disconnection. Notably, Wallerstein says of the adult children of divorce in her study that "no one cited a demanding career as a reason not to have children," which challenges a current popular assumption.[32]

[30] Wallerstein et al., *Unexpected Legacy of Divorce*, 67.
[31] Ibid., 68.
[32] Ibid.

The incomplete road map of love that ACODs received, combined with unhealthy self-protective behaviors they may find themselves exhibiting, makes it more difficult for them to achieve what is perhaps their most dearly cherished dream: forging a stable, joyful marriage and family life and breaking generational dysfunction once and for all. Let us pause and reflect that saying "yes" to marriage and being open to welcoming children are not just intellectual or "head" issues of agreeing with Church teaching (or not), or even issues of the will, definitively choosing for or against commitment and children. These issues also have much to do with the heart and the psyche, impacted by past pain and trauma. Without addressing those wounds, exhortations about the goodness of marriage and family can be quite literally incomprehensible.

As we'll discuss in the next chapter, ACODs who *do* achieve the dream of a stable marriage and happy family life are *excellent* witnesses to the joy of love. They have overcome so much to get to a place that many from healthy intact homes take for granted. And they are often remarkably committed to making their marriages last. This is a beautiful way in which their wounds can become truly life-giving!

8

Life-Giving Discernment and Love

Love is patient and kind . . . . Love never ends.

—1 Corinthians 13:4a, 8a

Remember Joanna from the last chapter? She was the adult child of divorce who had sworn off marriage in favor of single parenthood, haunted by her mother's experience and the lack of good marriages around her. But her story didn't end there. She did marry, and wrote, "Unlike my mother, I walked out of the church knowing that this was God's plan and not a mistake." She goes on to say: "Marriage has brought me so much joy and peace, more than I ever thought possible. God knew what I needed in order to heal, as he knows what each one of us needs. New difficulties and experiences continually reveal where I need more work, but at least now I know that healing is possible and is happening every day in my heart."[1]

What a remarkable change, moving from being fearful of marriage to proclaiming proudly how much joy, peace, and healing it has brought her! What made the difference?

[1] Joanna A. (pseudonym), "Healing a Mountain of Relationship Fears," *Life-Giving Wounds* (blog), September 25, 2019, https://www.lifegivingwounds.org/blog/stories-of-healing-a-mountain-of-marriage-fears.

For Joanna, the key elements in this change were deepening her life of faith and finding mentors and guides "to talk to and to offer advice as you work through your wounds and discern God's will." Her testimony illustrates why we opened with chapters about faith and identity and only now are looking at the impact divorce can have on a child's future relationships. It is important to heal *all* of our underlying wounds in our pursuit of love. And we need others on this journey who can guide, encourage, correct, and simply be with us.

In the first part of this chapter, we will discuss the hidden strengths ACODs can bring to relationships, and (re)discover God's vision for marriage, love, and discernment. In the second part, we will share practical advice for ACODs to overcome unhealthy self-protection and succeed in their relationships. While this chapter is primarily geared toward intimate relationships, much is applicable to friendships as well.

A Hidden Superpower

Often adult children of divorce come to marriage keenly feeling their lack. They may feel "less than" their peers from loving, intact homes, or feel that they bring too many problems to be worth a partner's trouble. They question whether love can last and whether *they* are capable of lasting love. They can feel empty-handed.

We know ACODs who were told they were not "marriage material" or were not asked out on dates because of their family's messy background. A friend of Bethany's once told her (not knowing Dan's family situation) that she would never have considered dating someone whose parents weren't still together.

Prejudgment like this is wrong, and we are sorry for anyone who has experienced this stigma. No one is reducible to his parents' mistakes (or his own), and we are always more than our wounds. In fact, many ACODs bring tremendous *strengths* to love, relationships, and marriage. They can possess an unshakeable conviction that marriage is *meant to last*, along with the fierce intentionality to make their own marriages enduring, healthy, and strong.

Consider that in Leila Miller's powerful collection of testimonies from adult children of divorce, *Primal Loss*, many contributors (the majority of whom are married) say things like this about the impact of their parents' divorces on their own marriages:

> The divorce has only strengthened my marriage. I don't want to repeat the mistakes of my parents. I work hard at our marriage and want so badly to model a holy, Catholic marriage for my kids.[2]

> [My parents' divorce] has made me *very* determined to have a God-filled relationship with my husband and to *always* think of how my children will be affected by everything I do. I will *never* divorce.[3]

> I vividly remember repeating the vow ... "for better or worse, in sickness and health, until death do us part." It was the only vow I've ever taken, and I meant it. *I meant it.* I was marrying for life. There was nothing, *nothing* that would change that. And nothing ever will. My marriage is the single most important thing in my life.[4]

[2] Leila Miller, ed., *Primal Loss: The Now-Adult Children of Divorce Speak* (Phoenix: LCB Publishing, 2017), 107.

[3] Ibid., 115

[4] Ibid., 123.

These men and women are *not* coming to marriage empty-handed. Instead, like undercover superheroes, whom the outside world may see as weak, they have a hidden superpower. They are showing up with a strong sense of purpose and the willingness to work, and to suffer, for the sake of their marriages, families, and children. The dedication by many ACODs to marriage is inspiring and should be seen as an admirable strength.

The Compass of Suffering

The suffering ACODs' experience is itself a witness to the nature of love and marriage. They suffer *precisely because* marriage is intended to be lifelong and parents are meant to be lovingly present together with each other and their children. The lack of this is keenly felt *because* it points to the truth of marriage's indissoluble, faithful, and loving nature. Suffering can be described as a *boundary experience* between two realities.[5] On the one hand, suffering makes us hyperaware of an injustice, a lack, or an evil. On the other hand, it points beyond itself to a great good that is worthy of defending when it is threatened and grieved when it is lost.

The suffering of adult children of divorce, far from being just a liability, is a compass for the roadmap of love.

The suffering of adult children of divorce, far from being just a liability, is a compass for the roadmap of love—a profound internal sense for, and affirmation of, the great good of lifelong love in marriage, a good often denigrated

[5] See John Paul II, apostolic letter *Salvifici Doloris*, February 11, 1984, no. 23; José Granados, "Toward a Theology of the Suffering Body," *Communio* 33, no. 4 (Winter 2006): 540–62.

today. Their suffering points to the truth of marriage and family in God's plan that they themselves and the world need to rediscover.

Rediscovering an Authentic Vision of Marriage

The difficulties experienced by ACODs in their own relationships often stem from having a damaged vision of marriage and defaulting to unhealthy self-protection, so we'll look at healing in both of those areas. In this section, we'll outline the Church's vision of what marriage and family are meant to be in God's plan and then look at three practical ways one's vision of marriage can be redeemed and healed.

Marriage and Family in God's Plan

Love is the "fundamental and innate vocation" of every human being.[6] Each of us is created by God out of love, and is called to love. Some of us are called to the vocation of marriage, which has a particular kind of love—conjugal or nuptial love. But all of us, no matter our vocation or state in life, are meant to love and be loved.

In Genesis chapters 1 and 2, Sacred Scripture presents God as the author of marriage, the union between a man and a woman. Marriage is not wholly a man-made institution but has divinely intended meaning and purpose.[7] When Jesus fielded questions about marriage and divorce during his public ministry, he pointed his listeners

[6] *Catechism of the Catholic Church* (CCC), no. 2392; John Paul II, encyclical letter *Familiaris Consortio*, November 22, 1981, no. 11.

[7] See also Second Vatican Council, Pastoral Constitution on the Church in the Modern World *Gaudium et Spes*, December 7, 1965, no. 48.

back to "the beginning," back to God's original plan for marriage—a plan that had been tarnished by sin and man's "hardness of heart" (Mt 19:8). In his "theology of the body" Saint John Paul II unpacks Christ's meaning in these few but weighty words, seeing in them a recovery of what he called the "original experiences" that form the foundation of authentic human love.[8] Jesus raised the covenant of marriage "to the dignity of a sacrament" when celebrated between baptized persons.[9]

Marriage must be entered into *freely*. The spouses' exchange of consent is "the indispensable element" that makes the marriage: "If consent is lacking, there is no marriage."[10] This consent must be given "free of coercion or grave external fear."[11]

Beyond the foundation of free consent, Saint John Paul II gives the following "summary" of what married (conjugal) love entails:

> Conjugal love involves a totality, in which all the elements of the person enter—appeal of the body and instinct, power of feeling and affectivity, aspiration of the spirit and of will. It aims at a deeply personal unity, a unity that, beyond union in one flesh, leads to forming one heart and soul; it demands *indissolubility* and *faithfulness* in definitive mutual giving; and it is open to *fertility*.[12]

[8] See John Paul II, *Man and Woman He Created Them: A Theology of the Body*, ed. and trans. Michael Waldstein (Boston: Pauline Books & Media, 2006), 131–223. For two helpful and accessible secondary resources on the theology of the body, see Jason Evert, *Theology of the Body in One Hour* (Scottsdale, Ariz.: Totus Tuus Press, 2017), and Carl Anderson and Jose Granados, *Called to Love: Approaching John Paul II's Theology of the Body* (New York: Image, 2009).

[9] *CCC*, no. 1601; *Code of Canon Law*, can. 1055.

[10] *CCC*, no. 1626; *Code of Canon Law*, can. 1057.

[11] *CCC*, no. 1628; *Code of Canon Law*, can. 1103.

[12] John Paul II, *Familiaris Consortio*, no. 13 (emphasis in original).

Married love is *total*. Bride and groom "give themselves definitively and totally to one another. They are no longer two; from now on they form one flesh."[13] Marriage's totality springs from the nature of love itself: love "demands a total and definitive gift of persons to one another."[14] Love naturally desires to give *everything* to the beloved, which includes *receiving* everything from the beloved too—receiving the other as a gift. The beautiful "all-ness" to love is illustrated in Saint Paul's "hymn to love": "Love bears all things, believes all things, hopes all things, endures all things" (1 Cor 13:7). The totality of married love is shown in Genesis when Adam and Eve "were both naked, and were not ashamed" (Gen 2:25). This represents both a pure love *and* a love that is willing to give *everything* to the beloved.

Married love is meant to be *faithful*, and a valid sacramental marriage is *indissoluble*. God did not give multiple Eves to Adam or multiple Adams to Eve, a truth that was lost in subsequent generations, as recounted in the stories of polygamy and infidelity in the Old Testament. Jesus reaffirms God's original plan for man and woman to be faithful in lifelong marriage, saying: "What therefore God has joined together, let not man put asunder" (Mk 10:9). The marriage bond, when "concluded and consummated between baptized persons," not only *should not* be broken; it *cannot* be broken until "death do them part," hence the term *indissoluble*.[15]

Again, this has to do with the nature of love itself: "Love seeks to be definitive; it cannot be an arrangement

[13] *CCC*, no. 2364; Mk 10:8.

[14] John Paul II, *Familiaris Consortio*, no. 80.

[15] *CCC*, no. 1640. For the Church's teaching on declarations of nullity (annulments), when a presumably valid marriage is determined by the marriage tribunal not in fact to have been contracted validly, refer to chapter 1.

'until further notice.'"[16] Love desires to say "forever" to the beloved. Marital fidelity witnesses to God's love, his fidelity to his covenant with his people, and Christ's fidelity to his Church.[17] This is an amazing honor for married couples, as well as a responsibility.

Married love is also *fruitful.* The first commandment given to the first married couple is "Be fruitful and multiply" (Gen 1:28). "Fecundity is a gift, an *end* [that is, *purpose*] *of marriage*, for conjugal love naturally tends to be fruitful."[18] Married love is both unitive (bonding the couple) and procreative (open to new life). While not every marital act results in a new child, married couples are called to be open to life and embrace children as a gift. Infertile couples "suffer greatly,"[19] but they too are open to life and can live out the call to fruitfulness by uniting themselves to the Cross and giving of themselves generously to others.

Parents are "the first and most important educators of their children,"[20] including formation in the faith. Every family is called to be a "domestic Church." Families are meant to teach spouses and children how to be fully human. In the Church's vision, it is in the family where a child "receives his first formative ideas about truth and goodness, and learns what it means to love and to be loved, and thus what it actually means to be a person."[21]

Pope Francis poetically describes marital love as "craftmanship" for the spouses: "Might we say that the greatest mission of two people in love is to help one another

[16] *CCC*, no. 1646.

[17] Ibid., no. 1647. See also Ephesians 5:32.

[18] *CCC*, no. 2366 (emphasis in original).

[19] Ibid., no. 2374.

[20] John Paul II, Letter to Families, February 2, 1994, no. 16.

[21] Pontifical Council for Justice and Peace, *Compendium of the Social Doctrine of the Church* (Washington, D.C.: United States Conference of Catholic Bishops, 2004), no. 212.

become, respectively, more a man and more a woman? Fostering growth means helping a person to shape his or her identity. Love is thus a kind of craftsmanship."[22] In sum, the family is a "school for human enrichment," where all members learn "endurance and the joy of work, fraternal love, generous—even repeated—forgiveness, and above all divine worship in prayer and the offering of one's life."[23]

In light of this overview of the Christian vision of marriage and the family, we can understand what some "offenses" against the dignity of marriage are.[24] The two most pertinent for this book are adultery and divorce. Adultery violates the call to fidelity in marriage,[25] while divorce (when there is not an extreme, grave circumstance) violates the indissolubility of marriage.[26] Divorce also tends to undermine fidelity due to the erroneous but widespread perception that divorce automatically renders a person free to enter into a new relationship. The Catechism speaks about the destructiveness of divorce in a passage worth quoting at length:

> Divorce is a grave offense against the natural law. It claims to break the contract, to which the spouses freely consented, to live with each other till death. Divorce does injury to the covenant of salvation, of which sacramental marriage is the sign. Contracting a new union, even if it is recognized by civil law, adds to the gravity of the rupture: the remarried spouse is then in a situation of public and permanent adultery.... Divorce is immoral also because it

[22] Francis, apostolic exhortation *Amoris Laetitia*, March 19, 2016, no. 221.

[23] *CCC*, no. 1657.

[24] Ibid., nos. 2380–2391.

[25] Ibid., nos. 2380–2381.

[26] Ibid., nos. 2382–2386. For an overview of when the Church tolerates civil divorce as morally licit versus sinful, see Leila Miller, "When Does the Church Tolerate Divorce?" *Catholic Answers*, June 29, 2018, https://www.catholic.com/magazine/online-edition/when-does-the-church-tolerate-divorce.

> introduces disorder into the family and society. The disorder brings grave harm to the deserted spouse, to the children traumatized by the separation of their parents and often torn between them, and because of its contagious effect which makes it truly a plague on society.[27]

Married couples are not "left to their own devices" when seeking to live a marriage according to God's plan. Even Jesus' disciples, after they heard his teaching on the indissolubility of marriage, questioned its feasibility: "If such is the case of a man with his wife, it is not expedient to marry" (Mt 19:10). But God gives spouses the grace they need to be faithful to their vows: "By coming to restore the original order of creation disturbed by sin, [Jesus] himself gives the strength and grace to live marriage in the new dimension of the Reign of God. It is by following Christ, renouncing themselves, and taking up their crosses that spouses will be able to 'receive' the original meaning of marriage and live it with the help of Christ."[28]

Lifelong, faithful marriage is therefore not something only possible for "elite" Christians or the most holy among us. Thanks be to God, the Lord gives husbands and wives what they need for their conjugal love to be free, total, faithful, fruitful, and lasting until death. God helps all Christian families, who cooperate with his grace and mercy, to take up the invigorating exhortation of Saint John Paul II and "become what you are."[29]

Dwell in the truth.

God's plan for marriage and family can be difficult to understand and accept today, especially for those who have

[27] *CCC*, nos. 2384–2386.
[28] Ibid., no. 1615.
[29] *Familiaris Consortio*, no. 17.

been hurt by relationships. One pathway toward healing our vision of love and marriage is to return again and again to the authentic sources of the truth about them: Scripture and Church teaching, especially the *Catechism of the Catholic Church* and the teachings of the popes and saints. This constant return necessitates *dwelling*, or making a "home," in this truth and not just being a consumer of it. A "truth consumer" scrolls incessantly, seeking quick and easy answers. There is very little relationship with the truth, nor contemplation of it. In contrast, a "truth dweller" recognizes that the truth we are seeking requires us to have a personal relationship with Christ, which entails spending time contemplating the truth and engaging in a two-way dialogue with Christ.

A truth dweller understands that internalizing Church teaching is a matter of the head *and* the heart. The head seeks understanding. It gains and retains the language and descriptions the Church gives us about marriage—free, total, faithful, and fruitful—and replaces false views of marriage with those true words. But the heart is essential as well, and that's where an adult child of divorce—especially one who tends toward cynicism—may question or resist the words on the page: "Can marriage *really* last a lifetime? Not in my experience." It is an act of trust at times to *believe* that what the Church tells us about marriage is true and not a fairy tale. These teachings can touch a tender area in the heart that has been wounded by experiences contrary to what God intended for love, and can trigger grief about what should have been. We encourage ACODs to pray for the gift of faith to believe that marriage *really is* free, total, faithful, and fruitful. As we'll see later, having actual flesh-and-blood people in our lives who are happily married can help overcome distrust about marriage.

Meditating on Scripture helps us dwell in the truth and renew our vision of marriage as God intended. One fruitful passage is Jesus' discourse about marriage in Mark 10 and Matthew 19. We can take an Ignatian approach to Scripture and imagine ourselves *there*, in the crowd, hearing Jesus' words directed *to us*. We can take all of the hurt, questions, and confusion in our hearts to Jesus in that moment, entrusting ourselves to him and asking for the faith to believe that what he says is true. We can talk to Jesus and apply to our own lives what he lovingly says to us through these Scriptural words.

The Wedding Feast of Cana (Jn 2) is another Scripture passage that can help heal our vision of marriage. On our retreats, we meditate on this passage together, and it is included in this book's appendices. This meditation emphasizes the *new wine* the Lord brings, wine that restores and heals human love. It is no accident that Jesus' first miracle of his public ministry was at a wedding. He is present in all human love, and we can place ourselves *there*, beside him at the wedding feast, as he renews the joy of love and our own vision of it.

Develop a "joy within growth" mindset.

As we have said, many ACODs tend to view marriage through either a cynical or overly romantic lens. Both are attempts to protect our hearts from further hurt, either by preemptively distancing ourselves from intimacy, or refusing to see or address anything other than the fun, happy parts of a relationship. Instead, we need to pray for a vision of marriage as a sacrament meant for our joy *within* sanctification and growth, and a tremendous pathway of healing. *Every* marriage will experience suffering and pains, both externally imposed and self-generated.

Every marriage will require ongoing conversion of heart (a truth those inclined to a romantic view of marriage may need to work to accept). As Pope Francis says, "No family drops down from heaven perfectly formed; families need constantly to grow and mature in the ability to love."[30]

But *in the very difficulties of married life*, the Lord meets us and sanctifies us further. "Iron sharpens iron, and one man sharpens another" (Prov 27:17). Nowhere is this truer than in marriage, where daily interactions provide spouses ample opportunities to "sharpen" each other—giving and receiving forgiveness after offenses and acting in charity no matter what. In this way, husband and wife can become better people, and better Christians, than they could have been without each other.[31] (This same growth also occurs in lasting friendships and among religious and lay consecrated communities.) Moments of suffering and conflict can become opportunities for sanctification and growth, and for deepening communion. Recall Shaina's struggle with a romanticism mindset that thought "anything less than a perfect marriage spells disaster." She describes how she cultivated a "joy within growth" mindset:

> The truth is, healing [in marriage] is work. It's not just the work of therapy, it's the work of everyday living and praying. It's making the choice to exert my will over my emotions. It's choosing to stay instead of running away. It's being vulnerable, uncomfortable, and staring the ugly in the face .... The work I put in, the necessary grace I ask for and receive from God, does not mean I will no longer

[30] Francis, *Amoris Laetitia*, no. 325.

[31] For many examples—often humorous—of how growth can occur in marriage, see Edward and Beth Sri, *The Good, the Messy, and the Beautiful: The Joys and Struggles of Real Married Life* (West Chester, Pa.: Ascension Press, 2022).

hurt. Rather, it means that my hurt will be transformed into the means by which I am saved .... And even more, there is a joy that comes with acceptance, one that is all the more treasured because it is hard-won.[32]

In his final exhortation to families in *Amoris Laetitia*, Pope Francis said, "May we never lose heart because of our limitations, or ever stop seeking that fullness of love and communion which God holds out before us."[33]

Couples seeking to develop holy and healthy expectations of marriage should remember that for spouses married validly and sacramentally, there is *literally nothing* they can do to destroy their union. No mistake, no blunder, and certainly no "irreconcilable difference" can render their union void. There is a great comfort in that! Lifelong marriage is possible not because two particular people are blessed with great virtue and good circumstances, but rather because Jesus promises that marriage in him lasts. He is the foundation of all love.

Lifelong marriage is possible not because two particular people are blessed with great virtue and good circumstances, but rather because Jesus promises that marriage in him lasts.

Those who struggle with cynicism about marriage may need to recover the joy and healing nature of marriage. Marriage cannot solve all of a spouse's problems or heal every wound, but it can contribute to healing when spouses embody Christ to each other in their love.

[32] Shaina Pia, "The Less than Perfect Marriage Does Not Equal Disaster: Godly Expectations for Love," *Life-Giving Wounds* (blog), September 2, 2019, https://www.lifegivingwounds.org/blog/stories-of-healing-the-less-than-perfect-marriage-does-not-equal-disaster.

[33] Francis, *Amoris Laetitia*, no. 325.

Dan has found moments of forgiveness in our marriage to be very healing. He knows that he can make mistakes and Bethany will still love him and see him as more than those mistakes. Marriage has also given him the stability needed to do a deeper dive into his healing. Our marital unity includes taking on each other's wounds—this "unity of woundedness" deepens our communion and, perhaps paradoxically, brings joy because we share each other's burdens together.

For the cynic, recovering an expectation for joy and healing keeps the "downs" of a marriage from defining or dooming it. There *are many* genuine joys that the Lord wants us to discover in marriage. And the romantic can take heart that even in the tough, messy parts of marriage, Christ is there to help us sanctify our love and *deepen* our communion.

Discernment and "Staying in the Herd"

Discernment of relationships can feel daunting for anyone. Single and dating ACODs can feel at a loss when trying to decide whether and how to move forward with a particular relationship, given their lack of successful role models or of an authentic vision of marriage from their family. They may feel like poor judges of these matters because of their background.

For example, one young woman raised the question of how to distinguish between "red flags" about a relationship, signs that the person is not a good fit for marriage, and more minor faults or annoyances that could cause problems but are not insurmountable. For some children of divorce, *everything* can seem like a red flag because even seemingly innocuous annoyances apparently contributed to their parents' divorce. For others who come from a background of high conflict, or extreme anger, even hints of discord can feel triggering. Many have not seen what it looks like for partners to put up with each other's faults instead of calling it quits. There can be a fear of committing to the "wrong" relationship that will end in heartache and even divorce.

It can be challenging, too, for an ACOD to know when he himself is ready to commit to a serious dating relationship or marriage. How much healing is enough?

We encourage any ACOD who is discerning a relationship first and continually to pray for courage and wisdom: courage even to *try* a relationship despite the inherent risk involved, and wisdom to see the other person and situation—and yourself—clearly. During a time of discernment, it is important to look as objectively as possible at the other's character, principles, ways of handling conflict and suffering, healing from past wounds, willingness to apologize and forgive, faith and commitment to Christ, and whether the person's vision for the future and marriage aligns with your own. Thinking about and examining the relationship in these areas is a healthy "testing" of the relationship. This thorough discernment cannot occur after only a few dates but takes place over time.

As another part of discernment, you should be attentive to how the other individual, if from an intact home, reacts to your more complicated family dynamics. Is he willing to support you in your healing? Does he see you as more than your background? Is he willing to accept graciously the added hardship that could come from navigating a fractured extended family?

For your own self-discernment, examining any tendencies toward self-protection is valuable for insight about where personal healing is still needed. A time of discerning a relationship can benefit from having wise friends and mentors offer real-time advice; nothing can replace the personal, "on-the-ground" guidance from someone who knows you well. A healthy relationship is not isolated from others; you need to "stay in the herd" of those who can guide you.

"Staying in the herd" was crucial for us while we were dating. We often asked our friends and mentors what they thought about our relationship. This was especially helpful prior to our engagement when we encountered a difficult moment. Initially Bethany's parents said "no" to Dan when he asked them for permission to marry her, to his shock and dismay. This reinforced his worst fears about his capacity to love. On top of that distressing event, Dan's parents were in the final stages of their divorce, bringing up all of the old fears again. We are convinced that if we didn't have the support of a wise spiritual director to lean on during this time, we might not have married. With the aid of his wise guidance and advice, things got better and Bethany's parents eventually came to support the marriage. Now we are all good friends. Praise God we "stayed in the herd" for our discernment and did not try to figure things out on our own!

Moving from Unhealthy Self-Protection to Authentic Self-Giving

As we saw in the last chapter, self-protective behaviors—like keeping people at arm's length, or leaving someone before he leaves you—can be, first, *honored* as ways that children of divorce survived the emotional chaos of their families. But in healthy, mature relationships, ongoing self-protection prevents the intimacy that relationships need to thrive. The goal is to move from unhealthy self-protection to love as total self-gift, an ever-deepening, reciprocal *giving* and *receiving* of love. We offer four practical ideas for moving toward this goal.

The "Holy Risk" of Intimacy

One place to start is to work on believing deep-down that relationships, intimacy, and vulnerability are *worth the risk.* Love, and the vulnerability it requires, are always inherently risky, as C. S. Lewis says in this memorable passage from his book about love:

> To love at all is to be vulnerable. Love anything, and your heart will certainly be wrung and possibly be broken. If you want to make sure of keeping it intact, you must give your heart to no one, not even to an animal. Wrap it carefully round with hobbies and little luxuries; avoid all entanglements; lock it up safe in the casket or coffin of your selfishness. But in that casket—safe, dark, motionless, airless—it will change. It will not be broken; it will become unbreakable, impenetrable, irredeemable.[34]

To love is to be vulnerable. For ACODs who have experienced the pain of abandonment, broken promises, or unforgiveness, it can take tremendous courage to choose to seek out love again rather than wall up their hearts. This is a "holy" risk because God is a God of love and has given each of us a vocation to love.

Developing the courage needed to accept the risk of relationships can take time, depending on how deeply the injury goes. Starting small can help, even with—as Lewis alluded to—a pet to love. (We know more than one child of divorce—Dan included—for whom a pet was

[34] C. S. Lewis, *The Four Loves* (New York: HarperCollins, 1960), 155–56.

a profound source of affection and comfort during their family turmoil.) Vulnerability can grow and develop in friendships, which are genuine forms of love without the same level of commitment or intimacy as marriage. Finding a good friend to open one's heart to is a treasure and a step toward trusting love again.

Most fundamentally, ACODs can cultivate the foundational relationship that is always trustworthy: a relationship with our Lord. Greater intimacy with God increases the capacity of our hearts for greater intimacy with others. They go hand-in-hand.[35] When we know as a bedrock truth that we are loved by our Creator (who, after all, knows every detail about us), we can have greater confidence to take the holy risk of loving and of being loved by others.

Recall Sandy's story from the last chapter about struggling with abandonment fears in relationships. She sought healing by first addressing her underlying fear that she was unloved, unlovable, and unworthy of love:

> In my case I had to adopt a prayer mantra that I made up, holding my hand over my heart and telling myself over and over "you are loved, you deserve love, you are worthy of love, you are capable of love, you can receive love." ... As children of divorce, we can take heart that we *are* lovable and loved, no matter how many times we've felt abandoned by people in our lives. And we can rest in the fact that our Lord will never abandon us, no matter what. That can give us the confidence we need to begin to trust in others again, and in so doing find the joy that comes from authentic, trustworthy love.[36]

[35] This theme is examined by Pope Saint John Paul II in his reflections on original solitude. See *Man and Woman He Created Them*, 146–56.

[36] Sandra Howlett, "How Fear of Abandonment Can Affect Your Relationships," *Life-Giving Wounds* (blog), May 15, 2021, https://www.lifegivingwounds.org/blog/abandonment.

Precision Work of Virtue

A way to grow beyond unhealthy self-protection is proactively cultivating virtues that *counteract* whatever self-protecting behavior we want to change.[37] These are concrete, practicable ways to become the kind of person who can and does love freely and fully. It is precision work, directed at specific tendencies we notice in our way of relating to others.

Someone who tends toward cynicism and doubt about relationships could strive to cultivate the virtues of *hope* and *joy* and develop a stance of gratitude and praise for good things. Small daily exercises like delighting in something about the relationship or keeping a gratitude journal can help heal a tendency to fixate on the negative.

Someone who has fallen into habits of bitter criticism or uncontrolled anger could work on the virtues of *meekness* and *gentleness*. Coming up with a plan for handling disagreements and conflict in a constructive way can de-escalate anger (and the deeper fear of the relationship failing), while encouraging vulnerability and growth.

Someone who tends toward romanticism in relationships, and who avoids interpersonal conflict out of fear, could strive to cultivate the virtue of *courage* to engage in difficulties and work through them, rather than fleeing from them.

Someone who resists being dependent in a healthy way in relationships could strive to cultivate the virtue of *humility*, recognizing his interrelation with others and the importance of receptivity in love.

[37] We're aware that for those who have been deeply traumatized or are struggling with addictive behavior, it can be necessary to seek professional, Catholic psychological help for those serious challenges as an essential complement to striving for greater virtue, and in order not to fall into either despair or scrupulosity.

Sandy gives an example of counteracting possessiveness and jealousy through developing the virtue of gratitude: "We can often admit to a lot of other faults more easily than jealousy. It seems so petty and embarrassing. But understanding and admitting this to myself has given me new insight into the effects of divorce on my feelings, reactions, anxieties, and relationships. If I can stop operating out of fear and give thanks for the people I have in my life instead of jealously guarding them, I can improve these relationships."[38]

The list could go on. After identifying your own pattern(s) of unhealthy self-protection (perhaps with the assistance of wise friends or mentors), and thinking about counteracting virtues, choose concrete ways to practice those virtues daily. Remember that progress can be slow. Patterns of unhealthy self-protection were likely developed over many years in response to family chaos and dysfunction. Dropping them can make you feel vulnerable. Much grace and patience are needed, and small steps, like persevering in a relationship rather than running away at the first sign of distress, should be celebrated.

Chastity at the Service of Communion

The virtue of chastity deserves special mention. Its connection with love often resonates deeply with us ACODs because we know all too well its importance not only before marriage, but also afterward. Many of us went through the heart-wrenching experience of infidelity by one or both parents that contributed to breaking up our family. Research has also found that pornography plays a key role in a substantial number of divorces.[39] The lack of

[38] Howlett, "How Fear of Abandonment Can Affect Your Relationships."

[39] See, e.g., Jill C. Manning, "The Impact of Internet Pornography on Marriage and the Family: A Review of the Research," *Journal of Treatment and Prevention* 13, nos. 2–3 (2006): 131–65.

chastity in our childhood home, and its disastrous effects on our family, can be a powerful motivator for living chastely in our own life. But recognizing the connection between unchastity and divorce can also cause additional shame for those who struggle in this area. This shame must be trustfully surrendered to God's mercy, and the healing of any underlying wounds contributing to unchaste behavior should be pursued. We need to remind ourselves that we are not doomed to repeat our parents' mistakes and that struggles with chastity often stem from the deep hurt we felt from our parents' divorce.

Chastity is self-mastery of sexual passions and thoughts ordered toward giving ourselves as a total gift to another.[40] It expresses our faithfulness to our current or future spouse, and entails viewing and treating our bodies and the bodies of others with great dignity, as worthy of love as total self-gift. Chastity is not just saying "no" to certain activities, but saying "yes" to love in its fullness. "Our bodies are so noble. The infamous carnal sinners of history are not those who loved their bodies too much, but those who loved their bodies too little. They are those who failed to respect or perhaps even to understand the dignity of that masterpiece of the Father, the human body."[41]

Struggles with chastity can overlap with struggles with self-esteem, making chastity a necessary virtue for our healing because it builds up self-esteem and personal dignity. Living chastely and refraining from too much physical intimacy with a dating partner can aid our discernment of marriage, since physical intimacy can cloud our judgment or influence our decisions about the relationship's future.

[40] *CCC*, nos. 2337–2359.

[41] Mother Mary Francis, *Anima Christi: Soul of Christ* (San Francisco: Ignatius Press, 2001), 22.

It's never too late to be chaste; a renewed commitment to chastity is always possible, no matter what mistakes have been made.

As an aid in the practice of chastity and to test if your vision of sex or physical intimacy is correct, ask yourself this question: "Do I use sex or false intimacy, such as pornography and masturbation, to solve a problem? Do I use it to alleviate loneliness, find affirmation or feel wanted, resolve problems in a relationship, or help me forget or escape a problem in my life?" If the answer is yes, then sex is being used in an inappropriate and unhealthy way. Sex is not meant to be a solution to a problem, but rather a *gift* to your spouse as an expression of your total self-giving and receiving of love from your spouse. Sex is meant to be an expression of your wedding vows for love and openness to children.[42] If you are using sex as a solution to a problem, then you should choose other ways of solving that problem and find healing for any underlying wounds that drive that problem.

Domestic Churches

We began the previous chapter with a quote from an adult child of divorce: "I fully expected that when I got married, I would be very unhappy .... After all, I hadn't met anyone who was in a happy marriage, as far as I could tell."[43] It is a sad reality that many people, like Joanna, have never seen a healthy, loving marriage up close. In our ministry, we have often heard, "Where do I turn to find a healthy example of marriage? Who will help us learn to love?"

Holy married couples can play a crucial role as mentors for ACODs who want to "do" relationships differently

[42] See *CCC*, nos. 2360–2379.

[43] Joanna A., "Healing a Mountain of Relationship Fears."

than what they saw in their homes. Loving, healthy, intact families have a beautiful opportunity to open up the doors of their domestic churches, especially to young men and women who come from broken families and are craving a living witness of love that lasts.

We have benefited from mentor couples in significant ways. Dan was blessed with several mentors as a teenager, during the tumultuous years of his parents' separation. Both sets of his grandparents had marriages that lasted over fifty years, and his mom's parents became (and still are to this day) the model that we want to emulate in our own marriage. We have a professionally recorded video of his grandparents' advice that has become a yearly ritual to watch and learn from. Dan also had a youth minister who opened up his home to Dan. He got to see firsthand a loving, prayerful family, serving as a blueprint for what he wanted someday.

As we were preparing for marriage, we sought out several couples whom we admired, and asked if we could learn from them (more or less inviting ourselves over for dinner). Those candid conversations remain some of the best premarital lessons on family life, finances, communication, and much more. We have also been blessed by friends and peers who are also striving to live marriage well, including a couples' group that met monthly for years. These couple "mentors" are more equally situated to us in age and life stage but have still guided and shaped us, giving us fresh ideas about tough situations and offering living examples of marriages striving to go the distance. Cultivating friendships with people who care as deeply about lasting marriage as we do is important because there is a "contagiousness" to divorce: the risk of divorce rises 75 percent if a family member or close friend divorces, and 33 percent if a friend of a friend divorces.[44] The Catechism identifies the "contagious effect" of divorce, too.[45] In contrast, friendships with successfully married couples spread a different type of contagion, that of virtue and of being supported in your own holy pursuit of lifelong love.

We realize that not everyone is fortunate enough to have mentors or peer companions in easy supply. Nonetheless, we always advise adult children of divorce to seek out and find "open domestic churches," even if it is awkward or takes time to find them. It could be a married couple at church, neighbors, relatives, coworkers, or others. Many elderly couples are delighted to share their time and wisdom with young people. With a prospective mentor, share a bit about your background from a broken home and that you are looking for guidance on relationships from someone whose marriage you admire. Who would not be honored by that?

Mentoring is something that can start before marriage, or even before dating. Some now-married couples have expressed to us that having a mentor during engagement was helpful, but too late and not enough. Many singles and dating couples want to know healthy married couples *now*, to learn anew how to love. Real flesh-and-blood spouses who have weathered crises together give a living witness to everything the Church says marriage is.

Heroic "Standers"

A beautiful witness to marriage is given by heroic abandoned spouses who were divorced against their will but

[44] Rose McDermott et al., "Breaking Up Is Hard To Do, Unless Everyone Else Is Doing It Too: Social Network Effects on Divorce in a Longitudinal Sample," *Social Forces* 92, no. 2 (2013): 491–519.

[45] *CCC*, no. 2385.

who choose to "stand" for (stay faithful to) their vows in the sacrament of Marriage—they remain chaste and do not remarry. Such "standers" are too infrequently acknowledged by society or the Church, but we have personally learned a great deal about love from them and are profoundly grateful for their witness.

These men and women embrace sacrifices like living alone and often dedicate themselves to praying for their estranged spouses and to being generous to their children and grandchildren. They demonstrate the fruitfulness of marital vows even in the midst of suffering and a lack of reciprocity from their spouses. "Standers" teach us much about married love in good times and bad, including the importance of faithfulness to marital vows no matter the circumstances. Amazingly, many "standers" are profoundly joyful, animated by a deep faith. Their holiness and witness can be profoundly healing in the lives of their children and others around them.[46]

Fail into Forgiveness

A final pathway for healing the tendencies toward unhealthy self-protection is to embrace forgiveness in our relationships. It goes without saying that many divorces involve the unwillingness of one or both spouses to forgive. Something has happened that seems so insurmountable that forgiveness either appears impossible or is rejected as an option.

As an antidote to this, ACODs can help heal their own relational wounds and disrupt the cycle of generational brokenness by striving to become *people who give*

[46] See also ibid., no. 2386; Leila Miller, "The Hidden Martyrs for Marriage," *Catholic Answers*, March 23, 2023, https://www.catholic.com/magazine/online-edition/the-hidden-martyrs-for-marriage.

and receive forgiveness. Forgiving someone and offering him mercy, or asking for and receiving forgiveness, requires vulnerability. Self-protective behaviors include withholding forgiveness, refusing to apologize, or avoiding the painful subject altogether.

As we will discuss later, forgiveness can and should coexist with healthy boundaries; forgiveness does not mean allowing another to continue to hurt us. In healthy, mature relationships, frequent forgiveness and reconciliation are essential for intimacy because we will *all* make mistakes in love. Divine Mercy—offering and receiving forgiveness through the grace of Christ—is crucial for lasting love.

When we or the person we love fail at something in the relationship, it does not have to be the end. Instead of "just" failing, we can *fail into* forgiveness and grace. Instead of criticizing with harsh accusations, avoiding discussion of the failure out of fear, or allowing the failure to be the last word, we can allow that mistake or failure to lead to a deeper communion through offering or asking for forgiveness. Forgiveness affirms that we are loved despite our mistakes, an affirmation that deepens communion. And learning from our mistakes helps us become holier people. Failure is often one of the best teachers of what to do (or what not to do) next time.

When we do not *feel* like forgiving, we can pray for the grace to *want* to forgive. When we do not *feel* like apologizing, we can pray for the grace to *want* to apologize. Developing forgiveness as a habit and frequent practice—repeating words that Pope Francis says are essential to a family, "I'm sorry" and "I forgive you"[47]—is a radical answer to the hardness of heart at the root of so much

[48] See Francis, *Amoris Laetitia*, no. 133.

relational brokenness. Making an effort of the will to forgive and to receive forgiveness, again and again, helps our hearts be more open and receptive. It helps us become more generous, loving people, instead of people with walls up at every turn.

A Non-ACOD Spouse's Perspective: Joy within Growth, Together

BETHANY: As the wife of an adult child of divorce, one of the best things I can do for Dan is affirm his ability to love me and our children well. So many ACODs struggle with a sense of inadequacy in relationships. But while Dan isn't perfect (and neither am I!), he is a *good* and loving husband and father. I look for opportunities to build up his confidence. He is not his parents' worst mistakes, and our marriage is not the same as his parents' marriage. I try to affirm the strengths he brings to our marriage, especially his intention to invest in and nurture our love. Affirmation helps us be more vulnerable and open with each other, creating momentum for helping each other overcome any unhealthy self-protective tendencies in our relationship.

As we have said in this chapter and the previous one, self-protective behaviors that adult children of divorce can express are often habits generated by simply trying to survive a chaotic or dysfunctional family environment. It can be easy to take those behaviors personally (I know I can!) but a certain relief comes in remembering that, for example, a spouse's difficulty with vulnerability or intimacy isn't because of something you or your spouse did or didn't do, but likely traces back to a wound deep in the past. It is now a *common* wound that we can tackle together, since in marriage we take on each other's pain, as Christ did on the Cross for those he loved. We try to cultivate this "common-good, common-wound" thinking within a larger "joy within growth" mindset. As a married couple, our common goal is ever-deepening communion, and our common enemy is anything that hinders that. Facing difficulties *together* makes a tremendous difference in the way we approach conflicts; it's not him against me or me against him. We are on the same team, even if it doesn't always feel that way when conflicts first arise.

9

The Wounds of Anxiety, Anger, and Sin

Make every effort to supplement your faith with virtue .... For whoever lacks these things is blind and shortsighted and has forgotten that he was cleansed from his old sins.

—2 Peter 1:5, 9

Divorce and separation can have serious emotional effects on the children involved. Compared with children from intact families, children of divorce are more likely to "experience lower emotional well-being,"[1] to have "many worries,"[2] and to be unhappy or depressed.[3] These difficulties are especially pronounced for those children who

[1] Paul Sullins, "The Case for Mom and Dad," *Linacre Quarterly* 88, no. 2 (2021): 184.

[2] Paul Sullins, "The Tragedy of Divorce for Children," in *Torn Asunder: Children, the Myth of the Good Divorce, and the Recovery of Origins*, ed. Margaret Harper McCarthy (Grand Rapids, Mich.: Eerdmans, 2017), 26.

[3] Laura Di Manno et al., "Family Dissolution and Offspring Depression and Depressive Symptoms: A Systematic Review of Moderation Efforts," *Journal of Affective Disorders* 188, no. 1 (2015): 69. See also Centers for Disease Control, *Family Structure and Children's Health in the United States: Findings from the National Health Interview Survey: 2001–2007*, Vital and Health Statistics, series 1, no. 246 (Washington, D.C.: U.S. Department of Health and Human Services, 2010), https://www.cdc.gov/nchs/data/series/sr_10/sr10_246.pdf.

live apart from their fathers[4] and whose parents persist in conflict after the split.[5]

In this chapter, we will look at two common emotional struggles adult children of divorce experience: *anxiety* and *anger*.[6] We will also reflect on how sin committed in response to our wounds furthers the fractures to our emotional life, wholeness, and relationship with God and others. In the next chapter, we will reflect on ways to get "unstuck" from the negative effects of these emotions and sin, particularly by growing in virtue.

Anxiety

We can describe *anxiety* as a feeling of fear, worry, nervousness, or unease, rooted in possible or perceived danger to our life or well-being, or concern about something with an uncertain outcome.[7] Different people can feel anxious

[4] Sullins, "The Tragedy of Divorce," 27. See also Matthew D. Bramlett and Stephen J. Blumberg, "Family Structure and Children's Physical and Mental Health," *Health Affairs* 26, no. 2 (March 2007).

[5] Kit Elam et al., "Non-Residential Father-Child Involvement, Interparental Conflict and Mental Health of Children Following Divorce: A Person-Focused Approach," *Journal of Youth and Adolescence* 45, no. 3 (March 2016): 581–93.

[6] Another common emotional struggle of adult children of divorce is depression, which is a complex condition with many causes that we cannot adequately address here. To learn more about depression and ways to combat it from a Catholic perspective, see Aaron Kheriarty, *The Catholic Guide to Depression: How the Saints, the Sacraments, and Psychiatry Can Help You Break Its Grip and Find Happiness Again* (Manchester, N.H.: Sophia Institute Press, 2012).

[7] At times, the feeling of anxiety can become so pervasive and life-disrupting that it is diagnosed by a psychological professional as an *anxiety disorder* that requires treatment and perhaps medication. For our purposes here, as non-psychological professionals, we are focusing on a broader, more general sense of anxiety that may or may not rise to the level of a diagnosable mental health disorder. We encourage anyone who relates to the struggles described in this chapter to consult with a psychological professional about whether treatment or medication would be beneficial in his particular situation.

about different things, but we can identify several common ways that anxiety impacts ACODs both at the time of the divorce or separation and far into the future.

A Sense of Foreboding

First, ACODs, especially those from low-conflict marriages, may have experienced their parents' split as a complete shock, the family "suddenly" falling apart (even if it was something the parents had been considering for a while). This can provoke an ongoing, generalized feeling of anxiety and foreboding that *anything* good or presumably stable can end without warning.[8] We have heard ACODs verbalize this as: "If something as important as my parents' love and marriage together can end, then anything good can end."

One of the ACODs interviewed by Judith Wallerstein described her anxiety in this way: "Part of me is always waiting for disaster to strike .... The truth is that I live in dread that something bad will happen to me. Some terrible loss will change my life, and it only gets worse as things get better for me .... I've learned to contain it. I no longer wake up in terror when I go to sleep happy, but this feeling does not ever go away."[9] This heightened anxiety at moments of joy and happiness has been aptly described by popular author Brene Brown as "foreboding joy."[10] That is, a feeling that just when things are going right,

[8] See Paul Amato et al., "Parental Divorce, Marital Conflict, and Offspring Well-Being during Early Adulthood," *Social Forces* 73, no. 3 (March 1995): 895–915.

[9] Judith Wallerstein, Julia Lewis, and Sandra Blakeslee, *The Unexpected Legacy of Divorce: A 25 Year Landmark Study* (New York: Hyperion, 2000), xxii.

[10] Brene Brown, *Daring Greatly: How the Courage to Be Vulnerable Transforms the Way We Live, Love, Parent, and Lead* (New York: Penguin Random House, 2015), 117–22. Interestingly, to our knowledge, Brown never makes the direct connection between parental divorce and foreboding joy.

disaster is *most* likely to strike. An ongoing feeling of distrust toward joy can impede one's ability to rest in a good and healthy relationship without constantly scanning for potential disaster. For example, the same adult child of divorce quoted above said that whenever her husband is late, "my first thought—and I hate myself for this—is that he's going to leave me."[11]

An ongoing feeling of distrust toward joy can impede one's ability to rest in a good and healthy relationship without constantly scanning for potential disaster.

Anxiety about impending disaster can also impact parenting. For example, often when Dan is playing with our daughters at the playground, instead of enjoying the moment with them, he will be thinking about all the possible bad things that could happen: they might be hurt, bullied, or kidnapped. He finds himself continuously scanning the environment for all possible dangers. To some extent, all parents (including Bethany) do some "scanning," since children are not always aware of potential dangers. But this is different than distrusting joy due to ongoing anxiety, which can impede Dan from delighting *at all* in pleasant times with our children. Through the healing work he has done, he recognizes the connection between this tendency toward anxiety in parenting and his parents' anxiety-provoking divorce. He is trying to "unlearn" this reaction and work toward re-trusting joy with a peaceful heart.

Even when things are going well, it can still be hard to shake the creeping sense that *this won't last*. As Wallerstein puts it, "no matter what their [ACODs] success in

[11] Wallerstein et al., *Unexpected Legacy of Divorce*, 61.

the world, they retain some serious residues—fear of loss, fear of change, and fear that disaster will strike, especially when things are going well."[12] One ACOD expressed it this way: "What divorce does is shatter [the child's] universe in a drastic and traumatic way … It even changes the way you perceive reality—you become anxious, nothing ever feels safe or predictable, and you're always waiting for the piano to fall."[13]

Financial Anxiety

Financial circumstances often deteriorate after a parental split, especially for newly single mothers and their children. Single-mother-led households are five times more likely to live in poverty than married households.[14] Wallerstein notes that "divorced mothers as a group earn a lot less than divorced fathers" and they "are not only poor after divorce but remain poor for many years."[15] Single-father-led households, too, are more than twice as likely to be in poverty as compared to married households.[16] Faced with suddenly distressed circumstances, perhaps falling from the middle class into poverty, relocating to a smaller house or apartment, going without small luxuries or even necessities, children can feel anxious about their material needs being met. They can also feel a heightened sense of responsibility to provide for their struggling parent and siblings (a kind of "parentification," which

[12] Ibid., 301.

[13] Leila Miller, ed., *Primal Loss: The Now-Adult Children of Divorce Speak* (Phoenix: LCB Publishing, 2017), 132.

[14] Emily A. Shrider et al., "Income and Poverty in the United States: 2020," U.S. Census Bureau, September 14, 2021, https://www.census.gov/library/publications/2021/demo/p60-273.html.

[15] Wallerstein et al., *Unexpected Legacy of Divorce*, 163.

[16] Shrider et al., "Income and Poverty in the United States: 2020."

we discussed earlier). This can continue into adulthood as elevated anxiety over finances and never feeling like "enough is enough."

Financial anxiety can influence choices about education and career. Compounding this, college-aged ACODs are far less likely to receive financial support from their parents for their education: in one survey only 30 percent of ACODs versus close to 90 percent of children from intact homes reported receiving at least some financial support for college.[17] Financial anxiety can also influence decisions about when or whether to marry.

For married ACODs, financial anxiety can also influence discernment about whether and when to have children, and how many to have. Some recoil at the idea of putting their children in daycare, having experienced long isolating hours there themselves. They delay having children until they are financially comfortable enough for the mother to stay home full-time. For others, however, having seen their mother (and themselves) suffer post-divorce without access to an independent source of income, they cannot imagine both parents not earning a separate income. One ACOD said that a reason behind not having many children was because "in the event of a divorce, I would not want to ... find myself unable to work and provide for myself. My mom lacked job skills and was financially dependent on my dad .... I learned that I have to be able to take care of myself no matter what, because I might otherwise be homeless!"[18]

As their parents age, ACODs face a possible additional financial challenge of being asked to support (or feeling the need to support) parents in two different households

[17] Wallerstein et al., *Unexpected Legacy of Divorce*, 249.
[18] Miller, *Primal Loss*, 121.

because neither has the assistance of the ex-spouse. This can cause further financial anxiety (as well as emotional challenges), especially if one of their parents becomes sick or needs long-term care.

Unmet Emotional or Spiritual Needs

Children whose parents' attention was taken up with rebuilding their own lives (including investing in new relationships) can feel anxious about whether their emotional needs will be met or even recognized. They can also wonder whether their big spiritual questions about what's happening will be answered adequately, or even heard. Loneliness is a common experience for children from broken homes: children of divorce are three times as likely as children from intact homes to agree with the statement, "I was lonely a lot as a child."[19] Researcher Marquardt elaborates: "Some of us felt lonely not only because we were often alone but also because we were isolated by intense and unacknowledged emotions."[20]

For some children of divorce, anxiety about having their emotional needs met can manifest as "acting out" to secure desperately desired parental attention. But others suppress their emotional needs. Marquardt found that children of divorce were less likely to turn to one or both parents for comfort during difficulties than were children from intact homes.[21] This self-protective behavior of not sharing emotions makes mutually vulnerable and self-giving relationships more challenging later. ACODs may

[19] Elizabeth Marquardt, *Between Two Worlds: The Inner Lives of Children of Divorce* (New York: Crown Publishers, 2005), 139. See also Nazmiye Civitci et al., "Loneliness and Life Satisfaction in Adolescents with Divorced and Non-Divorced Parents," *Educational Sciences: Theory and Practice* 9, no. 2 (2009): 513–25.

[20] Marquardt, *Between Two Worlds*, 49.

[21] Ibid.

find it difficult to trust that *any* relationship will meet their emotional needs. Indeed, Wallerstein says this about adult children of divorce: "Anxiety about relationships was at the bedrock of their personalities and endured *even in very happy marriages*. Their fears of disaster and sudden loss rose when they felt content. And their fear of abandonment, betrayal, and rejection mounted when they found themselves having to disagree with someone they loved."[22] Unmet emotional needs can also lead to "relationship-hopping" or settling for sub-par romantic partners out of a desire to have an emotional connection with someone after feeling deprived of that human need.

Health Effects

The anxiety adult children of divorce can feel, including a persistent fear of abandonment, has been found to predict future mental health problems.[23] And, as Vicki Thorn persuasively argued,[24] the anxiety and stress that children of divorce experience can impact their *physical* health as well. Thorn notes that ACODs are at greater risk for stroke and more likely to smoke.[25] She says that the emotional and psychological difficulties children of divorce go through "can disrupt the development of brain architecture and other organ systems, and increase the risk for stress-related disease and cognitive impairment, well into the adult years."[26]

[22] Wallerstein et al., *Unexpected Legacy of Divorce*, 300 (emphasis added).

[23] Karey L. O'Hara et al., "Longitudinal Effects of Post-divorce Interparental Conflict on Children's Mental Health Problems through a Fear of Abandonment: Does Parenting Quality Play a Buffering Role?" *Child Development* 92, no. 4 (July/August 2021): 1476–93.

[24] Vicki Thorn, "Biological Effects of Divorce on Children," in *Torn Asunder*, 41–50.

[25] Ibid., 42, 44.

[26] Ibid., 48. See also Bessel van der Kolk, *The Body Keeps the Score: Brain, Mind, and Body in the Healing of Trauma* (New York: Penguin, 2014) for an extended treatment of the physical-health consequences of trauma and emotional distress.

Anger

Anger is also common after divorce as children react to losing the love of their parents together and all the other losses that this entails. We can describe *anger* as a strong feeling of animosity, dislike, or enmity toward something or someone who has wronged you or toward an unjust situation. Anger is a complex topic. At times it can be righteous and merited, while at other times it is a sin.

Righteous Anger

As a reaction to an injustice or sin, anger can be *righteous* and even an expression of love for the victims. The Catechism says that anger plays a role in *resisting evil.*[27] We can picture Jesus overturning the tables of the money-changers in the Temple (Jn 2:13–17): "His disciples remembered that it was written, 'Zeal for your house will consume me'" (Jn 2:17).

Anger about our parents' divorce or separation can fall squarely in this category. Divorce is an offense against the dignity of marriage.[28] (Again, some spouses are unjustly abandoned and "innocent victim[s]" of a divorce;[29] and spousal separation and even civil divorce are permitted by Church law in extreme, grave circumstances.[30]) Actions and choices related to a marital breakdown may also have been wrong and unjust: neglect of parental duties and abandonment of the family (financially, emotionally, et cetera), adultery and affairs, harsh words and unkind actions toward the other spouse or children, and of course violence,

[27] *CCC*, no. 1765.
[28] See ibid., nos. 2380–2391.
[29] Ibid., no. 2386.
[30] Ibid., no. 2383.

neglect, abuse, et cetera. All of these situations rightly merit righteous anger at their sinfulness and injustice.

One ACOD found himself growing *angrier* about his parents' divorce over time: "As an adult, knowing better God's teachings on marriage and divorce, and being a husband and father myself, my emotions have changed from sadness to anger. I'm angry that the divorce happened and the ways in which it affected me and my family forever."[31] Another expressed her anger at missing out on the family she desired: "I always wish I had the life where everyone ate dinner together and vacationed as a family—and it left me very angry inside."[32]

At times, ACODs are told (explicitly or implicitly) that feeling angry about their family's dissolution is simply and always wrong. This oversimplification feeds into the "wound of silence" that overlooks or ignores the serious trauma divorce and family dysfunction cause children and abandoned spouses. It is an example of "divorce happy talk" that only allows for positive feelings following the divorce. And, as we will see in the chapter on forgiveness, it is a *false* sense of forgiveness that says that feeling continued anger at the divorce and problems caused by it means we haven't "actually" forgiven. One adult child of divorce pushed back against this misusage of forgiveness, saying: "Wow, the audacity of sinning terribly against your kids and then telling them that kids should handle it perfectly by just forgiving and not being

> Anger is normal after our family has fallen apart and can be an initial step in the healing and forgiveness process.

[31] Miller, *Primal Loss*, 87.

[32] Ibid., 51.

angry? I think that the way to heal sometimes includes getting angry at an injustice, at being sinned against, before true forgiveness can occur."[33] Anger is normal after our family has fallen apart and can be an initial step in the healing and forgiveness process. But we do not want to stay "in the anger" forever. We want to work toward lessening anger's hold on our hearts, letting it go little by little. And we always want to ensure that our righteous anger does not slip into sinful anger toward our parents or anyone else.

Sinful Anger

Church teaching is clear that anger can also be a sin. In fact, it was one of the first sins, as seen in Cain's hateful murder of his brother Abel (Gen 4:8–12). *Wrath*—extreme anger desiring revenge and ruin to befall someone—is one of the seven deadly sins. Saint Paul lists sinful anger as one of the "works of the flesh" and says that "those who do such things shall not inherit the kingdom of God" (Gal 5:19–21).

Anger is a mortal sin when it manifests as a "desire for revenge" and reaches a point of "a deliberate desire to kill or seriously wound a neighbor."[34] And anger that becomes hatred of another is a sin "when one deliberately wishes [another] evil."[35] In his book *The Seven Deadly Sins Today*, Henry Fairlie gives this helpful description of sinful anger: "Anger as a deadly sin is a disorderly outburst of emotion connected with the inordinate desire for revenge .... It is likely to be accompanied by surliness of heart, by malice aforethought, and above all by the determination to take

[33] Ibid. 167.
[34] *CCC*, no. 2302.
[35] Ibid., nos. 2302–2303.

vengeance."[36] Father T. G. Morrow gives three examples of sinful anger in his book *Overcoming Sinful Anger.* The first is passive-aggressive behavior, the angry person "shutting down," perhaps agreeing to something but not doing it, or giving the other the "silent treatment". The next example is explosive uncontrolled anger and rage, with insults or acts of violence. Finally, Father Morrow lists *perpetual* anger that holds onto past hurts and wields them against the other in an act of revenge or malice.[37]

In the Sermon on the Mount, Jesus "raises the ante" on anger, so to speak, by adding these words to the commandment "you shall not kill": "I say to you that every one who is angry with his brother shall be liable to judgment; whoever insults his brother shall be liable to the council, and whoever says 'You fool!' shall be liable to the hell of fire" (Mt 5:21–22). Clearly anger is not something to be treated as always neutral or inconsequential; it can have deep effects on our souls and spiritual health. Anger is sinful when directed at the wrong *thing* (something true, good, and beautiful, instead of an actual injustice or sin), expressed in the wrong *way* (with wrath, rage, insults, violence, passive aggressive behavior, et cetera), or for the wrong *reason* (desiring revenge, wishing the person harm, and the like). Careful discernment is needed to determine when merited, righteous anger slips into the realm of sinful anger.

Anger as a Mask

Discernment is also needed about whether a feeling is actually anger (at least at its deepest core). We'll share an

[36] Henry Fairlie, *The Seven Deadly Sins Today* (Notre Dame, Ind.: University of Notre Dame Press, 1979), 88.

[37] T. G. Morrow, *Overcoming Sinful Anger: How to Master Your Emotions and Bring Peace to Your Life* (Manchester, N.H.: Sophia Institute Press, 2014), 7–12.

example from a difficult period in our life: at a challenging time during our experience of infertility, we sought professional advice from a Catholic therapist. One emotion we were dealing with (especially Bethany) was anger at not receiving the blessing of children, and at times anger toward other women who had been blessed with children. Our therapist gave us some great wisdom about anger. She said that anger often *masks* emotions associated with vulnerability. An initial burst of anger at a situation (in this example, perhaps receiving another pregnancy announcement) could be hiding—"protecting"—a deeper feeling of vulnerability that might come with hurt, sadness, or loss. At times, our therapist said, it can feel "easier" to express the bright flame of anger, as an outlet to express our intense emotions. But that flame will burn out, leaving behind the "underneath" emotions that must be addressed and healed.

With this in mind, it's important to evaluate whether anger is the emotion in play, or the *only* emotion, and whether other, hidden emotions lie underneath that need attention, processing, and healing. One self-aware child of divorce described anger as a "protective force field" against other more challenging emotions.[38] Other ACODs have said they felt both angry and sad about their parents' divorce, and upon reflection discovered that sadness was the predominant emotion. Anger arose in part out of the sorrow of losing their intact family. They discovered that what they needed was not so much "venting" their anger but rather *grieving* their losses.

Consequences of Anger

Anger is a strong emotion. It takes a fair amount of energy to sustain the feeling of *being angry*. And when anger

[38] Miller, *Primal Loss*, 187.

becomes sinful, occupied with revenge, or when it is deliberately stoked and maintained, a number of consequences can result.

Anger can be misdirected at people who are not the true object of our anger. An ACOD's unaddressed anger at his parents, for example, can leech over into angry, aggressive behavior toward his spouse or children, provoked by seemingly small annoyances. Those small annoyances provide an excuse to unleash misdirected anger that hasn't found an appropriate outlet as yet.[39] This could help explain, at least in part, why a married adult child of divorce is more likely to escalate conflict, argue frequently, shout, or even physically assault his spouse when arguing.[40]

Unaddressed and unhealed anger can also lead to a buildup of bitterness and willful unforgiveness against the offender that, as we will see in the chapters on forgiveness, can steal our peace and joy and trap us in a prison of resentment. Even when anger is righteous and merited, it is not an emotion one wants to feel for long stretches.

Compounding Pain by Coping in Sinful Ways

Adult children of divorce, like all people, sometimes cope with their suffering, pain, and emotional upheaval in sinful ways. Sinful, rageful anger is one of those ways. In addition, when trying to assuage their hurt, pain, and loneliness, ACODs may turn to excessive alcohol use or other drugs, masturbation, pornography, promiscuity (sometimes

[39] See Richard P. Fitzgibbons, "Children of Divorce: Conflicts and Healing," in *Torn Asunder*, 51–65.

[40] Ibid. See also Pamela Webster et al., "Effects of Childhood Family Background on Adult Marital Quality and Perceived Stability," *American Journal of Sociology* 101, no. 2 (1995): 404–32.

resulting in abortion), self-harming behaviors, or addictions to work, video games, eating, and so on. These are all false comforts because they do not satisfy and instead make us thirstier, hungrier, sicker, et cetera. In an effort to feel emotionally safe, ACODs may also develop a hardened selfishness, turning away from people or God.

From heartfelt conversations we have had with adult children of divorce, we have learned that many of them know these behaviors are wrong and are ashamed of their choices. Nevertheless, they may struggle for a long time with sins that have become habitual. Sadly, for some it is hard to believe that God would welcome back such a terrible sinner or someone who still falls and struggles. Perhaps this is because some ACODs have only experienced a parent as an unmerciful judge. Some also struggle with a deep fear of rejection if their sins become known. Sadly, some come to believe they are unworthy of God's love or anyone else's love, especially if they struggle with habitual sin. But these false ideas couldn't be further from the truth! God has an especially tender heart toward those who are struggling for sanctity.

A false feeling of unworthiness is part of sin's injurious effect on our lives. Sin injures us far more than we typically realize. It is a self-inflicted wound that turns us away from God, the Church, others, and makes it difficult to have an integrated, whole sense of self that is not controlled by our passions and pleasures.[41] The Catechism defines sin as "an offense against reason, truth, and right conscience; it is failure in genuine love for God and neighbor caused by a perverse attachment to certain goods. It wounds the nature of man and injures human solidarity. It has been defined as 'an utterance, a deed, or a desire contrary to the eternal

[41] *CCC*, nos. 817, 953, 1849–1876.

law.' "[42] The effects of sin—especially repeated sin—go beyond the effects of simply choosing a bad action. Sin damages our capacity to believe, our freedom to love, our ability to choose what is right, the *way we think* (especially about ourselves), and even our *desires*. Sin separates us from the love of God and others by leading every aspect of ourselves further away from God and the things he desires for us in our lives, which makes living virtuously and coming back to God more difficult. Sin attacks our human dignity. "When we sin, God does not love us less, but we love ourselves less."[43]

John shared his story about why and how he fell into sin after his parents' divorce:

> Trapped in my self-isolation with no one beyond MTV to speak into my questions about sex, I found the pleasure [of masturbation] to be a means to escape from the strain of my parents' divorce .... But things quickly escalated. What started out as a survival mechanism for the unbearable moments of my childhood became a near-daily ritual to numb even the most minor inconveniences .... Pornography ... gave me the illusion of control. I couldn't get my parents back together. I couldn't end the chaos. But with pornography I could dictate the outcomes .... That simply wasn't true though. Porn began to warp the way I viewed and interacted with the women in my daily life. All the while, the one thing that failed to actually exist—the one thing I remained powerless to effect—was authentic love .... My parents' divorce not only built the emotional stage upon which my addiction began. It also created the circumstances where it could thrive .... I'm not making the argument that I would have never become

[42] Ibid., no. 1849.

[43] Augustine Institute, *Study Guide for Forgiven: The Transforming Power of Confession* (Greenwood Village, Colo.: Augustine Institute Press, 2017), 9.

> addicted to pornography had my parents stayed together. However, the breakdown of my family played an important role in my particular story.[44]

John eventually found healing for his addiction, and his life is a great example of courage, virtue, and faith that can develop out of suffering and struggles with sin. We will share in the next chapter what helped him.

In order to have deep healing, we need to stop any cycle of sin we are caught up in, and deal with its debilitating effects in our lives, by humbly acknowledging the areas where we have been hurt, admit to the ways we have sinned in response to our pain, and accept responsibility for those sins. We can seek outside help when we feel unable to break free from the behavior on our own. This may sound overwhelming, especially for sins that have become habitual or even addictions, but do not be discouraged: God loves you and is with you.

[44] John McLain, "Overcoming Pornography Addiction as an ACOD: Part 1," *Life-Giving Wounds* (blog), April 24, 2022, https://www.lifegivingwounds.org/blog/overcoming-pornography-addiction-as-an-acod-part-1.

10

Life-Giving Virtue, Hope, and Meekness

Cast all your anxieties on him, for he cares about you.

—1 Peter 5:7

In the previous chapter, we looked at two of the most common emotional consequences for children of divorce: anxiety and anger. In this chapter, we will reflect on ways that these emotions can be appropriately processed, especially through growth in virtue, so that they release their strong grip on our lives. We will also look at ways to overcome temptations and sin in general as ACODs.

Keep in mind that if you have experienced trauma or struggle with an addiction, and as a consequence feel stuck in a cycle of unhealthy "knee jerk" reactions to certain triggers, professional support and faith-based therapy may be needed before embarking on a robust attempt to grow in virtue. We do not want the following discussion about growth in virtue to discourage anyone trapped in addictions and trauma, which affects the entire person—psyche, heart, body, and soul.

Emotions, Identity, and Virtue

To have healing in our emotional life, we need to have the right perspective about emotions in general. Too often people equate their identity with their emotions. "I'm just an angry (or anxious) person." But no one can be reduced to his emotions. God gives us the great capacity to feel emotions as a *part* of our identity, not the whole.

A healthy approach to emotions understands them as a gift from God with many benefits: they give us a way to enter another's emotional world through empathy, as with a friend in times of great sadness or great joy. Emotions also give us insight about what is going on in our lives and our hearts; they can be "alarm bells" about our interior world. For instance, feeling angry or anxious could alert us to something wrong that is happening or may happen and spur us to work toward a response. We need not fear our emotions nor try to repress or internalize them (an approach that can lead to withdrawal, isolation, and—ironically—out-of-control emotional outbursts). Emotions—including anger and anxiety—are in themselves morally neutral.[1] They happen *to us* and are not of our own creation.

At the same time, while we are not morally culpable for the emotions we feel, we *are* responsible for our voluntary actions, including those we do "out of" or based on a particular emotion: "I yelled out of anger" or "I drank too much out of anxiety," for example. The Catechism's treatment of *passions*[2] emphasizes that passions, emotions, and feelings incline us toward actions that can be good or evil. Emotions enter the realm of moral culpability when

[1] See *Catechism of the Catholic Church* (CCC), nos. 1767–1768.

[2] Ibid., nos. 1762–1775.

we engage them with our will and reason. At this point, our emotions can be either "taken up into the *virtues* or perverted by the *vices*."[3]

Indeed, virtue is necessary to regulate our emotions properly and order them toward love and communion with others. Virtue is "an habitual and firm disposition to do the good .... The virtuous person tends toward the good with all his sensory and spiritual powers; he pursues the good and chooses it in concrete actions."[4] Virtues "order our passions" and "make possible ease, self-mastery, and joy in leading a morally good life."[5]

As we grow in virtue, we find that our emotions do not so readily master us, but we can more peacefully master them. Again, this does not mean that we suppress our emotions, but instead, when a powerful emotion arises—such as anger or intense anxiety—we are more capable of pausing, examining the emotion, exploring its roots and origin, and "sitting with" the feeling, all before we act in any way. We can entrust the emotion to the Lord and ask for assurance of his presence in that moment. A virtuous approach to emotion helps us have a measured *response* to the emotions we feel, guided by reason and truth, instead of a knee-jerk *reaction* to an emotional stimulus.

Further, we can train our emotions to incline us toward what is good. The virtuous man does not just choose what is good consistently, but in choosing the good repeatedly trains his thoughts, will, and emotions to desire or direct him toward the good. In this way, doing the good over time becomes not just easier, but also natural, like second nature.

[3] Ibid., no. 1768 (emphasis in original).

[4] Ibid., no. 1803.

[5] Ibid., no. 1804.

The possibility of growing in virtue should give us great hope and encouragement! No matter the tidal wave of emotions we may feel at times, we can have confidence that we are not doomed to be enslaved to our emotions. Poor behavior based on intense emotions is not "just the way we are"; everyone is capable of change and growth. No matter what is happening in our lives, and no matter what strong emotions or inclinations we feel, with the help of God we are always free to respond with virtue. What freedom and healing that brings!

Growing in Virtue and Overcoming Sin

Before we discuss specific virtues that can help us with anxiety and anger, we want to give some general, practical tips about how to heal through growing in virtue and overcoming sin, which is often influenced by emotion. After all, anxiety and anger are not the only emotions that ACODs struggle to manage properly and integrate into a virtuous life. The adage "hurt people hurt people" contains much truth. While children of divorce are *never* responsible for their parents' divorce or separation in any way, we have to accept responsibility for how we may have hurt ourselves or others.

The four main tips we recommend for growth in virtue can be remembered by the acronym "WASH": Wounds, Act of Hope, Spiritual Plan of Life, and Holiness.

W—Wounds

We need to understand the dynamics of sin—especially the "cycle" of sin—so we can confront it at multiple points. The wounds caused by our parents' divorce can affect this cycle and contribute to feeling caught in patterns of sinful behavior. In *Clean Break: New Hope for Freedom from*

Unwanted Habits, Brother Sam Gunn describes the habitual sin cycle in four phases—elation, deflation, compulsion, and revulsion, punctuated by four transitions—the trigger, the turn, the actual sin, and the dawn.[6] According to Gunn, first is the "phase of elation," feeling good, worthy, loved, and at peace. A trigger leads to the second phase, deflation. Triggers are anything that attacks your worth and identity, or negative circumstances summed up by the acronym BLASTED—bored, lonely, angry, sad, tired, empty, or dysregulated (difficulty in managing emotions). During the "deflation phase," Gunn says, a person feels "increasingly incapable, unconfident, unworthy, and unacceptable."[7]

After "deflation" comes "compulsion": "As anxiety and insecurity grow, your thoughts go to your habitual action. The turn happens when you make up your mind to do it."[8] In the compulsion phase, good resolutions and moral reasoning are lost, identity lies are believed, and sinful behavior that promises to satisfy one's needs is succumbed to. During the fourth stage, "revulsion," a person feels guilt, shame, and self-condemnation.[9] A final transition—the "dawn"—brings hope. This is the feeling that "you may rise burdened but in the hope that now, at last, you can get your life back on track."[10]

Gunn does not discuss how wounds could impact the cycle of sin, but it is not difficult to envision their possible effects. The "trigger" that moves a person from elation to

[6] Brother Sam Gunn, *Clean Break: New Hope for Freedom from Unwanted Habits* (Boston: Brotherhood of Hope, 2021), 5–16. For Gunn, the cycle of sin is elation, the trigger, deflation, the turn, compulsion, the actual sin, revulsion, and the dawn.

[7] Ibid., 8.

[8] Ibid., 14.

[9] Ibid., 15.

[10] Ibid., 16.

deflation could be a difficult feeling related to his parents' divorce or a subsequent feeling of rejection or abandonment. For instance, John, whose story we mentioned in part in the last chapter, shared that when he went through a breakup, pain from his parents' divorce would resurge and would lead to relapses with pornography.[11] Indeed, for ACODs, breakups are a common trigger for compulsive, unhealthy behavior, since they can be reminders of the rejection and abandonment we felt in our families growing up.

Our wounds can also make the deflation and revulsion phases more pronounced because they are often at the root of lies we believe about our identity, or patterns of thinking that make us feel unloved, unworthy, and self-condemning. For example, John discovered while doing healing work that at the root of his pornography and masturbation addiction was unprocessed trauma from his childhood and an unhealthy commitment he had made against dating and marriage in response to his parents' divorce. This avoidance of intimacy drove him further into the fantasy realm of pornography during moments of difficulties and deflation.

Gunn notes that the compulsion phase is often fomented by anxiety and insecurity, two common emotional situations for adult children of divorce. Having lost the secure base of their parents' love together, it can be tempting to grasp at a sinful behavior for a false sense of security. Lastly, the "dawn" transition, where hope is rekindled, can be affected by our wounds because they can tempt us to believe that we'll always just be "damaged goods,"

[11] John McLain, "Overcoming Pornography Addiction as an ACOD: Part 2," *Life-Giving Wounds* (blog), May 8, 2022, https://www.lifegivingwounds.org/blog/overcoming-pornography-addiction-as-an-acod-part-two-pathways-to-healing.

incapable of changing. To heal and grow in virtue, we need to see ourselves both as wounded *and* as always more than our wounds (and more than our sins, no matter how often we fall).

A—Act of Hope

Hope is an essential virtue for overcoming sin. If we cannot envision a better future *with hope* for ourselves, free from whatever sin, unwanted behavior, or suffering that affects us, then we will lack both motivation for change and a clear plan for the future with concrete goals. In *Making Hope Happen*, Dr. Shane Lopez provides concrete suggestions for predisposing our hearts to receive the theological virtue of hope. Dr. Lopez says that hopeful people have four core beliefs: "the future will be better than the present, I have the power to make it so, there are many paths to my goals, and none of them is free of obstacles."[12] Hope is different from "wishful thinking" because the hopeful man strives to *make hope happen* through his own efforts, coming up with multiple ways to accomplish his goals. Hopeful people "are realistic because they anticipate and plan for difficulties, setbacks, and disappointments," which gives them "momentum and staying power" for making that future happen.[13]

We can deepen Lopez' view from a Christian perspective. Hope does not just have natural dimensions but is also a theological virtue that comes from God. As a theological virtue, hope is lived only insofar as we *cooperate*

[12] Shane J. Lopez, *Making Hope Happen: Create the Future You Want for Yourself and Others* (New York: Atria Paperback, 2013), 18–19. We are grateful to Dr. Mario Sacasa for bringing this book to our attention, and note that Dr. Sacasa's podcast *Always Hope* is also an excellent resource for understanding and cultivating hope.

[13] Lopez, *Making Hope Happen*, 19.

with Christ's grace; this theological dimension unleashes a new power to the virtue of hope. The Church teaches that hope is the virtue by which we *desire* God as our happiness, place our trust in Christ's promises, and come to rely on grace from God rather than our own strength alone.[14]

> Hope in Christ can be the anchor of our healing to overcome fears, keep us still and peaceful when we are tossed by the waves of life, and help us to live differently.

To awaken hope and enlist its aid in overcoming sin and the effects of injuries, we need to envision our new future with Christ.[15] Pope Benedict XVI says in his encyclical on hope, *Spe Salvi*:

> Only when the future is certain as a positive reality does it become possible to live the present as well .... In our language we would say: the Christian message was not only "informative" but "performative." That means: the Gospel is not merely communication of things that can be known—it is one that makes things happen and is life-changing. The dark door of time, of the future, has been thrown open. The one who has hope lives differently; the one who hopes has been granted the gift of a new life.[16]

[14] See *CCC*, no. 1817.

[15] With the theological virtue of hope, envisioning the future is not presumption about God's specific plans for the future for me ("I know God wants this career for me"). Instead, it emphasizes trust and reliance on God who knows the way and fosters a healthy detachment to any specific future envisioned, realizing that often God only illuminates one step or a few steps at a time or may be asking me to do something different from what I initially hoped for.

[16] Benedict XVI, encyclical letter *Spe Salvi*, November 30, 2007, no. 2.

Scripture describes hope as being an "anchor of the soul" (Heb 6:19). Hope in Christ can be the anchor of our healing to overcome fears, keep us still and peaceful when we are tossed by the waves of life, and help us to "live differently." For this hope, we need to commit to prayer, which is a "school of hope,"[17] and can help us "become capable of great hope, and ... become ministers of hope for others."[18]

S—Spiritual Plan of Life

Developing a spiritual plan of life is the third main component to overcoming habitual sin. Many elements could be included, but at bare minimum the plan should include daily and weekly rhythms of prayer, regular reception of the sacraments, and perhaps journaling with the Lord and other prayer practices. A spiritual plan should also have concrete goals for living the particular virtues we need to counteract our sins. We can respond to patterns identified in the cycle of sin with virtuous thoughts and actions at *every point*, not just at the point of sin, until virtue replaces the *entire* old pattern little by little.[19]

Here is John's insight about his healing journey, recognizing sinful patterns, and adjusting these patterns toward virtue:

> Honestly the most impactful adjustments [toward virtue] are often what seem indirect ones. Maybe that's changing your sleep, diet, prayer, exercise, work, or spending habits to promote better self-care. Maybe it's going on a

[17] Ibid., no. 32.

[18] Ibid., no. 34.

[19] Brother Sam Gunn's book *Clean Break* has several helpful suggestions about different virtuous responses to the cycle of sin.

> Life-Giving Wounds retreat or seeking counseling regarding childhood trauma. Maybe it's studying the beauty of human sexuality in its intended framework in order to replace the damaging view that porn or masturbation are bad because sex is bad.[20]

Each of these practices—and more—can animate a spiritual plan of life and make acquiring virtue a reality. At the beginning, it can be helpful to focus on a few goals, rather than trying to tackle every aspect of our lives that needs a virtuous adjustment.

H—Holiness, Accountability, and Patience

After coming up with a plan, it is time to live it out and become more holy! To make sure we are making progress, it is helpful to do frequent checkups and share about our progress or challenges with a trusted friend, spouse, mentor, or spiritual director to keep the momentum going. Therapy with a compassionate Catholic or Christian psychological professional can also be tremendously helpful, especially for dealing with traumatic experiences and unwanted entrenched habits. Friendship with accountability also helps with growth in virtue, and this was true in John's story. To undo the "vow" against intimacy he made, John had to seek connection with others, including an online recovery group of Catholic men and a recovery coach. Advice for finding and living out accountable friendships is in Gunn's *Clean Break*.[21]

Finally, it is necessary to have patience with ourselves as we try to live out our spiritual plan of life. "We tend to think of patience as waiting, but it's much more than that.

[20] McLain, "Overcoming Pornography Addiction as an ACOD: Part Two."
[21] Gunn, *Clean Break*, 55–64.

In the Bible, patience is long-suffering and endurance. It's the strength to handle hardship well, not giving in to discouragement or self-condemnation."[22] Patience is both the commitment to persevere until virtue happens and extending *kind* motivation toward ourselves when setbacks occur. Pope Francis says patience is akin to being "slow to anger," not acting on impulse, and exuding God's mercy.[23]

Spiritual Direction

Receiving regular spiritual direction can also be a tremendous aid to growing in virtue and overcoming temptations to sin based on difficult family circumstances. Sister Kalin Holthaus, AVI, who is both an ACOD and a spiritual director, describes spiritual direction as "the art of guiding someone or being guided to greater growth in the spiritual life and ultimately the goal of becoming the saint that God has created each one of us to be."[24] Spiritual direction is not simply friendship, says Sister Kalin, but is more akin to "spiritual motherhood and fatherhood."

Another ACOD well-versed in spiritual direction, Graciela, identifies the three main benefits of spiritual direction as "interior freedom, encountering your own identity, and the experience of living in God": "Your inner freedom will start to increase as you are guided by the Holy Spirit .... The result of finding that interior freedom will lead you to encounter your own identity .... [And] by living in God's presence you will allow yourself

[22] Ibid., 41.

[23] Francis, General Audience, January 13, 2016.

[24] Sister Kalin Holthaus, A.V.I., "A Religious Sister's Advice about Spiritual Direction for ACODs," *Life-Giving Wounds* (blog), August 12, 2021, https://www.lifegivingwounds.org/blog/a-religious-sisters-advice-about-spiritual-direction-for-acods.

to be found, to be healed, to be freed, and to be able to act in Him."[25] Graciela writes that the image of three chairs in a circle is a symbol of spiritual direction because the Holy Spirit is an essential member of the process. Spiritual direction (as well as therapy) takes time: "There is no rush .... It took time to get where you are, feeling pain, sadness, anguish and distress, so don't feel you have to rush through these processes."

The Sacrament of Reconciliation and the Examen

We are all sinners in need of God's great mercy; for ACODs, perhaps there are particular sins related to our family's breakdown and how we reacted to it or coped with it. The sacrament of Reconciliation (or "confession") is a powerful instrument of God's mercy and healing for our souls. Christ forgives our sins through the priest (this is known as "in persona Christi"), restores and strengthens our relationship with him and others, and offers us "spiritual strength against sin."[26]

One of sin's most nefarious effects is that it leads us to hide from God and even from ourselves, but through confession we bring all of our weaknesses and sins into the light. With God's help, we take responsibility for the areas we need to change instead of blaming others or rationalizing the behavior. We make a commitment to amend our ways, and we grow in love. As Saint John Paul II, then Karol Wojtyła, said, "The more the sense of responsibility for the person, the more true love there is."[27]

[25] Graciela Rodriguez, "Are You Seeking Inner Peace? Spiritual Direction Can Help," *Life-Giving Wounds* (blog), April 20, 2021, https://www.lifegivingwounds.org/blog/spiritualdirection.

[26] *CCC*, no. 1496.

[27] Karol Wojtyła, *Love and Responsibility*, trans. Grzegorz Ignatik (Boston: Pauline Books, 2013), 113.

Receiving the sacrament of Reconciliation should remind us of our identity as God's beloved and restore our self-esteem. In this sacrament, God tells us that we are loved despite our failures and mistakes. The form of the sacrament—in which we hear the words of absolution from the priest "in persona Christi"—can help us reject the lies we may tell ourselves like, "I can never be forgiven," "I'm a worthless sinner," or "I don't deserve this mercy." The sacrament of Reconciliation should not be looked upon as a dreadful obligation, but truly as an immeasurable liberating gift of Christ's love and healing.

In addition, we encourage adult children of divorce to undertake faithfully a frequent examination of conscience. This practice—known in Ignatian spirituality as an *examen*—helps us see both our weak points where we need God's grace, as well as where we have cooperated with God's grace and are progressing in a life of virtue.[28] A good examen should recall words, thoughts, actions, and acts of omission. A daily or weekly examen helps prepare us to receive the sacrament of Reconciliation in all its fullness, having prayed and consulted with God in advance about what sins we need to confess and why. It also helps us grow in responsibility for our sins, and it strengthens us to "go and sin no more."

Therapy

To overcome habitual sin or unwanted habits and pursue virtue, we may need professional therapy and expert psychological guidance from a compassionate Catholic or Christian psychological professional. This is especially important for overcoming addictions and certain forms

[28] See Timothy M. Gallagher, O.M.V., *The Examen Prayer: Ignatian Wisdom for Our Lives Today* (New York: Crossroad, 2006).

of childhood trauma, such as abuse. Many ACODs have found great support, insights, and ongoing mentoring through therapy, especially with a compassionate Catholic or Christian therapist who integrates spiritual truths and practices with sound psychological principles.[29]

Countering Anxiety

After the above reflections on general ways of growing in virtue and overcoming sinful patterns of behavior, we now turn toward the two major emotional challenges we identified for ACODs in the last chapter, anxiety and anger.

Cultivating the virtue of hope and a childlike trust in God can help decrease anxiety. As a theological virtue, hope places "our trust in Christ's promises" and "keeps man from discouragement ... it opens up his heart in expectation of eternal beatitude."[30] In much of the anxiety that adult children of divorce feel, there is an expectation that things will become worse or even fall apart. Hope says the opposite: no matter what travails happen, no matter what suffering takes place, God is faithful in his promises and will not abandon his children. As Saint Paul says so beautifully, "hope does not disappoint" (Rom 5:5).

Catholic psychologist Dr. Mario Sacasa, who has specialized in research on hope, suggests several strategies for increasing hope.[31]

[29] For some tips on how to approach therapy as an ACOD, see Cafea Fruor, "Seeking Therapy as an Adult Child of Divorce," *Life-Giving Wounds* (blog), July 9, 2020, https://www.lifegivingwounds.org/blog/seeking-therapy-as-an-adult-child-of-divorce.

[30] *CCC*, nos. 1817–1818.

[31] Dr. Sacasa's strategies for hope were delivered to a Life-Giving Wounds online support group in Spring 2022.

First, intentionally *savor* the good. This can help overcome the foreboding joy and distrust of joyful things that many adult children of divorce experience.

Second, seek out hopeful stories and spend time with hopeful people. If you struggle to be hopeful, choose to be around people who encourage you and who model hope in their own lives. Turn to art, music, books, stories, and movies that give you hope and encourage you.

Third, reexamine your future goals from time to time and take steps to accomplish them. Being hopeful *and* realistic about our goals can make progress more attainable. Taking even the smallest step forward can increase our hope in the possibility of growth and change.

Fourth, engage in memory exercises, where we process and submit certain memories to the Lord in prayer or through therapy. This is helpful because the memories of difficult events can continue for years to sap the hope out of our lives and make us more fearful and anxious.

Cultivating a childlike trust in God, too, helps push back against tendencies toward anxiety. In his poem *The Portal of the Mystery of Hope*, Charles Péguy describes hope as "infancy of the heart." Hope trusts that God will meet our needs. We therefore turn to him frequently with our needs, as a child turns time and again to a loving parent (something adult children of divorce may have to "relearn" with their heavenly Father). The simple mantra of "Jesus, I trust in you" can be a buoy throughout the day when anxieties threaten our peace.

In a passage with much consolation for those who struggle with anxiety, Saint Paul describes anxiety as a *summons to prayer*: "Have no anxiety about anything, but in everything by prayer and supplication with thanksgiving let your requests be made known to God. And the peace of God, which passes all understanding, will keep your hearts and your minds in Christ Jesus" (Phil 4:6–7). Another Scriptural touchstone for countering anxiety is the Old Testament story of manna in the desert (see Ex 16). After Moses (with God's help) freed the Israelite slaves from Egypt and led them into the desert, they grumbled against God, bemoaning their hunger and homelessness. In response, God gave them "bread from Heaven" (manna). Interestingly, the manna lasted *only for that day*. Stockpiling it was impossible, because "it bred worms and became foul" (Ex 16:20). We can see in this story—which foreshadows the Bread of Heaven, the Eucharist—God's desire for total, childlike dependence on him for all our needs, which he *will* satisfy each and every day. "Give us *this day* our daily bread..."

Anxiety is a summons to prayer.

A final aid for virtuously addressing anxiety are two prayers: a newer prayer called "The Litany of Trust" and the traditional "Act of Hope." "The Litany of Trust" was written by Sister Faustina Maria Pia, S.V., and was popularized by the Sisters of Life. This beautiful prayer includes lines that can bring much comfort to the anxious heart of an adult child of divorce:

> From anxiety about the future, deliver me, Jesus.
> From resentment or excessive preoccupation with
> the past, deliver me, Jesus.
> From restless self-seeking in the present moment,
> deliver me, Jesus.
> ...
> That You will not leave me an orphan ..., Jesus,
> I trust in you.[32]

[32] "Litany of Trust," Sisters of Life, August 21, 2023, https://sistersoflife.org/wp-content/uploads/2019/05/Mobile-Litany-of-Trust-English-1.pdf.

It is no small task for an adult child of divorce to endeavor to free his heart from the tentacles of anxiety that can ensnare it so easily. As with all growth in virtue, progress in developing the virtue of hope and childlike trust in God can feel slow at times. But what a joy it is to notice you are *not* constantly "scanning" for danger, or that the reaction to your spouse's unexpected delay is a shrug rather than an intense fear that the marriage is over. Many of the victories over anxiety will go unseen by anyone other than our Lord and perhaps a spouse or close friend, but the inner freedom gained by a lessening of daily worries is a tremendous gift.

In the Scriptures, we find a powerful image of great mental (and spiritual) strain when Jesus prays "in an agony" in the Garden of Gethsemane "and his sweat became like great drops of blood falling down upon the ground" (Lk 22:44). This episode in the life of Christ, which takes place after Jesus was "troubled in spirit" at the Last Supper (Jn 13:21), can provide fruitful meditation for those who struggle with anxiety. Our Lord, too, experienced great mental distress and anxiety during his Passion, and yet knew the closeness of his Father to bear this suffering.

Finding Freedom from Sinful Anger

The virtue of meekness, with its focus on peace, patience, calmness, and gentleness, can help us make progress in addressing sinful manifestations of anger. Being meek does not mean being a "doormat" to sin and injustice, but rather recognizing the wisdom in not "fighting fire with fire" and responding instead with love and kindness, especially when provoked. For those who struggle with sinful anger, three verses to memorize and internalize are these:

"Be angry but do not sin" (Eph 4:26); "Blessed are the meek, for they shall inherit the earth" (Mt 5:5); and "Let the peace of Christ rule in your hearts" (Col 3:15).

To respond in meekness when a wave of anger hits, we can *pause* to take it to the Lord before we respond in any way: "contemplate before you communicate." What our therapist from years past recommended was to *stop, drop, and roll* (as you would when on fire, an apt analogy for the burning passion of anger). She advised us to *stop*: resist reacting, take a deep breath, pause, perhaps even walk away if needed; then *drop* the "mask" that anger often is, in order to see any more hidden emotions underneath; and finally, *roll* with whatever emotions you're now aware of: sit with those emotions and truly feel them. Through this exercise, we can learn to break habits of anger leading to sinful behavior and also work toward genuine healing of whatever hurt is hidden by our initial angry response.

It can be tempting to think that if our anger is justified, so are our angry actions. But we are always responsible for what we *do* with anger; even righteous anger can become sinful by yelling, insulting, or violence. There are two heroic moments of any argument. The first is taking a break when anger is increasing and conflict is escalating; this is the heroic moment of de-escalation. During the break, you could pray, exercise, journal about your thoughts, practice what you want to say in a kind way, and so on.

The other heroic moment is *returning* to the conversation and talking in a constructive, calm, and kind way—the heroic moment of re-engagement. This moment can be particularly difficult for ACODs who have fears surrounding conflict, including the false belief that conflict always equals disaster. As far as kindly and constructively talking about something that makes you angry, ideally this would include much empathy and listening to understand truly what the other person says and feels, mutual apologies and acts of mercy if possible, and (if necessary) mutual discussion about how to solve or address the problem. Planning in advance what you will do if an angry conflict arises helps to prepare you for acting meekly in such moments.

If you struggle with *internalized* anger, pretending you are fine when you are internally seething, then in addition to meekness, the virtue of courage could be necessary to face up to and address the issue with charity and honesty. This can be particularly difficult for anyone who has long fallen into the role of either peacemaker or people-pleaser. Sharing your genuine emotions, especially when they're negative, is a risky thing to do. But bottling up your feelings indefinitely is never a better solution, because one way or another they will come out in an explosion, like a shaken-up pop bottle.

Lastly, we would be remiss not to mention here that *forgiveness* is another beautiful way of reducing and healing anger, including lessening the temptation to sinful anger. We will discuss forgiveness in depth in the next two chapters.

A Non-ACOD Spouse's Perspective: Growing in Virtue Together

BETHANY: Emotions are part of life, and they're certainly part of our shared life as a couple. Our emotions, and how we handle them, impact each of us individually and affect the health and happiness of our marriage and family. Dan used to struggle mightily with anger, but now struggles more with anxiety (as he shared earlier), and I struggle more with anger. Often our emotions have gotten the best of us and influenced our actions in ways that we later regretted.

We want to help each other grow in virtue, since our main task as a married couple is to get each other to Heaven! This is a delicate process: on the one hand, we want to encourage each other's growth, especially in moments when we feel stuck in certain patterns; on the other hand, we need to tread carefully as anxiety and anger are so often triggered by deep hurts and quickly lead us out of the realm of the rational. We bless each other when we look at each other with a gaze of love, knowing that even when we make mistakes and fail at acting virtuously, that's not the whole story or the whole of who we are.

We're both challenged and encouraged to seek God's healing of our emotions and our responses to them by wanting to set an example for our children of how to handle emotions appropriately and in a holy way. We are very aware of how much our girls need to grow in acting virtuously and not being prisoners to moods and emotion swings! We know this takes time, and we seek healing and growth ourselves so as to be best able to guide them, too.

11

The Wound of Unforgiveness

And forgive us our trespasses, as we forgive those who trespass against us.

—Matthew 6:12

In his classic overview of the Christian faith, *Mere Christianity*, C. S. Lewis writes that one Christian virtue is even more unpopular than chastity: the "terrible duty of forgiving our enemies." Indeed, Lewis continues, "Every one says forgiveness is a lovely idea, until they have something to forgive .... And then, to mention the subject at all is to be greeted with howls of anger."[1] (The original listeners to Lewis' radio addresses, which formed the basis of *Mere Christianity*, certainly had something to forgive: they were experiencing the horrors of the Nazi Blitz.)

In a similar vein, to modify a famous line from Dostoevsky, forgiveness in action is a harsh and dreadful thing when compared to forgiveness in dreams.[2] Forgiveness in a fairy tale, especially if it ends with a theatrical reconciliation just before the curtain drops, brings joyful tears to our eyes. But the prospect of forgiving a particular person who

[1] C. S. Lewis, *Mere Christianity* (New York: Harper Collins, 1952), 115.

[2] The original quotation, from *The Brothers Karamazov* by Fyodor Dostoyevsky, book 2, chapter 4, is "Love in action is a harsh and dreadful thing compared to love in dreams."

has hurt us—especially someone as close to us as our family members, who are supposed to love us more than anyone in the world—can cause an immediate and strong reaction of dislike, or even revulsion.

Forgiveness may not be a natural impulse or our first reaction to being deeply hurt, but it *is* a commandment from the Lord and a great aid in our healing. Jesus' words in the prayer he teaches his disciples are among the most challenging in all of Scripture: "Forgive us our trespasses, *as we forgive those who trespass* against *us*" (Mt 6:12, emphasis added). When Peter asks Jesus a question many of us have wondered about—"Lord, how often shall my brother sin against me, and I forgive him? As many as seven times?"—Jesus responds with what must have sounded like an impossible number: "I do not say to you seven times, but seventy times seven" (Mt 18:21–22). Biblical scholars note that "seventy times seven" is symbolic for "without limit."

In this chapter, we will look at why ACODs may find forgiveness (and particularly forgiving their parents) difficult, as well as the effects of unforgiveness (withholding forgiveness). We will talk in the next chapter about what Christian forgiveness is and what it *isn't*, and we will conclude with some guidance on *how* to forgive.

Why Is It Hard to Forgive?

Forgiving offenses and hurts is hard for anyone to do. But there are several reasons why forgiving can be particularly challenging for adult children of divorce.

First, *what* we need to forgive is particularly weighty. Parents have the God-given mission to be a stable source of support and guidance for their children, in one unified home if at all possible. Losing the love of our parents together is a significant loss worthy of grieving, no matter the circumstances or timeline. It is no small matter to forgive the people involved for their roles and behavior before, during, and after the divorce or separation that changed our life's trajectory forever. Also, the closer someone is to us and the more foundational a relationship is, the more deeply felt an offense is and the more difficult it can be to forgive. There is no more foundational relationship than that with our parents, from whom we trace our very life.

> It is no small matter to forgive people for the divorce or separation that changed our life's trajectory forever.

Second, as adult children of divorce, we usually desire a relationship with our parents. Forgiving someone means acknowledging that he has caused harm, and acknowledging that (even to ourselves) can feel scary, threatening to the relationship, or disloyal to our parents. We may strive not to do anything that could risk destabilizing our relationship with our parents any further. Or we might fear that offering our parents forgiveness means blaming them too much or not honoring the sacrifices and loving actions they did make.

Third, it's not uncommon for an adult child of divorce to hear distorted messages about forgiveness from his parents or other adults involved that can seem more self-serving than beneficial to his healing. He might be encouraged to "forgive and move on" on a timetable faster than he feels ready for, without an honest acknowledgement of the deep and lingering effects of the family's breakup. Or forgiveness might be equated with condoning the situation: "It's really okay, no big deal, your parents did the best they could." Here forgiveness is treated like a tidy wrap-up maneuver, after which the adult child's negative feelings and the truth of his ongoing difficult situations are not welcome. "Forgiveness" in such a scenario reinforces the "wound of silence" that can lock adult children of divorce in pain and grief. Sometimes this type of false forgiveness is even weaponized to shame the other (e.g., "If you have any problems, it's because you are unwilling to forgive"). Understandably, ACODs can resist such an approach to forgiveness that seems to imply that it is a quick and easy endeavor after which everything is fine or "over," when there still remains genuine hurt and lasting negative effects from the family's breakdown.

Finally, it can feel challenging or even impossible to forgive a parent who refuses to accept any responsibility for the divorce or separation, or refuses to express any remorse about the pain it has caused. Here a misunderstanding of forgiveness may occur that equates forgiveness with reconciliation, which it is not. A related fear around forgiveness can be that it may encourage more bad behavior, giving the offender another chance to cause pain.

Why Forgiveness Is Essential

While it can be tempting to think that withholding forgiveness somehow empowers us or gives us control over the situation, unforgiveness *wounds us*. It traps us ever more deeply in our pain and impedes the deep healing that Jesus wants for us. Reflecting on how unforgiveness hurts us highlights *why* we should forgive those who have hurt us, even if interiorly we feel ourselves rebelling against this "terrible duty," to use Lewis' phrase.

Unforgiveness Cuts Us Off

Returning to Jesus' words in the Our Father, we forgive others because God forgives us and commands us to forgive as well. Saint Paul says, "As the Lord has forgiven you, so you also must forgive" (Col 3:13). None of us deserves God's forgiveness, but he showed his radical love for us "in that while we were yet sinners Christ died for us" (Rom 5:8). From the Cross, Jesus prayed, "Father, forgive them; for they know not what they do" (Lk 23:34). Mercy is an unmerited and unearned gift. *While we were yet sinners*, Christ loved us.

We are *all* imperfect and have sins that must be forgiven by Christ. The experience of having received forgiveness ourselves should strengthen our desire and ability to offer forgiveness to others. Perhaps this is why the Our Father first asks for our *own* forgiveness before praying for the grace to forgive others. We forgive not because the other party deserves it or has earned it through apologies and amends, but because we too are recipients of the unmerited gift of forgiveness from the Lord.

When we hold on to unforgiveness, we forget our own need of forgiveness, falsely believing we are superior to others. We may think, "Well I'm not as bad as *him* because I didn't do *that*." Such comparisons are not helpful. While it is always admirable not to sin, we are all sinners in need of a savior. Withholding forgiveness is itself a serious sin that distances us from God and others. Knowing this effect of unforgiveness, Christ makes forgiveness a *commandment* and removes any gray area or uncertainty about it. "Should I forgive X? Even though he did Y?" The answer is always, yes. No matter how hard it is, yes. And Jesus *gives us the grace* to forgive.

Unforgiveness Forgets Our Shared Human Dignity

In addition to following the Lord's commandment, we forgive because of the other person's dignity. No matter the seriousness of the sin he has committed, or the hurt he has caused, he is still a child of God, beloved by the Father just as we are. God loves him just as lavishly as he loves us. Here we should always distinguish between the sin committed (the action) and the sinner (the person). In his short book *Real Mercy*, Father Jacques Philippe writes, "This person [whom I struggle to forgive] did something bad, he or she committed a wrong act, but I don't want to identify the person with the bad action because God still loves this person who has done something bad."[3] When we hold on to unforgiveness, we reduce a person to his bad actions, and this has a boomerang effect on our own lives; when we fail or sin, we will be tempted to reduce our own human dignity to the sin and fall into patterns of self-condemnation.

Father Philippe teases out another aspect of human dignity: the potential for change. He describes forgiveness as a *beautiful act of hope*, saying: "God is working in this person's heart. Perhaps this person will convert. This person I'm judging and condemning will perhaps one day be a great saint. When we look at the lives of the saints, there are assassins, adulterers, criminals, but grace changed their hearts."[4]

What a striking (and challenging) image, but one indeed borne out in the lives of many saints who lived seemingly irredeemable, selfish lives before experiencing a dramatic conversion to the ways of God. We don't know whether the person *we* are struggling to forgive will end up a saint, but *dare we hope*! Unforgiveness cuts off this hope and doubts God's power to redeem all situations. We mimic the prodigal son's elder brother, grumpy and resentful that his younger brother returned home at last to such rejoicing. Instead, we should emulate the hopeful yearning of

[3] Father Jacques Philippe, *Real Mercy: Mary, Forgiveness, and Trust* (Strongsville, Ohio: Scepter, 2016), 33.

[4] Ibid.

the father. He never gave up scanning the horizon for his lost son.

Unforgiveness Makes Us a Prisoner of the Past

Unforgiveness doesn't mean, simply, that we still feel hurt by the person's actions or still feel angry toward him. Our feelings are not the main barometer of forgiveness; feeling hurt or angry can coexist with forgiving someone, although forgiveness can help loosen the hold of these emotions on our hearts. "Not forgiving" is not a feeling but a choice. Father Philippe describes unforgiveness in this way: "It means that I'm holding a grudge, a judgment, sometimes a hatred in my heart."[5] While we are not in control of what happens to us, we do have a say in how we react to it. Actively *not* forgiving or *harboring* resentment or hatred is one possible reaction. It's a "doubling down" on feeling hurt or wronged, and nursing or dwelling upon it to an unhealthy level. Unforgiveness is moving from that initial feeling of anger to the choice of sustained bitterness, revenge, or hatred.

This choice—to harbor and even feed resentment in our hearts—may seem like it gives us power or control over the situation, or protects us from future hurt by that person. But what it really does is keep us tied to the other at the point of the hurt. Unforgiveness keeps us from being free and hardens our hearts, making us less capable of loving others.

Charles Dickens gives us a vivid illustration of the prison of unforgiveness in the character of Miss Havisham in *Great Expectations*. Jilted on her wedding day by a fiancée who conspired to rob her of her inheritance, the spinster continues to wear her wedding dress and refuses to have

[5] Ibid., 36.

the wedding foods cleared from the room. For years, she makes herself a prisoner in her darkened and cobwebbed room, with the clocks all set permanently to the hour of her ruin. Her pain-turned-unforgiveness makes the worst moment of her life into her defining feature. And she teaches her ward Estelle to resent men and seek revenge against them; the unhealed wound continues on into the next generation.

Being actively unforgiving and resentful toward another person is emotionally and mentally exhausting. As Father Philippe says, "We often think as much about somebody we despise as we do about somebody we love .... I'm dependent on the person I can't forgive."[6] Consider the concept of revenge, and the extreme example of gang violence. Rival gangs can spend much of their time plotting revenge on each other for the most recent offense. Indeed, their very identities become focused on rejecting and hurting the other gang.

But fixating on revenge isn't just for gangsters. Jennifer shared how she learned a cycle of vengeance from her parents:

> Although my mother and father were still present in my life, their hearts grew distant from mine as they separated themselves from truth and lived in vengeance, division, unforgiveness, and unfaithfulness toward one another .... Since I was not yet formed as a Catholic, I repeated their behavior in all of my relationships. I was divisive, unforgiving, vengeful, and unfaithful with friends, coworkers, classmates, roommates, and boyfriends.[7]

[6] Ibid., 37.

[7] Hidden Daughter of Carmel (pseudonym), "My Parents' Divorce Left Me an Orphan, but God Became My Refuge," *Life-Giving Wounds* (blog), July 16, 2020, https://www.lifegivingwounds.org/blog/my-parents-divorce-left-me-an-orphan-but-god-became-my-refuge.

In contrast, when we choose to forgive, we gain a newfound freedom from the grinding weariness of bitterness. As Lewis Smedes says, "When we genuinely forgive, we set a prisoner free and then discover the prisoner we set free was us."[8] Forgiveness softens our hearts both toward the person who hurt us and by extension toward all others, making us more capable of loving tenderly and mercifully. We no longer exhaust ourselves by tallying up offenses committed and debts owed; we entrust that burden to our Lord, the one who judges all in righteousness. This leads to greater peace and less anxiety about "settling the score."

Unforgiveness Traps Us in Relational Brokenness

When we forgive, we can break the cycle of relational brokenness. It is sobering to think about how many divorces can be traced in large part to an unwillingness by one or both parties to forgive the other after hurt or betrayal. The opposite could also be said: it is hard to imagine many divorces happening in marriages where both spouses forgive each other deeply and often. Looked at from this perspective, our willingness to forgive those who have hurt us is a powerful *antidote* to the ubiquity of family breakdown. Saint Paul tells us, "Do not be overcome by evil, but overcome evil with good" (Rom 12:21), and choosing to forgive is one tangible way that the evil of divorce can be overcome with good.

> When we forgive, we can break the cycle of relational brokenness.

Forgiving those who have deeply hurt us, and making forgiveness a habit in our lives, also fortifies our other

[8] Lewis Smedes, *The Art of Forgiving: When You Need to Forgive and Don't Know How* (New York: Ballantine Books, 1996), 178.

relationships. It's striking that Jesus' clear teaching on the indissolubility of marriage in Matthew 19 is preceded by his equally clear teaching on the importance of forgiveness in Matthew 18, in the parable of the Unforgiving Servant. Forgiveness makes us better able to be in loving communion with others, which can motivate us to forgive the "hard cases" in our lives. We want our hearts to be occupied with peace, joy, and love for others, not debilitating anger, desire for revenge, or resentment. Forgiveness increases our capacity to love.

Lastly, we forgive out of a desire for integrity. As an ACOD friend puts it, "We forgive the other not because of who they are right now, but because of *who we are*." Or, we forgive others because of who we *want to be*. There is no need to wait for the other person to become better or change in order for us to improve. To do so would give him too much control over who *we* are. Instead, we should forgive because we are Christians, called to treat everyone with the same dignity and love and to leave a lasting legacy of mercy in the world.

Divine Mercy Changes Everything

Despite these laudable reasons to forgive and to avoid the injury that unforgiveness causes us, forgiveness is a "death," a sacrifice that goes beyond our own power and necessitates grace and an encounter with God's Divine Mercy. This was Dan's journey with forgiveness. After his parents separated when he was eleven, he was very angry for six and a half long years. He nursed anger into bitterness and resentment, primarily directed at his father. While he would get into angry fights with his dad from time to time, Dan mostly kept his anger hidden from the outside world, opting to scream in his bedroom when no one was home. He would sing along to heavy metal music, especially the song *Broken Home* by Papa Roach, which he thought perfectly captured his angry feelings toward his parents' split.

Outwardly, Dan appeared to be a happy, carefree teen who worked hard at getting good grades. But inside, his perpetual anger with no outlet was very toxic. Dan was tempted to cut off his relationship with his father completely, thinking he would be free from the pain. At his lowest point, he felt hatred toward himself. Even though the reason for his anger should have been obvious, tied to his parents' separation, the expectation from everyone around Dan seemed to be to "get over it" and move on, which left him feeling crazy for still feeling angry.

A turning point came when Dan attended a high school retreat. His chaplain, Father Larry Richards, shared a personal testimony about Divine Mercy. Father Larry's father was an alcoholic and had abandoned the family, yet he eventually offered mercy to his father and reconciled with him on his deathbed.[9] This was a powerful witness of mercy from someone who knew problems and pain similar to what Dan was facing.

Father Larry's witness inspired Dan to go to the sacrament of Reconciliation for the first time in a long time. Leading up to his confession, he had the insight that he needed to confess the sin of sinful anger and of deliberately *withholding* forgiveness from his father. In confession, Dan shared with Father Larry that he hated himself for being so angry. Father Larry said, "I don't see an angry kid. I see a hurt kid. And that hurt doesn't define you. God

[9] A version of Father Larry's inspiring story can be found on YouTube under the title "A Story about Love." You can find more about his life and work at *thereasonforourhope.org*.

loves you." Father Larry also encouraged Dan to learn the Divine Mercy Chaplet and pray it for his father.

From that point on, Dan embraced God in a deeper way, intentionally seeking to live out his Catholic faith and form Christian relationships with peers to help him in his newfound journey of discipleship. Beginning to forgive his father and having his grief compassionately acknowledged by Father Larry lessened the hold anger had on his heart. Dan reclaimed his true identity as God's beloved son, a recipient of God's unearned mercy. This motivated him to give this same mercy to others as much and as often as necessary. This included trying to deepen his relationship with his father to be defined not by anger, fighting, and withholding forgiveness, but instead by as much patient truth, love, and mercy as possible. Was the relationship perfect and free from conflict and anger from that point forward? No, but something notable did change, especially on Dan's part, and he noticed both gratitude and love for his father growing.

12

Life-Giving Forgiveness

Be kind to one another, tenderhearted, forgiving one another, as God in Christ forgave you.

—Ephesians 4:32

What Christian Forgiveness Is—and Isn't

There are many ways in which forgiveness can be misunderstood and misrepresented, some of which we mentioned in the last chapter. These distortions can contribute to a hesitation to forgive others, to the detriment of our own peace.

Here are some examples of what forgiveness is NOT:

- passive acceptance or approval of the sin or hurtful behavior
- excusing or condoning an injustice that was done
- being weak or a doormat
- *forgetting*, in the sense of removing the memories of the harm done and its lingering effects
- a quick fix to a painful situation or, for the more difficult things we have to forgive, a "one and done" event
- dependent on the other individual's reaction, remorse, or willingness to reconcile

- removing all boundaries with someone
- something we should—or can—do without God's help

Forgiveness Names the Harm

Forgiveness is courageous. It takes strength to be willing to face a painful memory or difficult current situation, and it can require careful preparation in therapy for particularly painful incidents. C. S. Lewis describes this process well: "Real forgiveness means steadily looking at the sin, the sin that is left over without any excuse, after all allowances have been made, and seeing it in all its horror, dirt, meanness, and malice."[1] Like a skilled doctor, the one who seeks to forgive must first identify and diagnose the painful injury in need of healing. After all, if there was no harm done, no forgiveness would be needed. In this way, forgiveness does not excuse an injustice, but rather identifies it and brings it to light.

We see this theme of naming the harm with specificity in Jesus' conversation with the Samaritan woman at the well. When she tells Jesus that she has no husband, he replies by saying, "You are right in saying, 'I have no husband'; for you have had five husbands, and he whom you now have is not your husband" (Jn 4:17–18). This specificity both astounds her and leads to belief in Jesus as the Messiah: "Come, see a man who told me all that I ever did. Can this be the Christ?" she says to her fellow Samaritans (Jn 4:29). As painful as it can be to recall the details of uncomfortable parts of our lives or to examine thoroughly how we have been hurt by another, that specificity is a tremendous pathway for healing and makes forgiveness authentic.

[1] *The Business of Heaven: Daily Readings from C. S. Lewis*, ed. Walter Hooper (New York: Harper Collins, 1984), 63.

Naming the harm done is not the same as blaming others (e.g., our parents) unjustly or refusing them charity. We should distinguish between the ineffable dignity of every person, including those who have hurt us, and the objective harm that certain actions and choices cause us. When it comes to the breakdown of our parents' relationship, we likely do not know all the factors, nor do we need to. But we can state the truth of the harm done to us, even through well-intentioned actions; even if you do not mean to step on my foot, it still hurts! The ultimate judgment of a another's culpability is left to God, the perfect judge. We seek neither to blame nor condemn our parents, but to state as honestly as possible the hurt we have experienced.

The importance of naming the harm done helps us see why the platitude "forgive and forget" rings hollow. In his 1997 Message of Peace, Saint John Paul II reflected on the relationship between forgiveness and memory. Remember that this pope, who grew up in Poland, experienced the horrors and trauma of both the Nazi and the Communist regimes; he and all the Polish people had much to forgive from their history. In his message, he says:

> The truth is that *one cannot remain a prisoner of the past*, for individuals and people need a sort of "healing of memories," so that past evils will not come back again. This does not mean forgetting past events; it means re-examining them with a new attitude and learning precisely from the experience of suffering that only love can build up, whereas hatred produces devastation and ruin. The deadly cycle of revenge must be replaced by the new-found liberty of forgiveness.[2]

[2] John Paul II, 1997 Message for the Celebration of the Thirtieth World Day of Peace, January 1, 1997, no. 3.

We do need to remember and name the past, and past painful events, with specificity, but with an attitude of love and forgiveness that looks ahead to healing and restoration. This is different from dwelling in the past in self-pity, pointing fingers of blame at our parents out of vengeful anger, or reciting past harms from a position of victimhood. An honest examination of our hurts is part of the tough internal work of forgiveness that is necessary for deep healing. In this way, forgiveness allows us to let go of resentment and the desire for revenge, and helps us develop the attitude of love that Saint John Paul II describes above.

Forgiveness Is Ongoing

The effects of divorce on children don't end when the legal papers are signed, or, in the case of long-term separation, when mom or dad moves out. Rather, it is an event that has ongoing repercussions for the lives of all those involved. And in many cases the family situation leading up to divorce or separation was difficult, tumultuous, or dangerous. All of this means that forgiving your parents (or others involved) "for the divorce" means forgiving past hurts as well as fresh difficulties that arise as a consequence of the family's brokenness.

As your knowledge of your wounds grows, so does the number of hurts there are to forgive. It is not uncommon for ACODs whose parents split when they were very young to think for a long time that they had nothing to forgive. They never knew anything other than two homes, with mom and dad separated; that was their "normal." But in the process of healing they come to see that never experiencing their parents' being *together* was a tremendous loss and has deeply affected them. Something fresh to grieve and to forgive comes to the surface with this awareness.

In this way, forgiveness can feel at times like one step forward, two steps back. One adult child of divorce said it this way: "There are times when I think, 'Okay I'm good,' and that I'm past whatever heartache is there ... and then I turn over another stone and, *Whoa Nelly*, there's a whole nest of new grievances to overcome."[3] But rather than a mere setback, every new hurt we encounter can further refine our healing. The more we forgive, the better we get at forgiving. Our hearts are a muscle, both literally and figuratively, and forgiving and letting go of anger and resentment does get easier (although it doesn't usually feel *easy*) the more we do it.

ACODs may feel the effects of their parents' divorce throughout their lives, so forgiveness may never be *over* completely. They may have to forgive their parents again and again for the difficulties and inconveniences their split causes over time: for having to juggle two separate families at the holidays; for the tension brought to special events, like weddings and baptisms; for new unkind words in talking about each other; for the additional burden in caring for an abandoned parent in their later years; and so on. There's no "one and done" here, but rather practicing again and again the *virtue* of forgiveness.

Forgiveness Is a Virtue and a Habit of the Heart

At times, we might question whether we have *really* forgiven someone because we still feel angry with him or hurt by his actions. But forgiveness is an act of the will, not a

[3] Leila Miller, ed., *Primal Loss: The Now-Adult Children of Divorce Speak* (Phoenix: LCB Publishing, 2017), 179.

feeling. It is a virtue and a habit of the heart that we can seek to cultivate. As Saint John Paul II said, "Forgiveness is above all a personal choice, a decision of the heart to go against the natural instinct to pay back evil with evil."[4]

The fact that forgiveness is not equated with pleasant feelings is a liberating truth. It allows us to proceed with our efforts to forgive someone genuinely—wishing him well (which includes praying for his repentance and that God's will be done in his life) and absolving him of any "debt" we may feel he owes us—while processing through our feelings at our own pace. The angry or sad feelings we have about a person or situation can be used for our healing: when we feel a pang of anger or a wave of hurt, we can take that to the Lord, examine it with him, then proactively say, "I forgive so and so for *x* ..." At first, this might be said through clenched teeth, truly an act of the will out of obedience to our Lord's commandment to forgive. However, as we have seen personally and witnessed in others, choosing to extend forgiveness can itself help our hearts heal of their intense anger, giving us another layer of freedom.

Forgiveness as a habit of the heart is a process of slowly letting go of the anger, hurt, and resentment we carry. As Dr. Andrew Sodergren points out, this is a great paradox: "Forgiveness is deciding to give up anger and resentment, even though they are natural reactions to being hurt."[5] Part of this letting go means taking the time to acknowledge and work through the hurt feelings internally in the heart. We seek the peace of Christ that comes through forgiveness.

[4] John Paul II, Message for the Celebration of the Thirty-Fifth World Day of Peace, January 1, 2002, no. 8.

[5] Dr. Andrew Sodergren has shared this information via video presentations in Life-Giving Wounds support groups.

Forgiveness Coexists with Boundaries

Forgiving someone does not necessarily mean dropping all boundaries with that person, especially if he has a history of hurting us. A faulty understanding of forgiveness posits an almost magical quality that instantly transforms unhealthy relationship dynamics or erases all past bad behavior and its lingering effects. Forgiving someone does not mean you are necessarily ready to spend a lot of time with that person or allow him more access to your life.

We will discuss boundaries in detail in chapter 14, but suffice to say that boundaries are meant to keep the good in and the bad out, for the sake of maintaining healthy long-term relationships. We establish boundaries with people in our lives not to push them out, reject them, or ostracize them, but in order to continue being in relationship with them in a way that honors both their dignity and ours. When seeking to forgive someone, what exactly the relationship will look like going forward is a separate question. And this can change over time and as circumstances change, too.

Forgiveness May Be One-Sided

One of the hardest truths about forgiveness is that there are times when the person we seek to forgive expresses no remorse about his past actions. There may even be a fundamental disagreement on *whether* anything wrong has taken place. We know of a parent who had an affair but adamantly insisted that he did not do anything wrong because, in his eyes, his marriage was "already over" or the other parent had "stopped loving him." A parent might insist that the divorce was done *for the child's good* and therefore nothing exists to regret or to apologize for. Much of society's "divorce happy talk" consists of well-meaning "consolations" that deflect any responsibility for wrongdoing, allowing for no expressions of remorse or apology: "but you had two Christmases," "people go through much worse things," "at least you had two involved and loving parents," and so on.

It is painful when the person we seek to forgive is unrepentant because true *reconciliation* is not possible at this time. Reconciliation takes two people willing to offer apologies, forgive each other, make amends, and mutually deepen their relationship. While forgiveness is ordered toward reconciliation (when it is safe and prudent to do so), it must at times be *unilateral*, meaning forgiveness is offered but not received for various reasons. The other person may neither accept wrongdoing nor desire our forgiveness, or perhaps cannot comprehend his actions due to his own past trauma. Unilateral forgiveness can also take place after the offender has died. Depending on the circumstances, it may be necessary to offer unilateral forgiveness only internally, in our heart, but unspoken.

Does unilateral forgiveness "count"? Can I forgive someone who insists he has done nothing wrong? The answer is *yes*. In fact, this type of forgiveness is uniquely Christian: Jesus says "Love your enemies" (Mt 5:44). And on the Cross, Jesus forgave those who had tortured him and brought about his death before they asked for forgiveness or repented. His words provide a model for us: "Father, forgive them; for they know not what they do" (Lk 23:34). These can be our words too, in those painful situations when a parent or someone else close to us does not see, or chooses not to see, the hurt his actions have caused us.

It is an extra *layer* to forgive when the other one refuses to see our pain or acknowledge any role in that pain. But we should never feel blocked in our efforts to forgive by someone who accepts no blame. We are still free to forgive unilaterally, *always*, and to find that freedom of heart that comes from forgiveness.

Forgiveness Is a Gift from God

Finally—and most fundamentally—forgiveness is ultimately a gift from God. Yes, it is a virtue that we should cultivate, but as with all virtues, we can and should pray for the grace to forgive. At the very raw, initial stages of forgiving, we can pray for the grace *to want to forgive*. We can pray for a softened heart toward those who have hurt us—not to minimize the harm done, but to see them as God sees them, as his beloved children. Ultimately, the heroic forgiveness that we have just outlined is not something we can achieve by our efforts alone, and we don't have to. God generously gives us grace to help us forgive—and he set the precedent for forgiveness by forgiving us while we were yet sinners. We must cooperate with God's grace to offer forgiveness and his divine mercy to those who have seriously hurt us.

How to Forgive

Below is some guidance for embarking on the difficult but worthwhile effort to forgive. We recommend starting with the parent you believe to be most at fault for the divorce or the one you feel the most hurt by, and then repeat this process for the other parent, or other people.

Seek God's help.

Since the ability to forgive is ultimately a gift from God, seek his help first, second, and always. *Pray* for the desire to forgive. Ask God for insights into your hurt. Petition our Lord for a softened heart toward the guilty party. Pray for guidance about where you have made mistakes and need God's mercy. Ask to see meaning in your suffering. Pray for freedom from resentment, bitterness, and the intense anger that steals our peace. Pray, pray, pray!

One adult child of divorce expressed God's role in forgiveness in this way:

> Sometimes I do not want to forgive them; I feel justified in withholding forgiveness for *x*, *y*, and *z* reasons .... [Some] advice I received from a priest friend, is: Pray for them. Let God do the heavy lifting. Simply tell God that you haven't forgiven them and that you *need Him* to help you heal. Soon your simple prayer for them will deepen, and one day you'll realize the hurt isn't so bad anymore. The scars may always be there, but let God help you through it .... He really wants to![6]

Praying the Divine Mercy Chaplet can help soften your heart toward those who have hurt you. You can entrust the other person to God's perfect mercy and justice, placing yourself with him at the foot of the Cross. The three o'clock hour is traditionally the "hour of mercy," the hour when Jesus died on the Cross. A worthwhile practice is to say a short prayer—or the whole Chaplet—at three o'clock, praying for those who have hurt you and for the ability to forgive them.

Go to confession frequently.

To cultivate a forgiving heart, go to the source of forgiveness: the sacrament of Reconciliation (or confession). Adult

[6] Miller, *Primal Loss*, 179.

children of divorce are not responsible for their parents' divorce or separation itself, but may have responded to it in sinful ways. And in general, the more we ourselves receive God's mercy and humbly recognize our own need for it, the more we will be able to offer that mercy to others. Perhaps intentionally withholding forgiveness is a sin you need to confess, as Dan shared in the previous chapter. Confession can give us the sacramental grace we need to overcome bitterness, resentment, and our desires against forgiveness.

The more we ourselves receive God's mercy and humbly recognize our own need for it, the more we will be able to offer that mercy to others.

Examine motives.

Keeping the benefits of forgiveness in mind can help you forgive those who hurt you. This is not intended to be self-focused, but rather to acknowledge the graces God gives to you in forgiveness. Still, while forgiveness will positively impact your life, offering forgiveness to others may or may not produce any changed behavior in their lives. You should not seek to forgive *primarily* with the motive of wanting the other to change or repent, for your relationship to be healed, or to hear (at long last, perhaps) an apology. When improvements do occur and reconciliation happens, it is a reason for rejoicing! But another person's choices and behaviors are not under your control. You *can* steadfastly pray for his good and his repentance, knowing that his salvation is God's deepest desire and the pathway for his own freedom. And you can carry on with forgiving him no matter how he reacts or behaves.

Alex illustrates this with the story of his grandfather's deathbed conversion.[7] In Alex' family, divorce reaches back two generations: both his parents and his dad's parents divorced. He tried at various points to talk with his grandfather about their family history, in an effort to help him see the tragedy of the family's split; but these efforts seemingly went nowhere. It wasn't until Alex' grandfather was dying that he expressed his remorse, telling his children shortly before his death: "I never should have left your mother." Alex writes about this moment: "When I heard about this, I felt a tremendous sense of *relief*—not so much for me but for *him*. I realized in that moment that I had been hoping—for over sixteen years—for some small shred of remorse from Pappap for the good of his immortal soul." Alex goes on to say:

> I share this tale because I know many of us long to hear apologies from one or both of our parents for their own roles in the divorce. I just encourage you to pray for apologies and a sense of remorse *not for your own sake but for theirs*. If we forgive them in our hearts, we can find healing without their apologies. But apologies on their parts will do them a great deal of good when they stand before God at the end of all things.

Name the hurt specifically.

A thorough discussion about forgiveness comes so late in this book because we hope the previous chapters have given you a deep insight into yourself and how you may have been hurt by your parents' divorce or separation. Being

[7] Alexander Wolfe, "'I Never Should Have Left Your Mother': A Deathbed Confession," *Life-Giving Wounds* (blog), March 6, 2022, https://www.lifegivingwounds.org/blog/i-never-should-have-left-your-mother-a-deathbed-confession.

able to acknowledge and name that hurt is an important step in forgiving others for their role in it.

Journaling can play a fruitful role because it provides a private space to process your emotions through writing. Here you can be completely free and unedited with your thoughts and feelings. Writing can also help bring clarity to confusing situations: looking back at what you wrote, you may start to see a "thread" in the narrative, or put some pieces together about why a particular event impacted you the way that it did. At our retreats and in our support groups, we encourage attendees to write a letter of forgiveness or "forgiveness statement" to their parents. In this letter (which does not necessarily have to be sent), the writer names and forgives specific hurts in detail. It may take multiple attempts to write this forgiveness statement, especially as deeper aspects of the wound are explored. While this letter is mainly for the ACOD writer, some have found it helpful to share it with a trusted friend, spouse, spiritual director, or counselor.

You can also "name the hurt" through the "empty chair technique," placing an empty chair in the middle of the room and telling it what you would like to say to your parents. And many ACODs have also found it helpful to talk to peers who have been through similar experiences and are working on forgiveness.

Two extremes should be avoided in the forgiveness exercises of writing, processing, or talking with others. First, it is unhelpful if you or your confidant feels the need to censor your story or find the "silver lining" immediately. You need to acknowledge the deepest emotions of hurt, abandonment, and sadness. At the same time, to progress on the path of healing and forgiveness you want to avoid becoming stuck in venting or blaming. You share your hurt in order to forgive it.

Cultivate empathy and compassion.

Divorce, family brokenness, abuse, and other negative dynamics in families are often generational. If you are an adult child of divorce, it is likely that your parents experienced some family brokenness, too. This may have been exacerbated by the more common tendency in the past for the pain caused by divorce or separation to be overlooked, minimized, or otherwise not attended to.

Your parents' backgrounds do not excuse their choices or behavior, any more than your background excuses your own sinful choices. But realizing that your parents, too, may have experienced deep suffering in their own families can increase your empathy and compassion for them. It can help you see them as hurting children who also desired something better than they received. It can help you understand why they may have struggled in their own relationships, or struggled in parenthood. Growing in empathy toward your parents for difficulties they have faced can soften your heart toward them and aid you in forgiving them. And it can motivate you to end the cycle of brokenness and family dysfunction in your generation.

Recalibrate expectations and accept the limits of the relationship.

A difficult part of forgiveness is proactively freeing the other person from the "debt" you feel he owes you. This word is used in some translations of the Lord's Prayer: "Forgive us our debts, as we forgive our debtors" (Mt 6:12, KJV). A *debtor* is someone who owes something. As an ACOD, you have experienced a fundamental injustice, the loss of your intact family through the willful actions of one or both of your parents. The restoration of your family is a tremendous *debt* that you are owed, but tragically it is likely not a debt that will ever be paid. Even in the inspiring cases of parents who do reconcile, there remain losses and trauma from the family's temporary split. You may desire a deeper, more loving relationship with a parent that simply is not possible due to mental illness, obstinacy in sin, life choices, abandonment, or other obstacles. You may never have the kind of parent-child relationship that you desire.

As a step toward forgiveness, you can work on accepting that your expectations for a happy, intact family or an enriching and healthy relationship with a parent may never be met. Merciful acceptance of this fact can help you forgive a parent and even find joy in what he *is* able to offer you. Accepting the limits of the relationship ends the torment of constantly wanting things to be different and better in your family. It ends the wish for *repayment that is not forthcoming*. Your parents can never fully pay the debt that is owed or deserved, so if you want freedom, then you must forgive and accept the limits of the relationship.

A striking witness of this comes from an adult child of divorce whose mother died an untimely death in a car accident after years of struggling with alcoholism and mental illness.[8] In the midst of her grief, Rebecca wrote that she had decided years before to come to terms with the fact that her relationship with her mother would never be what she desired. Within that sadness, she was able to see that her mother, in her own way, was truly trying to love her: "It wasn't the love I needed, but it was the

[8] Rebecca Smith (pseudonym), "Coping with Death of a Parent as an Adult Child of Divorce," *Life-Giving Wounds* (blog), August 5, 2021, https://www.lifegivingwounds.org/blog/coping-with-the-death-of-a-parent-as-an-adult-child-of-divorce.

love she could give." Rebecca wrote about cleaning out her mom's apartment after her death and finding "picture after picture of me and my brother framed on the walls, a quilt she was making for my birthday that wasn't quite finished, a box of every card I sent her over the years." She saw these things as signs "that she loved me immensely ... she loved me as she knew how."

It is a *heroic* act of mercy for an adult child of divorce to be willing to receive the love that his parents *can* give. One expression of mercy is simply continuing in relationship with someone who has hurt you (within whatever boundaries are needed to be healthy and safe). You "forgive our debtors" by releasing the people in your life from the debts they owe you but will never be able to repay. You forgive not because you think you will get something from the other individual, but despite the fact that you never will.

It is a *heroic* act of mercy for an adult child of divorce to be willing to receive the love that his parents *can* give.

Discern sharing our hurt.

Forgiving your parents does not *require* sharing your hurt directly with them. Forgiveness, which you can give regardless of the other's response, is different from reconciliation, which takes two people who wish to heal the relationship. At the same time, some ACODs have found that sharing their authentic feelings with a parent has brought both additional healing and a deepened relationship with that parent. Whether and how to go about this takes prudence and discernment of God's will; there is no absolute right or wrong here.

A good initial question to ask is, "Am I ready to take this step?" Sometimes there may be an urgency to share your pain, such as when a parent is considering divorce during a period of separation. (But remember that the decision to divorce is *always* that of one or both of your parents, regardless of what you say or do.) In general, though, sharing your hurt with your parents should ideally occur after internally working on your wounds and striving to forgive your parents for any hurt they have caused. You will then be better prepared for an honest and deep conversation on the specific ways you have been hurt, better prepared for genuine reconciliation (having cultivated forgiveness in your heart) and, come what may from a particular conversation, you can have peace of heart knowing you have already advanced in your own healing. You will also be in a better place to handle any rejection of you or what you have shared.

It takes careful discernment and prayer to determine whether sharing your hurt with your parents is prudent, safe, and conducive to deepening the relationship and fostering reconciliation, or whether it could further negatively impact the relationship. Of course, even "risking" the latter outcome could be worth it if you have discerned the need for *yourself* to be honest and forthright with a parent, perhaps after a long period of "going along" with the situation.

Consider this advice from Catholic therapist Dr. Andrew Sodergren:[9]

- *Discern your motives.* Healthy motives include the desire to be heard and understood, to advance in

[9] Dr. Sodergren has shared this information via video presentations in Life-Giving Wounds support groups.

healing, and to improve the relationship. However, we have to remain conscious that we may be seeking something that the other won't or can't give us, such as validation, understanding, or compassion. If one of your motives is the desire to hear an apology from him, keep in mind that that's not something he may be able or willing to give at this time.

- *Pray for the ability to speak truth in love, and pray that your parents can receive your words and feelings.* Also, consider how similar conversations have gone in the past, as an aid to your discernment on approaching this topic again.
- *Prepare what you want to say before the conversation*, perhaps by writing it out.
- *Forewarn your parents that you want to talk about this*, and set a time and place to do so. Set a timeframe for the conversation so that your conversation won't be interrupted by other activities.
- *Begin the conversation with gratitude.*
- *Show preemptive empathy for them, putting yourself in their shoes.* For example, begin with a statement like "I know you tried to make it work for a long time . . ." and resist adding a "but" to this statement. Let it stand on its own and then if and when you sense the other person taking it in and softening a bit, talk about your own experience.
- *Speak subjectively about the objective truth of your situation* (i.e., how the situation impacted you: "When *x* happened, I felt *y*. This is how it affected me.").
- If you choose to speak about the present relationship, *share about how you hope things could be different without dictating or demanding any changes* (e.g., "For the future, I hope for *y*.").
- *Evaluate throughout the conversation their ability to receive what you're saying*, and feel the freedom to stop

if the conversation is becoming too difficult or overwhelming.

- Above all, *show love and respect.* Expect them to do the same. (If either party seems to be having difficulty remaining charitable, it may be prudent to end the conversation for now.)
- Because your parent(s) might be thinking, *What does my child want from me?*, consider telling them something like: "Mom and Dad, I don't expect you to be able to go back in time and fix this. It's just become increasingly important to me to share my experience with you, with the hope that you can understand and appreciate how all this has affected me."

Some parents will be able to receive their children's expression of hurt, which can provide a beautiful opportunity for deepening the relationship, expressing forgiveness, and experiencing reconciliation. But not all parents can receive their children's hurt in this way. When a parent is either unwilling or unable to accept his children's experiences from the divorce, you can grieve that lack, strive to forgive him, and seek to have the relationship he is capable of having.

If the situation seems to merit it, another strategy is to send a scripted video (preparing in advance what you want to say) or to write a letter to your parent(s) and ask them for a written or video reply. This could be in lieu of an in-person conversation or in preparation for a conversation later. This may be a particularly helpful method for adult children of divorce who have not been in contact with a parent for several years or more.

You should never stake your healing "success" on a conversation with your parents, or feel like you must do this. It can be a powerful *part* of your healing journey, but ultimately it is just one of many means for healing.

Seek therapy.

A reliable, well-grounded Catholic therapist can be a tremendous help in forgiving parents or others. This is particularly the case if your background includes abuse, trauma, neglect, or other serious situations. A therapist can help if you are feeling "stuck" or unable to "go there" in examining past wounds. And therapists can help with the sometimes-challenging process of setting boundaries with the people in your life you are seeking to forgive. There's no shame in seeking out professional help, and it can avoid many years of headache and hardship.

Study examples of forgiveness.

Our Lord himself, of course, would top the list of heroic examples of forgiveness; meditate on the mercy he shows throughout the Gospels. And the lives of the saints are replete with acts of heroic forgiveness, including Saint Maria Goretti, who forgave the man who tried to rape her and eventually killed her; Saint Stephen, the first martyr, who prayed for those who were stoning him: "Lord, do not hold this sin against them" (Acts 7:60); Saint Edmund Campion, an English priest and martyr, who forgave the man who betrayed him; and many more. We can call on our heavenly friends in moments when forgiveness seems difficult.

We also have many modern-day examples of radical forgiveness. Saint John Paul II forgave his would-be assassin; Rwandan genocide survivor Immaculee Ilibagiza forgave her family's murderers; and several Amish families whose children were murdered in the Nickel Mines school shooting raised money to support the murderer's widow and children.[10] These examples help us see that forgiveness is possible even in the direst circumstances.

[10] For more inspiring, modern stories of forgiveness, we recommend Johann Christoph Arnold's *Why Forgive?* (Maryknoll, N.Y.: Orbis Books, 2009).

A Non-ACOD Spouse's Perspective: The Freedom of Forgiveness

BETHANY: Frequent forgiveness is essential for a strong marriage. Dan and I see the importance of forgiveness day in and day out, as we imperfect people find many opportunities to offer each other forgiveness! While the more painful offenses can take time to forgive after the initial intense swell of emotion has subsided, we have been intentional about making forgiveness a virtuous *habit* in our relationship, and this has borne much fruit.

One reason why forgiveness is so important to Dan and me is because he has worked so hard to forgive the people in his life who have hurt him or let him down. I can barely imagine Dan when he was intensely angry at his parents' divorce, because that's so unlike the husband I know. I have no doubt that working on forgiveness, and receiving it himself in confession, was foundational for finding freedom from intense anger and bitterness. That's been a tremendous blessing in our marriage and has made Dan a better husband and "forgiver" because of it.

I have also seen in our marriage that parental divorce provides ongoing opportunities to forgive. When a new difficulty or offense occurs, I can see Dan *pausing*, taking stock of his emotional state, processing it, and making the effort—again—to forgive. It's not easy to see him go through this, and that gives me something to forgive, as well. Now married to Dan, I have had to work on forgiving certain relatives for how they have hurt him. I'm not the main recipient of that hurt, but can find myself feeling angry on Dan's behalf, or experiencing a situation of brokenness together with Dan. So I too need to guard my heart against unforgiveness, and Dan and I can share together the hard but rewarding path of forgiveness.

Dan's efforts to forgive and not let his heart become bitter ensure that there is far more room in him for joyful love for me, our children, our extended family, and others. A spouse burdened with resentment and unforgiveness might take that frustration out on the people nearby, so forgiveness has a positive ripple effect: the spouse and family don't receive any collateral damage.

13

The Wound of Unhealthy Family Dynamics

Can a woman forget her sucking child, that she should have no compassion on the son of her womb? Even these may forget, yet I will not forget you.

—Isaiah 49:15

When parents split up, the family's fundamental geography changes forever. No longer does *home* denote one unified place where father, mother, and children live together. Suddenly children (no matter their age) must navigate a dramatically new landscape with new places, many transitions, and likely new people who may become new family members, and may later detach again. These new family structures and dynamics can bring both practical and emotional challenges, which will be outlined in this chapter. The experience of every adult child of divorce is unique, so these scenarios or difficulties may or may not apply to each and every situation but do remain generally common experiences. In the next chapter, we will take a close look at what it means to honor one's father and mother as an adult child of divorce, and what healthy boundaries are (and are not).

The Landscape

A bird's-eye view of family composition and structures in the United States today helps illuminate the life experiences of adult children of divorce or separation, which in turn can bring greater self-awareness and a sense of solidarity—you are not alone. For many people, the experience of family dynamics has been, among other things, *complicated* and *unstable.* As we have noted previously, *most* American children today will not live their entire childhood together with their original married parents in one unified home.[1] This is a marked change from 1960, when 75 percent did.[2]

Around 15 percent of all American children live in so-called "blended" families, with one parent and the parent's new spouse, and perhaps the stepparent's children, or half-siblings from the new marriage.[3] With 75 percent of divorced women remarrying within ten years,[4] most children of divorce will experience a stepparent situation at some point in their lives. And about 10 percent of all American children will experience more than one divorce during their childhood as one or both parents remarry and divorce at least once more, creating more family "branches" to navigate.[5]

[1] "Parenting in America," Pew Research Center, December 17, 2015, https://www.pewresearch.org/social-trends/2015/12/17/parenting-in-america/. See also Melanie Wasserman, "The Disparate Effects of Family Structure," *Future of Children* 30, no. 1 (Spring 2020): 55–82.

[2] "Parenting in America."

[3] Ibid.

[4] Paul Sullins, "The Tragedy of Divorce for Children," in *Torn Asunder: Children, the Myth of the Good Divorce, and the Recovery of Origins*, ed. Margaret Harper McCarthy (Grand Rapids, Mich.: Eerdmans, 2017), 27. See also Matthew D. Bramlett and William D. Mosher, *Cohabitation, Marriage, Divorce, and Remarriage in the United States*, Vital and Health Statistics, series 23, no. 22 (Washington, D.C.: U.S. Department of Health and Human Services, 2002).

[5] Paul Sullins, "The Case for Mom and Dad," *Linacre Quarterly* 88, no. 2 (2021): 186.

Children who live with neither their original, married parents nor in a stepfamily live either with a single parent (26 percent; most live with their single mother) or with a parent who is cohabitating (7 percent)[6]; both of these family arrangements have seen dramatic increases since the 1960s.[7]

The increased rate of cohabitation merits special mention. While, happily, the divorce rate has been on the decline for decades, reaching its lowest rate in over fifty years in 2019, the marriage rate has also declined, also reaching its all-time low in 2019.[8] Over the same time period, the number of couples cohabiting has grown. Today, more people have "ever cohabited" than have "ever married," and just over half of cohabiting couples are raising children.[9] Cohabiting-with-children is a highly unstable family structure: by age nine, half of the children in cohabiting households will have experienced their parents breaking up, as compared to one in five children in married households (a strikingly high number itself).[10]

Among children of divorce strictly speaking, meaning those whose parents married before splitting up, most divorces happen when children, if present, are young:

[6] "Parenting in America."

[7] Stephanie Kramer, "U.S. Has World's Highest Rate of Children Living in Single-Parent Households," Pew Research Center, December 12, 2019, https://www.pewresearch.org/short-reads/2019/12/12/u-s-children-more-likely-than-children-in-other-countries-to-live-with-just-one-parent/; Juliana Menasce Horowitz, Nikki Graf, and Gretchen Livingston, *Marriage and Cohabitation in the U.S. Pew Research Center* (Washington, D.C.: Pew Research Center, 2019).

[8] Wendy Wang, "The U.S. Divorce Rate Has Hit a 50-Year Low," *Institute for Family Studies* (blog), November 10, 2020, https://ifstudies.org/blog/the-us-divorce-rate-has-hit-a-50-year-low.

[9] Horowitz et al., *Marriage and Cohabitation in the U.S.*

[10] Gretchen Livingston, "About One-Third of U.S. Children Are Living with an Unmarried Parent," Pew Research Center, April 27, 2018, https://www.pewresearch.org/short-reads/2018/04/27/about-one-third-of-u-s-children-are-living-with-an-unmarried-parent.

13 percent of first marriages end in divorce within five years,[11] and a full 80 percent of divorces take place in the first ten years of marriage.[12] But family instability continues into couples' older years, with "gray divorce" on the rise. Among Americans over fifty, the divorce rate has doubled since the 1990s; for those over sixty-five, the divorce rate has tripled.[13] (Note that around half of these older marriages breaking up are remarriages, which are less stable than first marriages.)[14]

Transitional Family Life

One important takeaway from the foregoing data is the sheer number of transitions that a child of divorce or separation may undergo during his childhood. While it is statistically *possible* that a child experiences only the one split of his original parents (a scenario worthy of grieving in itself), neither of whom remarry, the *general* experience of children from broken homes involves navigating a variety of new family relationships and configurations, and major life transitions. As Andrew Cherlin notes in *The Marriage Go-Round*, "family life in the United States involves more transitions than anywhere else,"[15] and "nearly half of

[11] Yeris Mayol-Garcia, Benjamin Gurrentz, and Rose M. Kreider, *Number, Timing, and Duration of Marriages and Divorces: 2016* (Washington, D.C.: U.S. Census Bureau, 2021), https://www.census.gov/library/publications/2021/demo/p70-167.html.

[12] Sullins, "The Case for Mom and Dad," 187.

[13] Renee Stepler, "Led by Baby Boomers, Divorce Rates Climb for America's 50+ Population," Pew Research Center, March 9, 2017, https://www.pewresearch.org/short-reads/2017/03/09/led-by-baby-boomers-divorce-rates-climb-for-americas-50-population/. See also Bruce R. Fredenburg and Carol R. Hughes, *Home Will Never Be the Same Again: A Guide for Adult Children of Gray Divorce* (New York: Rowman and Littlefield, 2020).

[14] See, for example, Bramlett and Mosher, *Cohabitation, Marriage, Divorce, and Remarriage in the United States.*

[15] Andrew Cherlin, *The Marriage-Go-Round: The State of Marriage and the Family in America Today* (New York: Vintage Books, 2019), 19.

children who had experienced the breakup of their parents' marriage or cohabiting relationship saw the entry of another partner into their household within three years."[16] Changes in family relationships can be concurrent with changing houses, schools, or other foundational features of a child's life.

Research shows the deleterious effect of multiple major transitions during childhood. Summing up a meta-study of the effects of divorce on children, researcher Paul Amato says: "The number of family structure transitions during childhood has been shown to be associated with children's behavior problems, drug use, externalizing problems and delinquent behavior, academic achievement, psychological well-being, having a non-marital birth, and relationship instability in adulthood."[17] Beyond these important externally evident effects, the pattern of bonding with a parental figure or stepsibling, losing that relationship, then re-bonding with new parental figures and stepsiblings, can take a serious toll on a person's future relationships and can contribute to what we described earlier as unhealthy self-protective behaviors.

Common Challenges for ACODs in Reconfigured Family Structures

Reconfigured Families and Forced Intimacy

There is no perfect way to describe the kinds of reconfigured family situations that occur after an original parental relationship splits up and one or more new adults, and perhaps new children, are added to the original children's

[16] Ibid., 18.

[17] Paul R. Amato, "Research on Divorce: Continuing Trends and New Developments," *Journal of Marriage and Family* 72, no. 3 (2020): 657.

family orbit. Moreover, the language itself can cause discomfort or confusion to children of divorce or separation.

Stepfamily, *stepmom*, *stepdad*, *stepparents*, and *stepsiblings* are common, relatively neutral labels for the family relationships that follow a parent's new marriage or long-term relationship. Some ACODs have a stronger relationship with a more-present "step" parent than with their original parent, or with "step" siblings, and may opt to drop the qualifier altogether. At times this can cause a conflicted sense of disloyalty toward the original parent(s) or siblings. Others may feel that describing the new people with terms like *family, mom, dad, parents, or grandparents* rings untrue for individuals whom they barely know and with whom they have only a superficial or minimal relationship. The words can feel forced (or sometimes may actually *be* forced, their use insisted upon by the parent in the new relationship). This can be especially true for those whose parents remarried later in life.

It may feel awkward to use close, familial terms with stepfamily members if the relationships have felt strained from the beginning. Perhaps a new stepparent was involved in the affair which broke up the original marriage. The child faces an inner anguish: he wants to continue a relationship with his mom or dad, but he resents feeling forced into a relationship with someone who contributed to the breakup of the family. He also resents being asked to use terms of endearment for the people responsible.

Beyond "stepfamily," other descriptions of reconfigured families can strike some adult children of divorce as a kind of "divorce happy talk" and a forced positivity about the new family structure. "Blended" family can imply that the new family is perfectly and smoothly re-combined, with everyone feeling equally at home and centered. The reality can seem quite different for some children who question their place in the new family situation or feel keenly their loss of connection with the nonpresent parent. Relationships with new family members can feel anything but smooth or "blended."

"Bonus family" is more forthrightly, and even forcefully, positive, along with the adage "your family didn't end; it expanded!" Children of divorce who are grieving the loss of their original intact family could bristle at such descriptions, which proactively offer a positive "spin" on the new situation, and which may or may not fit with the child's own experience.

Ultimately, the difficulty in accurately naming the reality of complicated family structures demonstrates the difficulties awaiting the children involved in navigating the new relationships and dynamics that occur when one or both parents begin new relationships. It is simple for a child to say *family* and mean his own father, mother, and siblings. It is much more complicated to describe—let alone *live*—the variety of family structures and relationships that tend to follow a parental split. Language difficulties around reconfigured families also point to a phenomenon some researchers call "forced intimacy," where the expectation of bonding with new family members trumps the child's need to process his own losses at his own pace.[18] As the adults reboot their lives, they can forget the fact that the child's perspective is often quite different from that of the grown-ups.

Triangulation of Conflict

It is often assumed that a separation or divorce will end or reduce the parents' fighting and conflict, but this is not

[18] See the helpful discussion of "forced intimacy" in Ron Deal, *The Smart Stepfamily* (Minneapolis: Bethany House, 2014).

always the case.[19] Instead, what can happen is that the parents' contact with each other decreases (due to interacting less), but their disagreements continue *through* the child, triangulating the fray by making him part of it. Contention may even increase now that the parents need to navigate childrearing decisions, schedules, and so forth with less of a bond and perhaps new love interests that pull their attention elsewhere. For parents who have difficulty communicating directly with each other, it may seem easier to tell the child to pass along messages to the ex-spouse (and this may continue after the child has become an adult). Worse, one or both may speak disparagingly of the ex-spouse in the child's presence, may lie about the situation in an effort to win the child over to their perspective, may ask the child to keep a secret from the other parent, or act in other unhealthy and divisive ways. This triangulation causes the child, who is always the embodied unity of both parents, to feel torn between them and within himself.

> It is often assumed that a separation or divorce will end or reduce the parents' fighting, but this is not always the case.

Difficulty with Boundaries

A common struggle we hear from ACODs (and have experienced ourselves) has to do with setting and maintaining healthy boundaries with their parents and other relatives; this can be all the more challenging in complex family structures, complicated with more relationships—and

[19] Judith Wallerstein, Julia Lewis, and Sandra Blakeslee, *The Unexpected Legacy of Divorce: A 25 Year Landmark Study* (New York: Hyperion, 2000), 87–105. Wallerstein discusses this point at length.

relationships that are more complicated. ACODs may have never seen good boundary setting "in action" in their families. They may fear doing anything that would risk further relationship rupture, including establishing boundaries that the other may resist or use as an excuse to reject them.

Dr. Jill Verschaetse, a licensed clinical psychologist and ACOD herself, identifies three common boundary-issue scenarios that many ACODs experience, noting that "how we learn to relate to others early on in life has a direct bearing on how we relate to others later in life."[20] These boundary challenges can also be experienced by those whose parents divorce later in life, since that crisis entails a radical re-shifting of their family with deep impacts on their sense of identity and relating to others. Further, the same unhealthy parent-child dynamics that exist when children are young can, of course, continue into children's later years when left unaddressed.

The first potential boundary "imbalance" Dr. Verschaetse identifies is *overidentification*: a divorced or otherwise single parent may overly identify with a child in an attempt to fill the void left by a spouse. The parent may allocate the emotional investment otherwise given to a romantic partner to the child instead. A child in this scenario may lose a strong sense of self, become inappropriately enmeshed with the parent, and later on experience difficulties "leaving" the parent (see Gen 2:24) in order to give himself fully and freely in other relationships.

Second, *parentification*: a child may find himself taking on parental-type roles and responsibilities in the midst of the

[20] Dr. Jill Verschaetse, "Navigating Boundaries as an Adult Child of Divorce (Part Two: Typical Boundary Patterns of ACODs)," *Life-Giving Wounds* (blog), February 27, 2022, https://www.lifegivingwounds.org/blog/navigating-boundaries-as-an-adult-child-of-divorce-part-two-typical-boundary-patterns-of-acods.

family crisis, such as caring for siblings, providing emotional support to parents, and being privy to adult anxieties. The child may have his own emotions and needs sidelined as he seeks to take care of others. Later, he may gravitate toward relationships where he continues in a caretaker-type role, setting himself up to be taken advantage of without his own legitimate needs being attended to. He may struggle to be appropriately dependent in relationships, which makes vulnerability and intimacy more difficult.

Third, *avoidance*: due to serious dysfunction in the family, the child may erect strict defensive walls against one or both parents, cutting off either physical contact or emotional connection out of self-protection. At times this is called *alienation*, a complex phenomenon with a variety of motivations on both the parent's and the child's side. "Alienation" can be the expression of a healthy boundary, but it can also be an overreaction out of unhealed hurt, or a tragic consequence of one parent's rancor toward the other parent. Later in life, an avoidant approach to relationships can prevent deep, intimate relationships from forming, or make it difficult to extend consistent emotional intimacy and availability to another. The grown child could develop a pattern of establishing rigid and overly firm boundaries, rather than healthy and holy ones, and of cutting people off when relationships experience a difficult patch.

Scenarios like these make it both more difficult *and* more important for ACODs to set healthy boundaries with their parents and others in their lives as needed. We will spend time in the next chapter looking at what healthy boundaries are and how to set and maintain them.

Feeling like an Outsider

Often, especially in secular or legal sources, advice about helping children of divorce living in reconfigured families focuses on mitigating the outward effects of the family's split: what the ideal custody arrangement is, how "co-parents" can better ease their child's transition between homes, or ways to help the child "adjust" to his new reality. Unfortunately, such discussions can cause the goal to seem like making the child easier to handle for the adults involved, rather than truly to hear and acknowledge his pain and needs. They can also further the ideology of a "good divorce," namely that if former spouses do everything right after their split, the negative effects on the children will be negligible and not long lasting.

Divorce and separation have a profound existential impact on a child's identity, reaching deeply into his sense of self and his understanding of home.

While practical considerations certainly have their place, these do not address the *deepest* impact of living in a split, step, or "blended" family. Divorce and separation have a profound existential impact on a child's identity, reaching deeply into his sense of self and his understanding of home. Even after he is grown, he may not feel fully at-home in either mom's or dad's world. And if one or both parents enter a new relationship, the child of the original union can wonder whether he has a place in the newly configured family, or what that place is.

It is not uncommon for children of divorce to feel *displaced* by the new spouse or new children. They can even feel *replaced* when a parent spends more time, energy, and effort building up his relationship with a new spouse and new children than in maintaining the relationship with his original children. This can be felt particularly intensely if a child is born of the new union, someone with an equal connection to both parents in the home, which the child of divorce does not have.

In his work on stepfamilies, Christian therapist Ron Deal notes that stepparents have preexisting loyalties to the children of their former union, loyalties that may create issues of fairness with stepchildren, as well as an "insider/outsider" dynamic within the family. Originally united siblings and parents may become "insiders" and stepsiblings and stepparents "outsiders." While the preexisting bond cannot be ignored and should be honored, one can imagine how this situation might easily develop unhealthy rivalries and competition for love and affection.[21]

The feeling of displacement can be exacerbated further if a child has a joint custody arrangement such that he is not fully present in either family but travels back and forth between them. Recall the image we shared earlier, when one ACOD said she felt like a small Magna-Tile that *clicked in* to mom's house, then detached and *clicked in* to dad's house. In neither place did she feel essential, but rather peripheral to the heart of that family space. There may also be other siblings or new stepsiblings who have different custody arrangements, allowing them more time to bond with particular family members, which creates an imbalance in the sibling and stepsibling dynamic. A child may feel even more like an outsider to that family, as if he came from a different, off-brand magnet toy set compared to the others.

Holidays, Traditions, and Milestones

For many ACODs, holiday seasons and life milestones such as graduation, their own marriage, the birth of a child, family funerals, and so on, present potentially difficult scenarios to navigate with a split and reconfigured family.

[21] See Deal, *The Smart Stepfamily*.

These experiences are prime examples of how a parental split reverberates throughout the lifetime of the child. Every Christmas, every birthday, every moment when families traditionally come together can become both a painful reminder of their broken and dysfunctional family and potentially a stressful situation that requires advance preparation, discernment, and tact to navigate.

Divorced parents can have unrealistic expectations for their children's participation in holiday events; not all remember that because of the family's split, the adult children now have more households to visit and more events to attend in the same finite amount of time. If the split branches of the family are in different locations, difficult decisions can arise concerning whom to visit and when. This can be a source of sadness for the grown children, too, as they miss out on part of the time with their mom or dad, instead of enjoying everyone's company *together.*

Holidays, especially Christmas, can also cause pain for ACODs because of the family-focused aura of these moments. In a time lauded for making happy family memories and reconnecting with loved ones, the contrast between the hoped-for intact family and the reality of broken relationships and stressful dynamics can be particularly painful. Most families have holiday traditions, and for adult children of divorce, it can feel strange when long-standing, beloved traditions, which were done with both parents together, are now expected to be the "same" but with new, different family members. It becomes emotionally difficult to participate in such traditions, which feel like a shell of the past. Or new traditions from a new branch of the family could be added, sometimes in a forceful way.

ACODs can also face extra logistical challenges when preparing for big family events or celebrations of milestones—logistical challenges that in turn can cause emotional heaviness. For instance, consideration might be needed as to whether mom and dad will agree to attend the same event and if not (or if so) how to handle that. Or there may be stress in anticipating whether parental interactions will be peaceful or acrimonious, a stress heightened if there are new romantic partners in the picture as well.

The fact that adult children of divorce face difficult family complications and dysfunction around what should be the purely joyous times in their lives—their weddings, baptisms of their children, and other celebrations—can lead to anger and resentment. It can be something new to grieve for ACODs, who are lamenting the fact that planning special family occasions or preparing for holidays is laden with additional pain and drama thanks to their parents' split.

Talking to Your Children

A challenge for ACODs who are parents themselves is how to explain the broader family situation to their own children. It can be painful to have to introduce a child to the brokenness of the world at a young age. Here too is something else to grieve. Children's growing awareness of the family's brokenness reminds us of what was lost from not having an intact family.

Around age four, our older daughter started to ask us, "Why do we leave Grandma's house to go to Grandpa's house? Why doesn't Grandma come with us?" Her innocent assumption that Grandma and Grandpa should be in the same house, as a unit, broke our hearts. And her desire to be with them both together was good and holy. As with many difficult conversations we need (eventually) to have with our children, our approach has been to explain the situation with both truth and charity, being honest and not sugarcoating the situation, but without speaking harshly of those involved. We proactively counteract any fears in her mind of Mommy and Daddy divorcing, like her grandparents, and moving to different houses, too.

So, for example, we told our four-year-old daughter, "Grandma and Grandpa don't live in the same house because they got a divorce. This is a sad and tragic thing to happen, but we love them both. And don't worry: Mommy and Daddy are not ever going to get a divorce as we believe marriage is lifelong; we're going to live as a family, together, always."

Children will ask additional questions as they grow and will require increasingly detailed answers, something to be discerned in prayer. Michael Hernon, an ACOD and co-founder with his wife Alicia of the Messy Family Project, recommends telling all of the details of your family of origin as one of the "rites of passage" for your children as they enter high school. He recommends using this time both to share with them the honest wounds of the past *and* to foster love for the beauty of sacramental marriage that you are now living, and which they too can live in their own lives one day. This is also a chance to discuss the importance of mercy and love for the whole family, including those who have hurt you.

Helping Aging Parents

Coping with aging or ill parents is challenging for any grown child, but when one or both parents is alone during their older years and without their ex-partner's support, there is an additional layer of practical challenges for the children. It is also difficult not to feel resentment toward the absent spouse who has not fulfilled his promise to love and care "in sickness or in health ... until death do us part." If a parent has remarried, handling a time of illness or death together with a stepparent or stepsiblings may add complications, especially if there were already feelings of displacement, replacement, or hurt present.

An ACOD may become the primary caretaker of a solo parent, perhaps exercising that parent's medical power of attorney or general power of attorney. After the parent's death, he may be responsible for the myriad decisions about funeral plans, estate considerations, and more. In effect, he may be asked or expected to fulfill a spousal role in the absence of a spouse (who is still alive but not playing a spousal role). Unlike scenarios where the other parent has died or is himself ill or incapacitated, it can be hard to accept the fact that the other parent is alive and reasonably well but has abdicated his responsibility toward his former spouse.

14

Life-Giving "Honoring Your Parents," Sibling Relationships, and Boundaries

Honor your father and your mother, that your days may be long in the land which the LORD *your God gives you.*

—Exodus 20:12

Honoring Your Parents

In Exodus chapter 20, God delivers the Ten Commandments to the people of Israel. The fourth commandment he gives to them is this: "Honor your father and your mother" (Ex 20:12). This is the only commandment that comes with a concurrent promise: "that your days may be long in the land which the LORD your God gives you."

In other places in Scripture, especially in Proverbs and the book of Sirach, the exhortation to honor your parents is repeated, for example: "With all your heart honor your father, and do not forget the birth pangs of your mother. Remember that through your parents you were born; and what can you give back to them that equals their gift to you?" (Sir 7:27–28) Saint Paul says, "Children, obey your parents in everything, for this pleases the Lord" (Col 3:20).

For adult children of divorce, as well as for any child in a challenging relationship with a parent, these scriptural passages can seem problematic and may even cause a visceral reaction of anguish. We are often asked by adult children of divorce: "What does it mean to 'honor your father and mother' when one or both have repeatedly hurt you by their selfish actions and their decision to divorce or separate?" What does the fourth commandment require when a parent has abandoned the family, treated the family poorly, or otherwise not lived fatherhood or motherhood in an honorable way? What does honoring them look like, then?

These are valid questions. Here we will reflect on what the fourth commandment asks of children *and* of parents, and consider ways that ACODs can obey it, sometimes heroically, within the family situation they have received.

Mutual Honor

In a section of the Catechism called "The Duties of Family Members" (nos. 2214–2231),[1] we read that the fourth commandment requires children to show their parents *respect* (filial piety) and to *obey* them while under their direct care. Children should acknowledge with gratitude the gift of life received from their parents (ultimately a gift of God's Fatherhood). As children mature into adulthood, the obligation to obey their parents ceases, but not the obligation to respect them. Further, grown children have additional responsibilities toward their aging parents, to "as much as they can ... give them material and moral support in old age and in times of illness, loneliness, or distress" (no. 2218).

[1] This section is found within the larger treatment of the fourth commandment (nos. 2197–2257).

The Catechism then outlines the duties that *parents* have toward their children, devoting several more paragraphs to this topic than to the duties of children. Parents are reminded that their parental role does not end with procreation but their responsibility extends to their children's moral and spiritual education, including "education in the virtues" (no. 2223). The family is called to be a "school" of human formation and a domestic church. Parents are exhorted to regard their children as children of God and to respect them as human persons. They are encouraged to be good examples for their children and embrace their God-given role as the "first heralds" of the faith (no. 2225). Parents are exhorted to provide for their dependent children's material needs and, as their children grow, not to exert undue pressure on their children's choice of a profession or spouse.

The Catechism also makes clear that God, not the parents, remains the ultimate authority. Children are advised to obey their parents, but if "convinced in conscience that it would be morally wrong to obey a particular order, [they] must not do so" (no. 2217). Recalling Jesus' words in the Gospel, "He who loves father or mother more than me is not worthy of me" (Mt 10:37), we are reminded that "family ties are important but not absolute" (no. 2232). Children must be free to follow God's will and their God-given vocation, and parents should encourage their children to follow Jesus above all else.

Saint John Paul II says the following about the fourth commandment:

> If the fourth commandment demands that honor should be shown to our father and mother, it also makes demands of the parents themselves. You parents, the divine precept seems to say, should act in such a way that your life *will merit the honor* (and the love) of your children! Do not let

> the divine command that you be honored fall into a moral vacuum! Ultimately then we are speaking of *mutual honor*. The commandment "honor your father and your mother" indirectly tells parents: honor your sons and your daughters. They deserve this because they are alive, because they are who they are, and this is true from the first moment of their conception.[2]

The fourth commandment, then, is a call to *mutual* honor between parents and children. Children are called to honor their parents, and parents are called to act in an honorable way. Saint John Paul II goes on to say, "Honor is essentially an attitude of unselfishness. It could be said that it is 'a sincere gift of person to person,' and in that sense honor converges with love."[3]

Obedience, Respect, and Care

Given the above reflection, we can understand the fourth commandment as exhorting children under their parents' direct care to be *obedient* to their parents (unless to do so would be immoral, harmful, or against God's will), for children of any age to *respect* their parents, and for grown children to *provide* for their elderly, ill, or distressed parents' needs "as much as they can" (CCC, no. 2218). Concurrently, parents are called to the lofty vocation of raising their children well, meeting their needs, respecting them as persons, providing them a good and moral example, and helping them discover and follow their God-given vocation in life.

The fourth commandment does *not* entitle parents to hurt their children (far from it), nor does it envision parents

[2] John Paul II, Letter to Families, February 2, 1994, no. 15.
[3] Ibid.

as autocratic rulers. The heart of the commandment is *mutual* honor between children and parents. When you are an adult, honoring your parents does not mean doing everything they ask without exception, enduring poor treatment, or sacrificing or neglecting your vocation and family life in order to meet a parent's requests (or even, at times, their legitimate needs). Honoring your parents can—and often should—coexist with healthy, holy boundaries discerned through prayer, which we will discuss shortly.

The heart of the fourth commandment is *mutual* honor between children and parents.

At the same time, the fourth commandment *does* oblige children to *respect* their parents, always. This respect (this *filial piety*) is fundamentally rooted in *who* our parents are for us, and not in *what* they have (or have not) done for us, or what kind of people they are. In other words, children are commanded to respect their parents because these parents are made in the image and likeness of God, and because of the gratitude properly felt for their role in bestowing life (a role unique to those two particular people we call Mom and Dad). It is not because either parent is necessarily a good and virtuous person worthy of emulation. Praise God when that is the case! But even when it is not, respect is required by the fourth commandment. We could describe it as *unconditional* respect, no matter what—the unselfish act of love that Saint John Paul II said was at the heart of honor. And even when honor and unselfish love are not reciprocated by parents, that should not be used as an excuse not to show respect; two wrongs do not make a right.

Respecting your parents looks like acting with charity and goodwill toward them, speaking kindly to them and about them, refraining from "bad-mouthing" them (distinguished from constructive, charitable sharing of your own hurt in appropriate settings), not seeking revenge for offenses, and wishing them well and not ill. Respect also entails acting generously toward them and graciously receiving the love they *can* give, even if it is not the warm and reliable love that children desire from their parents.

Respect does *not* mean: always affirming, approving, or validating parents' choices (especially in regard to divorce, affairs, or subsequent relationships), following all of their directives, necessarily being in consistent contact with them, or seeing them as an example to follow.

Honoring your parents includes praying for them. Monsignor Charles Pope, commenting on the fourth commandment to a man asking for clarity concerning his abusive parents, wrote: "Your parents, perhaps especially due to their shortcomings, need your prayers. Even in situations where there is little to praise and where we cannot reasonably interact with parents or family members, we fulfill the Fourth Commandment by praying especially for them, for their conversion and spiritual well-being."[4] We can always pray for others, no matter what. And in situations where we have been hurt by someone, such as a parent, we can ask for the grace to follow Jesus' exhortation to "Love your enemies and pray for those who persecute you" (Mt 5:44).

Heroic Charity

In situations of broken homes and dysfunction, it can be heroic enough to fulfill the fourth commandment and

[4] Monsignor Charles Pope, "Honoring Father and Mother Means Praying for Them," *Our Sunday Visitor*, March 6, 2020, https://www.oursundayvisitor.com/honoring-father-and-mother-means-praying-for-them/.

honor your parents by treating them with respect. However, an adult child of divorce may at times be convicted through prayer to "go the extra mile" for his parents, and as Saint John of the Cross said, "Where there is no love, put love—and you will find love." Expressions of proactive charity provide a tremendous opportunity for growth in holiness.

Graciela gives an example of heroic charity toward her parents. She is an only child whose parents divorced when she was fifteen. As both she and her parents grew older, she reflected deeply on the fourth commandment and concluded that its call for her was to be generously charitable toward her parents, who needed her more in their aging years. She became the primary driver for both her father and her mother, taking them to their appointments and other activities. While embracing this role was not without personal sacrifice and moments of tension, the time spent with each of them toward the end of their lives was also a great gift.

Reflecting on that gift, Graciela writes:

> Thanks to trying to follow the Fourth Commandment and show love to my parents, I was able to recognize their own vulnerability and weaknesses. I also became cognizant that I wanted to be a better child of God. As I tried to work with my imperfections, I realized that my parents were also imperfect. I realized that they probably experienced their own silence and withdrawn emotions just like me. After much thought I decided to try to *honor my father and my mother* and allow God the opportunity to work with me.[5]

[5] Graciela Rodriguez, "Honoring Your Father and Mother ... As a Child of Divorce," *Life-Giving Wounds* (blog), October 29, 2020, https://www.lifegivingwounds.org/blog/honoring-your-father-and-motheras-a-child-of-divorce (emphasis in original).

The commandment to honor your father and mother *can be* an opportunity for radical growth in holiness by moving you beyond your natural inclinations toward resentment or even revenge, and instead finding concrete ways to love and care for your parents. Again, discernment is needed for what this looks like given your vocation and other responsibilities, as well as the particular dynamics of the relationship. The fundamental point remains: obeying the fourth commandment is a way that the wound of parental divorce can become life-giving. Brokenness and hurt can call forth generous and sacrificial love, transforming the evil into goodness through generosity.

Healthy Boundaries for ACODs

Healthy boundaries are important for any relationship, but (as we saw in the previous chapter) setting and maintaining them can be both particularly important *and* particularly difficult for adult children of divorce or separation.

> Healthy boundaries coexist with—and strengthen—love, forgiveness, and honor toward your parents.

It is first important to identify what relational boundaries are—and are not. Boundaries, rightly understood and lived, are not selfish. They are not equivalent to rejecting the other person or not loving him anymore. And when well-discerned boundaries are set with our parents, they are not a failure to obey the fourth commandment.

Instead, good and healthy boundaries have the purpose of keeping the good in and the bad out of relationships, in order to have the best chance of maintaining a lasting, healthy bond in sometimes tricky relationships. Boundaries are not walls, pushing people out. They are more like garden fences, which delineate a perimeter in order for the garden to flourish and not be overrun by weeds or foraging animals. Healthy boundaries coexist with—and strengthen—love, forgiveness, and honor toward your parents.

A Healthy Sense of Self

A first step toward establishing healthy boundaries with your parents and others is to cultivate a healthy sense of self and self-love based on your inherent God-given dignity. This is particularly important if you have fallen into patterns of unhealthy enmeshment with a parent to the neglect of your own legitimate needs or vocation. As Dr. Verschaetse notes, "In order to have healthy relationships with others, we must have a self. There is no relationship if two people are so enmeshed that they cannot be distinguished from each other .... You must have a sense of self before you can share that self in a healthy way."[6]

Developing a healthy sense of self means rejecting two extremes: first, total self-focus or "fierce independence," defined as making your self-care primary with little regard for others' needs or openness to healthy interdependence with others; and second, the other extreme: considering it selfish to care about your own needs. Rejecting both extremes, Jesus challenges you to "take up [your] cross and follow me" (Mt 16:24) *and* "love your neighbor *as yourself*" (Mt 22:39, emphasis added). You cultivate a

[6] Dr. Jill Verschaetse, "Navigating Boundaries as an Adult Child of Divorce (Part One: The Necessity of a Self)," *Life-Giving Wounds* (blog), January 12, 2022, https://www.lifegivingwounds.org/blog/navigating-boundaries-as-an-adult-child-of-divorce.

healthy sense of self by rejoicing in your existence and identity—an individual lovingly and intentionally created by God with legitimate needs to be honored and a purpose to be pursued. To know at the deepest level of your being that your self, your existence, is *good*, provides the necessary foundation for being in right relationship with others, including setting healthy and holy boundaries that help relationships thrive.

Mature Dependence

Grounded on the firm foundation of a healthy sense of self, the kind of relationship healthy and holy boundaries seek to support is one of *mature dependence*—a concept more or less interchangeable with *interdependence*. Mature dependence, or interdependence, stands in contrast to both *enmeshment* (an unhealthy dependence on others, even for a sense of self), and *fierce independence* (a rejection of depending on others in any way).

Psychologist Harry Guntrip describes mature dependence in this way: "Maturity is not equated with independence though it includes a certain capacity for independence .... The independence of the mature person is simply that he does not collapse when he has to stand alone. It is not an independence of needs for other persons with whom to have relationship: that would not be desired by the mature."[7] Mature dependence is very much at home in a Christian anthropology or understanding of the human person. We are always-already dependent on God, the source of our life and our continued existence. Further, several foundational aspects of our existence and identity were *given* to us, not chosen by us: our coming-into-being itself, the parents to whom

[7] Harry Guntrip, *Personality Structure and Human Interaction: The Developing Synthesis of Psycho-dynamic Theory* (London: Hogarth Press, 1982), 293.

we were born, our name, our identity as male or female, and other aspects of our identity such as our ethnicity and heritage, physical attributes and abilities, personality traits, and so on. We are far from being "self-made," but must instead *receive* our person and identity from God, mediated through our particular parents and all they contributed to our identity.

At the same time, we are given our existence as a gift *and a task*. When God placed Adam and Eve in the Garden of Eden, he commanded them to cultivate and care for it. Their handiwork contributed to the flourishing of paradise (see Gen 2:15). Several of Jesus' parables teach about the responsibility we have as men and Christian disciples to nurture our gifts and talents for the increase of the Kingdom of God (e.g., Mt 25:14–30). Further, every baptized Christian receives at his baptism the dignity of priest, prophet, and king, each with attendant roles and responsibilities toward God and his people. Men, then, are always-already dependent on God and others, but *also* always-already tasked with "becoming who we are," to borrow a phrase employed by Saint John Paul II in his exhortation to families.[8]

In terms of relationships and boundaries, then, remembering who we are as human persons can guide us to relate to others with a *mature dependence*—neither with an excessive dependence or enmeshment, nor with a cold, forceful independence that rejects our connection to others or our need for relationship with others.

Discern Boundaries

When considering how to establish healthy and holy boundaries with another for the sake of the relationship,

[8]John Paul II, encyclical letter *Familiaris Consortio*, November 22, 1981, no. 17.

Dr. Verschaetse advises considering your motives for doing so and asking the right questions. "Rather than simply inquiring, 'What do *I* need?,'" she says, "let the question instead be, 'Lord, what do healthy boundaries look like for me in this particular relationship?,' which necessarily includes your good and all of your deepest needs."[9]

Inviting God into the discernment of how to relate with the people in your life shows you trust him to guide you toward your deepest fulfillment. It also expresses a desire to live boundaries not as a way of controlling others (which is not possible) or *first* protecting yourself, but as a way of honoring both others and your legitimate needs and vocation. In this way, you are living the principle of mutual honor implied by the fourth commandment.

Dr. Verschaetse says that discerning boundaries in prayer "elevates the process of setting boundaries from simply a self-help and self-focused one, to a God-centered one that promises to bring the true and lasting healing for which we long."[10] Prayerful discernment of boundaries can be aided by outside guidance from a therapist, spiritual director, or trusted friend. Often a third-party mentor can bring needed objectivity and emotional distance to the question of how to navigate difficult relationships. And having a support team can also help when those boundaries are tested or have to be reevaluated over time.

Boundaries Are about *Your* Actions

A common misunderstanding about boundaries is that they are about controlling or mitigating another's behavior. But the opposite is true: setting boundaries is about *my own* behavior, and what *I* will do in certain scenarios. While

[9] Verschaetse, "Navigating Boundaries (Part One)."
[10] Ibid.

we can always encourage what is good for the other, we can never make decisions for him or control his actions.

In their simplest form, boundaries consist of deciding, after prayerful discernment, that "If he does *x*, I will do *y*." For example, "If my father starts speaking poorly of my mother, I will stop the conversation or leave the room." Or, "If my mother's request, short of an actual emergency, conflicts with a legitimate, preplanned investment of time in my own family, I will not respond to it immediately, but will follow up with her at a later time."

Boundaries direct and shape our own *time, space*, and *access*. They direct and shape the time we give to the people in our lives, our physical presence, and our availability to others. For those of us who are parents, boundaries also encompass our children as part of the family. A boundary could be, for example, "Mom, we will instruct our children to treat your new boyfriend with respect, but in order to honor the special relationship I have with just you and Dad, we will not insist that they call him 'grandpa'." Or, as a boundary of time for the whole family, "Dad, we are going to spend Christmas morning relaxing together with just our family at home. Then, if it suits, we'd love to come to your house for lunch and to exchange gifts. After that we have agreed to go to Mom's house for dinner and another gift exchange."

Sometimes it is helpful to communicate a boundary in advance, with as much kindness and respect as possible. This is particularly important when establishing a boundary that will change the typical or expected way of behaving. These are not effortless conversations and can be met with some resistance. Discernment is needed on whether and how to communicate boundaries, but communicating them establishes our expectations for the relationship, places those behavioral expectations in the open, and can then be referenced if a boundary violation takes place. For example, "Dad, I said that if you insulted Mom, I would leave the room; you're speaking unkindly of her, so I'm going to leave until you're ready to talk about something else." Then comes the importance of following through, since an unenforced boundary is no boundary at all.

In some difficult or even toxic circumstances, a boundary could look like cessation of contact. This is most common in situations involving abuse, where continuing contact would be physically unsafe or severely damaging to one's mental health.[11] Here, outside guidance is helpful for evaluating motives, discerning whether a boundary is necessary, and if so, providing the support and plan needed to establish such a boundary. As with any boundary, it should be remembered that ceasing contact with a particularly difficult or unhealthy person is not the equivalent of no longer loving him—sometimes it is a way to love him best.

Grace and Patience

At times, the person with whom we are establishing a boundary will resist the boundary, perhaps interpreting it as an attempt at control. But again, setting a boundary is about identifying what *I* will do in a certain scenario. I can communicate my boundary decision to the other person, which allows him to decide what his behavior will be.

In situations of enmeshed dependence, where a parent (for example) has long expected the child to be consistently present to him and attentive to his needs, it can take a period of adjustment (not always painless) if the adult child begins to establish boundaries of time and availability for

[11] See Appendix II for resources for psychological help to heal from abuse as well as guidance on how to report abuse.

the sake of his own legitimate needs or those of his family. It can *feel* unloving or selfish, even when objectively it is not. This can be particularly difficult to discern as a parent ages and has greater needs, without a spouse to help care for him. As with any relationship, sacrifices are needed at times, but caution should be exercised to make sure that legitimate needs or those of the family aren't *always and entirely* subsumed into a parent's needs. To do so can risk mental, emotional, and even physical well-being, which does not help anyone. It takes time, patience, prudence, and ongoing adjustments to establish healthy boundaries that achieve the goal of mature dependence with a parent or others.

When setting boundaries, remember that you are trying to *limit* the unhealthy dynamics in your family, but you will never succeed in rooting out *all* unhealthy dynamics and sin this side of Heaven. Even otherwise healthy intact homes can have ongoing unhealthy dynamics. When setting boundaries, you need to have realistic expectations of imperfection. With this in mind, you can focus on boundaries for the most distressing scenarios while surrendering other lesser problematic dynamics to God, or dealing with them further down the road.

Peace in Our Families

In addition to establishing healthy boundaries, here are some other ways of finding greater peace in the midst of complicated and possibly drama-filled family situations:

- *Steep yourself in the sacraments, especially confession, before and after family visits or big family events.* Confession fills you with God's mercy, which you can then offer more freely to others. As Sarah notes, "Filling yourself to the brim with the love of the Holy Spirit will allow [God] to abound in your thoughts and interactions."[12]

- *Reflect on your expectations.* Oftentimes pain results when your expectations of a family visit or encounter vastly differ from what actually happens. Taking the upcoming event to the Lord in prayer can help you release your hold on what you *hope* will happen (e.g., consistently pleasant family interactions or long-established family traditions) or how others will act, and re-centering your goals in what you can control (your own behavior, acting in charity, finding joy wherever possible, et cetera).
- *Continually remind yourself of the deeper purpose of the season or event.* The cliché-sounding phrase "the reason for the season" can truly be a balm and anchor, reminding you that the holidays and big life milestones are not *first* about making picture-perfect happy family memories or enjoying the external trappings of the season or event, but are rather occasions to re-encounter our Lord and celebrate new outpourings of sacramental grace.
- *Visualize with Christ responses to difficult situations.* Successful athletes spend time envisioning various game scenarios and how they will respond. You, too, can pray about potential scenarios or conversations that cause anxiety, and invite the Lord to show you how best to respond in charity. This includes reminding yourself that Jesus *is present* there, in whatever messy scenario you find yourself in.

[12] Sarah Hart, "8 Tips on How to Spiritually Survive the Holidays as Adult Children of Divorce or Separation," *Life-Giving Wounds* (blog), November 20, 2020, https://www.lifegivingwounds.org/blog/8-tips-on-how-to-spiritually-survive-the-holidays-as-adult-children-of-divorce-or-separation.

Sibling Relationships

Families reconfigured by separation, divorce, and remarriage can become quite complicated. In terms of siblings, a variety of scenarios can result after parents split up, with various children added to the family (or not) and with various degrees of relationship between them and with the parents in the households. Alongside the losses experienced when parents and parental-type figures leave the family are the losses experienced when siblings, half-siblings, or step-siblings leave for other houses or have different custody arrangements that reduce time together. Challenges can arise from new children entering the household, either by birth or a new relationship, and all the children can feel confusion and tension from the new relationship dynamics. Added to this may be pressure (explicitly stated or felt) to accept the new family members as "full and true" siblings, despite just having met them.

As we have seen, it is not uncommon for children of divorce to take on parental-type roles toward younger siblings in the midst of the family's chaos. This can be a tremendous act of love, but can also be a sad loss of childhood dependence. This dynamic can become unhealthy in adulthood if a sibling still takes on excessive responsibility toward a now-grown sibling. Siblings might also take up unhealthy roles and behaviors in an effort to survive, cope with the pain, or win whatever love they can from their parents. Parents may have contributed to these roles by choosing favorites or labeling the children.

While it is a blessing when siblings can be each other's first and foundational support in the midst of their family's breakdown, sometimes siblings disagree on what to think about the divorce, take sides with one parent or the other, or repeat other unhealthy family dynamics.

Everything said above about boundaries applies to sibling relationships. It is not a given that a relationship with a brother or sister will be healthy and warm; praise God when it is! But healthy boundaries can help sibling relationships survive and thrive for the long term. With sibling dynamics, it is all too easy to continue behaviors established in childhood into adulthood and lose out on a deeper connection to siblings. It is key to *rediscover* one another in adulthood and "reset" the relationship. For adult children of divorce, this includes acknowledging that each sibling shares a common wound from the parents' divorce or separation, and at the same time could have had very different experiences of the split and its aftermath. Perhaps siblings were different ages at the time of the family's breakdown, had varying levels of information, had different experiences vis-à-vis their parents, or had different responses due to personality and temperament,[13] coping strategies, roles taken on, decisions made, and so on.

It is beautiful when siblings can openly and honestly discuss the grief caused by their parents' divorce. But we are often surprised at how little siblings have talked about this topic with one another, or how they have treated the divorce as a distant wound in the past that has no bearing on their reality today. The wound of silence can creep into even very close relationships. We have heard astonishing stories about breakthroughs in sibling dynamics and closeness after an honest discussion of the past. Often a set of siblings attends a Life-Giving Wounds retreat together and discusses for the first time in many years—or perhaps

[13] See Art Bennett, "Utilizing the Temperaments for Adult Children of Divorce," *Life-Giving Wounds* (blog), October 8, 2021, https://www.lifegivingwounds.org/blog/utilizing-the-temperaments-for-adult-children-of-divorce-acods.

ever—the life-altering fact of their parents' divorce or separation and all of the effects it has had on their lives.

Attempts at honest and open discussion about wounds with siblings does not always go smoothly. Some siblings may continue to avoid the subject, harden into various positions or roles, or continue to compete for the parents' affection or attention. In these challenging cases, the forgiveness process that we discussed earlier may have to be extended to them as well. Above all, remember that we are our brother's "keeper" as the story of Cain and Abel reminds us (Gen 4). Let us try to limit the sprawling cycle of division and dysfunction among siblings by proceeding with empathy and love, grounded in a recognition of our kinship, mutual woundedness, and desire for healing (even if hidden at times).

A Non-ACOD Spouse's Perspective: Navigating Complicated Family Scenarios

BETHANY: As any spouse could tell you, it's no small feat to marry and become assimilated into the whole new ecosystem that is your spouse's family of origin. Every family has its own history, its own way of doing things, its own traditions, and its own expectations (often unspoken). When the family is fractured and reconfigured, there's another layer to learn of the unique dynamics, hurts, and stories behind these new people to whom you're suddenly related.

I remember the disorienting experience of visiting Dan's family over the holidays for the first time and traveling between his mom's house and dad's house. At each, it was as if the other half of Dan's parentage didn't exist; they truly felt like separate worlds, even though they were in the same town. Years later, the challenge of explaining the family complexities to our children looms large on the spiritual horizon.

A few things have helped us navigate this situation as a couple. First, we remember that we're in this *together* now that our families are joined; it's not "Dan and his family" or "Bethany and her family" but "us and our families," with all their good and ill. Second, we take each other's lead on thoughts and feelings about our particular family of origin, letting each of us be the "guide" and the primary setter of boundaries within our families. After all, each of us is more intimately connected and has more history with our parents and others. At the same time, we are open to each other's viewpoint because, as the one less emotionally involved, Dan can help me see a particular situation with my parents more clearly, and I can do the same for him. We discuss potential boundaries as a couple, come to mutual decisions, and let each other communicate our chosen boundaries with our respective families. And third, we keep the centrality of our own marriage and family life crystal-clear as our vocation, our main priority, and our touchstone for making decisions regarding relations with other family members.

I'm forever grateful that I didn't write Dan off as a prospective spouse because of his messy family situation. What a tragedy that would have been! I'm glad I was able to distinguish Dan in all his virtues (and flaws of course, just like me) from the challenging family situation he had been given. All the added difficulties cannot outweigh what a wonderful husband and father Dan is. I've seen firsthand that adult children of divorce can be some of the most committed, intentional, and holy marriage partners *because* of what they have been through. Dealing with complicated families is not always fun, but it's well worth it for a good spouse.

15

Life-Giving Wounds

By his wounds you have been healed.

—1 Peter 2:24

Throughout this book, we have been meditating on and discussing an underlying thread that is essential for healing. Every chapter entitled "Life-Giving ..." is a manifestation of it, and we aim to bring it into sharp relief in this last chapter. It is one of the most important—if not *the* most important—keys to healing. Mary, the saints, and the martyrs lived it out heroically, and it was the cornerstone of Jesus' mission and his Paschal Mystery. If you understand and live this truth, you will find deep healing in Christ, no matter the wounds caused by your family background. This truth has been crucial to Dan's healing from his parents' divorce, and to the joy and strength of our marriage, and it has been important for the healing of so many adult children of divorce whom we have had the privilege of accompanying over the years.

We are referring to the uniquely Christian grace and joy of *redemptive suffering* that is expressed by the paradoxical gospel-based concept of "life-giving wounds." In this chapter, we seek to answer a profound and notoriously difficult question that comes up again and again in the search for wholeness and healing: "Can I find meaning in the suffering I have faced from my parents' divorce or separation? What can I *do* with all of this pain?"

A Christian Approach to Suffering

As Christians, we believe that God is good and that he created a good world.[1] Evil, in fact, only persists as a *lack* or *absence* of some good God has created. As the Catechism says, the "scandal of evil" and "drama of sin" exist because God in his "infinite wisdom and goodness ... freely willed to create a world 'in a state of journeying' towards ultimate perfection."[2] The Church teaches that all moral evil comes from the free will of creatures' sins. God permits evil to exist out of respect for the great good of human freedom, since without freedom we could not love him or others.[3]

But leaving the conversation at "God permits evil and suffering" is only a partial answer of the larger salvation story. Worse, it can make God seem passive in the face of evil, not what we expect of a *good father*. But the truth is that every aspect of our Christian faith is a part of the answer to the question of evil, especially God the Father sending his only Son, "who died and rose to vanquish evil."[4] Jesus Christ not only *limits* evil in many ways (especially through the fullness of truth he brings), but also, through his triumph over death, he shows the astounding truth that God can bring an *ever greater good* out of the darkest evil.[5] We

[1] *Catechism of the Catholic Church* (*CCC*), no. 299.

[2] Ibid., nos. 309–10.

[3] Ibid., nos. 311, 324.

[4] Ibid., no. 324; see also ibid., no. 309.

[5] Ibid., nos. 312, 324.

hear in the Exultet at the Easter Vigil, "O happy fault / that earned so great, so glorious a Redeemer!" Saint Paul likewise testifies, "We know that *in everything* God works for good with those who love him" (Rom 8:28, emphasis added). Thanks to Christ's redemptive power and presence, made abundantly manifest in the sending of the Holy Spirit and his transformative work in and through the Church, evil does not have the last word, nor is suffering wholly meaningless. Instead, it can be transformed into a tremendous witness of faith, hope, joy, and love.

"By His Wounds You Have Been Healed"

Redemptive suffering is further illuminated by this Scripture verse: "By his wounds you have been healed" (1 Pet 2:24). This echoes the description in Isaiah 53 of the Christ-like suffering servant: "with his stripes we are healed" (v. 5). Here, wounds—suffering—are presented as a good that will bring healing and life. Reflecting on the central mystery of Christ's Passion, Death, Resurrection, and Ascension, we find the paradoxical reality of a "life-giving wound"—the result of the transformative work of redemptive suffering.

But *how* can wounds bring healing and life? Isn't suffering pointless, meant to be "fixed" at all costs? Let us recall again that suffering can be described as a *boundary experience* between two realities: suffering makes us both hyperaware of the grave injury being inflicted *and* points beyond itself to a good worthy of defending or regaining (we feel the pain of its loss).[6] Suffering is a trial, at times a very hard and painful one. Anyone who denies this reality is being untruthful and harms the victim by minimizing or

[6]John Paul II, apostolic letter *Salvifici Doloris*, February 11, 1984, no. 23.

ignoring his wounds. But while we should try to alleviate suffering as much as possible, the challenging truth is that there is some suffering that we cannot entirely escape, such as the effects of our parents' divorce, or certain illnesses, or the death of a loved one. In these situations of suffering beyond our control, lasting in a certain sense our entire lives, it is all the more important to recognize and embrace the *other* side of the "boundary" experience of suffering.

Saint John Paul II says that alongside the painful "trial" in suffering there is also a "birth of power in weakness."[7] Saint Paul attests to this reality as well, saying, "I will all the more gladly boast of my weaknesses, that the power of Christ may rest upon me" (2 Cor 12:9). This power made perfect in the weakness of suffering is most properly termed *love*. In humanity's darkest hours or in the last moments of a person's life, we often find the most eloquent expressions of love. Think of the martyrs, saints, and courageous men and women who died for a noble cause. Their greatest examples and lessons were given in times of suffering and death.

Saint John Paul II goes on to say, "Suffering is present in the world in order to *unleash love* in the human person."[8] This powerful love *unleashed* from suffering is the *life-giving* part of life-giving wounds. Our wounds start off as life-draining, but *they do not have to stay that way*. They can become *life-giving*. God can transform evil—can transform our pain—into the greater goods of faith, hope, love, and joy. This is the heroic work of everyday people doing everyday miracles of believing, hoping, rejoicing, loving, and forgiving in the midst of pain and distress. This is life-changing interior work for our own good and

[7] Ibid.

[8] Ibid., no. 29 (emphasis added).

for the good of all those we will meet and touch in this world. We continually need to learn from, receive, and rely on Christ's grace and the power of the Holy Spirit to do this redemptive work of suffering. We want to be his instruments, but that must begin with our own healing received from Jesus.

The Paschal Mystery and the Eucharist

Suffering can unleash great love when we unite it to Christ's suffering. In a certain sense, all suffering is a question addressed to God regarding human dignity and the meaning of life, and therefore can be answered only by God's ultimate answer to suffering—Christ's Cross and Resurrection. This is a new, unheard-of form of compassion (a word derived from Latin meaning *suffering-with*), the redemptive compassion of Christ on the Cross.

Through the dynamism of the Cross, Christ *suffers-with* everyone and for everyone. He invites those who suffer to join with both his suffering and his love. We see this in his dialogue with the good thief who was being crucified next to him (Lk 23:43). Human suffering now becomes in Christ's suffering a suffering *in* God, *with* God, and *for* God. Christ on the Cross transformed human suffering from sheer pain and meaninglessness into his work of redemption, love, and Resurrection. As Saint John Paul II beautifully says, "To suffer means to become particularly susceptible, particularly open to the working of the salvific powers of God, offered to humanity in Christ's cross."[9] He continues: "It is suffering, more than anything else, which clears the way for the grace which transforms human souls."[10]

[9] Ibid., no. 23.
[10] Ibid., no. 27.

Christ's Paschal Mystery—his Passion, Death, Resurrection, and Ascension to the Father—transforms suffering forever. He took upon himself all the pain we could possibly experience. He was forgotten, falsely accused, rejected, humiliated, abandoned and alienated, cursed and mocked, beaten, and tortuously killed with his body nailed on the Cross. Some of our wounds may need continual healing, but now, when united to Christ's glorified but not extinguished wounds, they can also become a continual font of love and grace. Jesus' resurrected body still bore the marks of his crucifixion. In his Ascension, Jesus brought those marks of suffering and his entire humanity to the Father, whereby the Holy Spirit was poured forth upon those who believed in Jesus and was promised to all who have faith and are baptized.

Jesus did not come to remove all suffering from this earthly life, but rather to fill it with his presence by the power of his resurrected and glorified body and by the Holy Spirit. The presence of Christ, who suffers with us, is not just something from the past but is an ongoing reality, especially through the Eucharist. In the Eucharist, "the sacrifice Christ offered once for all on the cross remains ever present."[11] In the Eucharist, we are called each time we receive the Lord in his Body, Blood, Soul, and Divinity to unite our suffering to Christ's suffering, and Jesus in turn suffers with us and fills that suffering with his love.[12] It is in the Eucharist, by virtue of Jesus' life-giving wounds bleeding on the Cross and glorified in the Resurrection and Ascension, that he makes *our* wounds life-giving.

The Eucharist is the privileged place—the source and summit of our faith—whereby Jesus encounters us in our pain and transforms the suffering, sin, and evil in our lives

[11] *CCC*, no. 1364. See also ibid., no. 1366.

[12] Ibid., no. 1368.

into greater faith, hope, joy, and love. Thus, the Eucharist is God's ultimate answer to evil and at the core of redemptive suffering. If we desire deep healing, we need to be Eucharistic people who pray before the Eucharist, love the Eucharist, and are nourished and transformed by the Eucharist.

In high school, Dan was introduced in a profound way to Eucharistic adoration while on a retreat, and later at World Youth Day in Toronto. When he is asked by ACODs what difference the Eucharist concretely makes to healing, his short answer is *everything*.

During Eucharistic adoration, Dan takes his wounds before the Lord. He journals about them, reads Scripture, and just listens to what the Lord has to say. Many of those conversations with God have informed this book. Dan even coined a little acronym about the importance of those prayer times in adoration: LIFE is Living In Full Eucharist. He feels most alive and healed when living in full communion with God during those intentional prayer times at Eucharistic adoration, knowing he is seen, known, loved, and understood by God. Those moments of prayer deepen Dan's interior conversion, and as part of that ongoing conversion God purifies his thoughts and outlook on life. God gives him a supernatural outlook and answers to his most burning questions. He gives Dan interior freedom in response to the wounds, as well as love in a deeper way than he ever imagined. (And all this is true for Bethany as well!)

Life-Giving Wounds: Faith, Hope, Joy, and Love

At times we may be tempted to think that when God heals a wound, we will no longer struggle with that situation nor feel pain from it. There's a certain truth to this, as healing does mean that our painful experiences have less and less of a hold on our hearts and lives. But the deepest level of healing God desires for us is to *transform* our wounds so thoroughly that they become vibrant *resources* for love, even if the pain remains.

Together with Christ, we can respond to the pain we feel with *greater* life-giving faith, hope, joy, and love than we feel capable of. In this earthly life, healing does not necessarily mean "having no more wounds" or the absence of pain. Instead, healing has more to do with our attitude, thoughts, heart, and embodying the virtues in *response* to the wounds. Healing is a *way of life* with Christ in response to our pain that eventually becomes a part of our daily spiritual life. Father Jacques Philippe beautifully teaches that the essence of interior freedom (so essential for happiness and peace) is to embrace the freedom to believe, hope, and love in response to any past, current, or future wound.[13] Every layer of the wound can become a lesson for love.

We have reflected throughout this book on *how* we can respond to our wounds with greater faith, hope, joy, and love, and we will summarize in broad strokes here. We hope this will serve as a guide for thinking about how the often life-draining wounds caused by our parents' separation or divorce can be transformed and become *life-giving* for ourselves and others. The theological virtues of faith, hope, and love are particularly important here because they "adapt man's faculties for participation in the divine nature" and "dispose Christians to live in a relationship with the Holy Trinity."[14] Faith, hope, and love are "infused by God into the souls of the faithful to

[13] Father Jacques Philippe, *Interior Freedom*, trans. Helena Scott (New York: Scepter, 2002), 24–25.

[14] *CCC*, no. 1812.

make them *capable of acting as his children* and of meriting eternal life."[15] Think about that for a moment. To realize fully our identity as beloved children within God's family, we must live out the theological virtues. They are the key to embracing the new childhood, our relationship with God, and the life-giving joy God wants to give us to heal our wounds.

Life-Giving Faith

Our wounds can strengthen our relationship with God, Mary, and the saints, and sharpen our discernment of God's will for our lives. They can become avenues of greater closeness with our Lord, his Mother, and the saints—points of intimacy with God, who meets us and loves us there. He is "waiting in the wound" for us, as our ministry "anthem" says (see below). We know many ACODs who find an extra joy and richness in adoration (like Dan), in the Divine Mercy Chaplet, and other devotions where they bring their own hurting hearts to Christ's Sacred Heart, and feel a bond with our Lord who also knew grief and pain. We can see in the life of Mary and the witness of the saints examples of living redemptive suffering to the full. We can take courage in knowing that Mary and the saints faced deep trials (including saints who knew the pain of broken families) but learned the art of *suffering well*, uniting all of their pain with God. Truly a saint is one who knows how to suffer well.

God gives every person who suffers a particular mission from within the wounds. What is *yours*? Dan believes he received the call to the vocation of marriage and family through his experiences as an ACOD. His suffering made him desire to live the truth of marriage as proclaimed by the

[15] Ibid., no. 1813 (emphasis added).

Church, as he knew (from experiencing the opposite) the need for vibrant marriages in the world today. Dan's wounds also led him to want to strengthen the marriages of others, which guided his education at the John Paul II Institute and our shared volunteer work (at times) in marriage preparation and mentoring. Maybe the Lord is leading you to your vocation through your suffering? We have heard beautiful stories of adult children of divorce discovering a call to marriage, consecrated life, or the priesthood at least in part through their wounds.

> God gives every person who suffers a particular mission from within the wounds.

Healing from Dan's parents' divorce also helped us face in a holier way the other great suffering we have experienced in our lives, infertility. We knew the importance of grieving and did not rail against the fact that we were both sad a lot when in the worst throes of infertility. And through seeing the pain that broken marriages bring, we were given a deep sense of the importance of marriage and family, come what may with children. We knew we had a gift to offer the world in our marriage bond and loving home, regardless of whether children came or not. We have striven to make our home a place of hospitality, meals, advice, and prayer for priests, religious, family, and friends, including those from broken homes. For a time, we served as "honorary family" to an elderly widow who had no immediate family and became like a grandmother to us. Best of all, we received the call to adopt children, to share our loving home with two precious girls who needed one.

Before you go down the path of helping to heal others or some other bold undertaking for the Lord, your first "mission" is always to seek your own healing. At the same time, you should not wait until you are "perfectly" or "fully" healed because there will always be more healing work to be done this side of Heaven. Finding a mission in your wounds is a powerful way to embrace redemptive suffering and, in cooperation with grace, to allow the Lord to transform your pain into life-giving faith in God's plan to bring something good out of difficulties and crosses.

Life-Giving Hope

Our suffering can help us develop greater hope that things can change and will work out for the good of those who love God. Hope-filled people believe that "with God all things are possible" (Mt 19:26). They aren't weighed down by pessimism, cynicism, and discouragement. The hard-won *hope* that maintains trust in God's goodness and promises through difficulties and disappointment is different from a blithe presumption, born of things coming easily, that the "right" outcome will continue to happen. How beautiful it is to see genuine *hope* manifested by those who have not experienced all happy outcomes but nonetheless have triumphed over despair and cynicism.

We can become people of hope who go through life's suffering with great perseverance, which is a beautiful witness in the face of adversity. Commenting on Romans 5:3–5, a great passage on hope, Saint John Paul II says the following:

> Suffering, as it were, contains a special call to the virtue of perseverance in bearing whatever disturbs and causes harm. In doing this perseverance, the individual unleashes hope, which maintains in him the conviction that suffering will not get the better of him, that it will not deprive him of his dignity as a human being, a dignity linked to awareness of the meaning of life.[16]

[16]John Paul II, *Salvifici Doloris*, no. 23.

Simply persevering with the Lord through suffering produces hope in yourself and others around you. Why? Because the act of persevering will build your character, and it aids in healing because it refuses to give up easily. You might fall, like Christ did carrying the Cross up Calvary, but you can get up each day and persevere.

A beautiful example of perseverance are the spouses who struggle in their marriages but stick with their commitment, believing that their marriage is worth the sacrifice of difficult years and that shared suffering has made them better spouses and people. They find themselves happy on the other end, and their children are richly blessed by their perseverance as well. We saw this example in Bethany's parents, who worked through serious difficulties to stay together. Steady perseverance inspires hope in others and persevering through difficulties strengthens us and helps us understand how to suffer well.

Life-Giving Joy

Our wounds can lead to life-giving joy. Joy is not just an emotion reserved for optimists or a byproduct of a particular temperament but is meant to be part of the regular fabric of Christian life and discipleship for all of us, as a fruit of the Holy Spirit (Gal 5:22). The Lord promises his followers that "no one will take your joy from you" (Jn 16:22) and Saint Paul tells us to "rejoice in the Lord always" (Phil 4:4).

ACODs often anticipate future suffering, which steals the joy from otherwise joyful moments or makes bad moments worse. We can struggle with trusting that joy is *real.* And we can fail to delight in the joy that God has given us to help us through the suffering, or to find joy *in* the suffering itself. To live redemptive suffering well, then, we need to be intentional about trusting the joy and doubting the doubt. We can strive to live out joy by intentionally delighting in the good gifts of life, allowing ourselves to be delighted in by others, and proactively practicing gratitude. We may need a spiritual plan not just for when things go wrong, but also for when things go *right*. How will we trust, receive, and cultivate the joy of love and blessings in our lives, so as to keep that joyful momentum going for as long as possible?

We can be joyful when there is suffering in our lives because true joy is not contingent on circumstances. It can coexist right alongside grief; in fact, one of life's greatest joys is being comforted in sorrow. We have found much joy in sharing our struggles with other ACODs and couples who face this together. Joy can also be present in suffering because it means choosing to delight in God's presence and trusting in his love, no matter the circumstances. Pope Francis says that even though joy is not expressed the same way in all circumstances, "It always endures, even as a flicker of light born of our personal security that, when everything is said and done, we are infinitely loved."[17]

Life-Giving Love

Lastly, we can turn our pain into compassion and greater love for ourselves, our family, and the world. Pope Benedict XVI said that "the capacity for loving corresponds to the capacity of suffering and for suffering together."[18] Suffering can increase our capacity to love because an essential part of love is to sacrifice and suffer for and on behalf

[17] Pope Francis, apostolic exhortation *Evangelii Gaudium*, November 24, 2013, no. 6.

[18] Benedict XVI, Letter to the Faithful of the Diocese and City of Rome on Educating Young People, January 21, 2008.

of others. Suffering purifies our intentions to love others for their own sake and not for an advantage they give us. Suffering also purifies us of our weaknesses, limited vision, and sinful tendencies so we can focus on what's most important in life and love. No one wants to suffer, but when it comes it need not be something that destroys and divides, but it can powerfully build up love.

Our wounds can increase our compassion and lead to a greater solidarity with all those who are hurting, especially those who share a similar wound from their parents' divorce or separation. For us, wanting to help other ACODs was a key motivation behind founding Life-Giving Wounds as a peer-based ministry. We have seen again and again on our retreats the uniqueness of peer-to-peer compassion as very healing and restorative. It is beautiful to see kinship develop between "fellow sufferers" because it is a sign that they are already allowing their wounds to be turned into loving resources for others like them.

We can also allow the suffering caused by divorce to strengthen our approach to loving others and loving ourselves, for increasing trust, and for the courage to forgive. As we receive healing in these areas, we can share the path of healing we have learned with others. It's like an exam, where it is through the struggle of learning the material that we truly know the answers. The struggle of learning how to heal gives us a unique knowledge and insight into healing that we can share with others.

As you deepen your healing, you should ask yourself with whom can you journey on the path of healing. Do you have a mission to love by being a wounded healer? As Pope Benedict XVI says, "The Christian's program ... is 'a heart which sees.' This heart sees where love is needed and acts accordingly."[19] We believe that your wound, when

[19] Benedict XVI, encyclical letter *Deus Caritas Est*, December 25, 2005, no. 31.

healed (or in the process of being healed), enables you to see more clearly where love is needed in people's lives—especially fellow adult children of divorce. *Every layer of the wound is a lesson for love* that can be applied to other people's situations, as well as other sufferings, problems, and circumstances that arise in your life. This is the fruitfulness of the Holy Spirit working through suffering in the lives of those who believe in God.

The Resurrected Christ

With Jesus' help, we can respond to suffering with greater faith, hope, joy, and love. By doing so, our pain can be transformed into something life-giving and redemptive. This reality of life-giving wounds is poignantly expressed in the Gospel portrayal of the Resurrected Christ *with* his wounds (Jn 20:19–27). Jesus appeared in the midst of his fearful disciples and "showed them his hands and his side" (v. 20). The marks of his injuries became the catalyst of belief for Thomas: Jesus said to Thomas, " 'Put your finger here, and see my hands; and put out your hand, and place it in my side' . . . Thomas answered him, 'My Lord and my God!' " (vv. 27–28).

> With Jesus' help, our pain can be transformed into something life-giving and redemptive.

The Resurrected Jesus shows us that wounds no longer *only* signify sin, evil, and suffering. If this were the case, then it would make no sense that the Resurrected Christ would still have his wounds since he triumphed over these realities. But Christ does not get rid of his signs of suffering because they too have now become part of His glory as God. They have been transformed, through the Resurrection and Ascension, into life-giving wounds par excellence that radiate God's love to the world by the Holy Spirit, the Spirit of Love.

When freely accepted, united with the Lord Jesus, and transformed by him into faith, hope, joy, and love for ourselves and others, our wounds lead to a surplus of love that cannot be outdone and far exceeds the original hurt inflicted, even if pain remains this side of Heaven. "Where sin increased, grace abounded all the more" (Rom 5:20). *Your* wounds can become life-giving like the Resurrected Christ's life-giving wounds. So *don't waste your pain.* Unite it to Jesus and pray to see the ways your suffering can be life-giving for yourself and others. You have already started to do this by reading to this point in this book, so keep going! Your wounds can become a grace-filled mission for love.

Waiting in the Wounds

We have an "anthem" for Life-Giving Wounds that we think expresses beautifully the deep truths of redemptive suffering and our Lord Jesus Christ's care for hurting hearts. It's a song called "Waiting in the Wound" by musician, artist, and retreat leader Michael Corsini.[20] This song is sung on all Life-Giving Wounds retreats and speaks deeply to many hearts:

> You are, the grain of wheat the falls on my awaiting land
> You are, the precious coin that I let slip from my hand
> You are, the pearl of greatest price on my ocean floor
> You are, mercy waiting just behind my door

[20] For more background on this song, and to watch a music video for it, see Daniel Meola, "Waiting in the Wound Song—Michael Corsini," *Life-Giving Wounds* (blog), July 21, 2019, https://www.lifegivingwounds.org/blog/waiting-in-the-wound-song-part-i.

And I love you for waiting
I love you for waiting

You are waiting in the wound
That I hide from you
You call me, to find you

You were there when I was weak
You were there when I sought light
And you were there when I brought fire in the garden

You were there when I lost hope
You were there when I took life
And you were there between the falling and the rising

The wait is over, the wait is over now.

A Non-ACOD Spouse's Perspective: Redemptive Suffering, Together

BETHANY: Every marriage faces its times of pain and suffering, whether one or both spouses come from a background of family brokenness or not. So, the beautiful truth of redemptive suffering's power is something precious for every couple. For us, having the mindset that the sufferings we would face within our marriage would not be simply meaningless or negative has helped sharpen our awareness of what the Lord is calling us to from *within* the difficulties.

Within the difficulty of navigating Dan's split family, the Lord calls us to greater charity, forgiveness, and commitment to our own marriage; within the difficulty of infertility, the Lord calls us to deeper fruitfulness and trust in his plan; within the difficulty of marital dryness or "distance," he calls us to a purified understanding of our marriage as a vocation, meant not solely for our own satisfaction but for the good of our children and others. Finding a meaning and purpose for all the big and small difficulties in our married life has been truly life-giving. Suffering doesn't become "easy" or effortless, but it becomes easier to bear and even, paradoxically, joyful. Looking back, we can see more clearly how the Lord has used the sufferings in our marriage to help us advance into greater faith, hope, joy, and love—a process of growth that will be ongoing our whole lives!

CONCLUSION

Beyond the Wounds

In this book, we have talked in depth about the wounds experienced by men and women whose parents have divorced or separated. We have named these various hurts and examined them in the light of faith, so that with Christ's help we can heal from them. We have had this in-depth discussion also in order to invite divorced or separated parents, the loved ones of ACODs, and Christian leaders to understand more fully what adult children of divorce experience.

We hope this book is a strong response to those in society who promote divorce and easy-to-dissolve marriage as a pillar of modern happiness, at times willfully or ignorantly denying that divorce harms children or that it has anything beyond a temporary effect on them. As we have endeavored to show, the wounds divorce causes for children run deep and are lifelong. Re-wounding occurs at various points in our lives because of the ongoing reality of our parents' separation. We have talked about the importance of grieving our hurts and acknowledging how they may affect our faith, identity, relationships, emotional life and pursuit of virtue, our approach to forgiveness, and our ongoing relationships within our family.

At the same time, we have tried to stress that *healing is real and possible in God's time.* We are always more than our wounds; they do not define us. As we progress in our healing and draw greater love and virtue out of our painful experiences, we go *beyond* the wounds, transforming them from life-draining to *life-giving*.

It is God's divine love that primarily defines us, not our parents' divorce or separation. Our fundamental identity is as children of God, not as children of divorce. While we may not know the particulars of our future, we do have a great future ahead of us, even if suffering remains. We come from God's love and are ordered toward a future of love with God. His love willed us into existence, sustains us through trials, and carries us forward to a glorious future. While we may struggle with our earthly families, we are going to the Father's house where there are many rooms (Jn 14:2). We are children of a perfect and everlasting marriage, Christ's union with the Church (Eph 5:21–33). By dwelling in *this* marriage and home, we learn to accept that we are beloved and capable of great love. Jesus calls each of us to a *renewed* childhood: "Unless you turn and become like children, you will never enter the kingdom of heaven" (Mt 18:3).

> Our fundamental identity is as children of God, not as children of divorce.

We believe we can bring about a great cultural rebirth of faith, hope, love, and joy in our society *through* the healing of adult children of divorce or separation, in part because of what we ACODs now see more clearly *on account of our wounds*. As our wounds heal, they give us grace-filled missions. So, we do our healing work not just for ourselves, but because our being healed will bless our friends, families, and society.

For our ACOD readers, as you go forth from reading this book, we offer three last pieces of advice. First, discouragement is never from the Lord. If you have setbacks, healing takes longer than you expect, or a negative voice says, "you can't do this," know that these are deceptions. God is a god of encouragement and praise, and the Holy Spirit is your Counselor (Jn 16:7–8), so seek out and listen attentively to his voice of truth and love. Remember the victories that you have had and will accomplish, to encourage you in your healing.

Second, trust in God's slow and steady work. The deeper the suffering, the longer the journey of healing. Parental divorce or separation causes deep pain, hitting you at the core of your existence and identity, so the journey to heal may be long indeed or longer than anticipated. And that is okay. Sometimes healing goes one issue and one step at a time, whereas at other times the Lord allows you to make a giant leap forward. But even if it is slow, and even if there is more work to be done, the Lord is always at work in you, and your healing is real.

Third, you cannot heal by your own strength alone. You must keep relying on Christ and his Cross *and* turn to the people he sends your way to help you heal and grow through their love and mentorship. We hope you can find your Simons, and perhaps also be a Simon to someone else.

With the Lord, let us dare to dream of a great future of joy, and trust that he will continue to give us the means needed to heal and thrive.

"By his wounds you have been healed" (1 Pet 2:24). With the Lord, let us dare to dream of a great future of joy, and trust that he will continue to give us the means needed to heal and thrive. As an expression of our reliance on the Lord's strength, we have composed an original prayer for healing as part of our Life-Giving Wounds ministry that sums up all of the key lessons of this book and keeps us centered on the most important things. The prayer begins with a profession of faith, then a promise to the Lord, and finally a request for God's intercession for our healing. It is intentionally Trinitarian because God as a Trinity is a God of Love.[1]

We conclude our book with this prayer and hope that it leads to greater healing in your life. We will continue to pray it for everyone who is an adult child of divorce or separation. We began this book discussing the "wound of silence," so let us end it with another type of silence: a silence that is joyful and tranquil, the holy silence of contemplating our Lord's love.

[1] These prayer cards can be found and purchased on our website, *lifegivingwounds.org*.

PRAYER FOR THOSE FROM A BROKEN HOME

O Eternal Father, You created me in your image and likeness and you long to hold me always in your loving embrace. Your love has sustained me in my trials and struggles.

Each day, I will live as a beloved child of God, confident in your divine mercy. I will place in you all my trust and hope, for you lift my gaze from shame, fear, and the pain of division to your unparalleled love for me on the Cross.

By the power of Christ's great wounds, heal the wounds left in my life by the tragedy of my parents' separation or divorce, or family brokenness. Help me love, despite the pain. Help me forgive, no matter how deep the hurt. Help me to have peace and virtue when old and new wounds arise. Remain with me, Holy Spirit, so that I may be a wellspring of healing for others.

In Jesus' Name, Amen.

APPENDIX I

Resources for Ongoing Healing and Joining the Mission of Life-Giving Wounds

Adult Children of Divorce or Separation

For the adult children of divorce who have read this book and are asking themselves, *Now what?*, we invite you to join us in the Life-Giving Wounds ministry and community. Our passion is giving voice to the pain of adult children of divorce or separation and helping them find deep spiritual healing in Christ. This book is one way of living out our mission, but we offer much more. Consider this a personal invitation to join us! We and our team of volunteer leaders would be honored to walk with you as you journey toward greater healing, joy, and peace.

Life-Giving Wounds ministry offers:

- *Retreats*: in-person weekend retreats run in partnership with a Life-Giving Wounds local chapter, and nationally available online seven-week retreats
- *Support groups*: locally run in person by a Life-Giving Wounds local chapter, and nationally available online support groups
- *Online resources*: a blog featuring over one hundred articles by ACODs and experts about all aspects of the ACOD experience and healing; unique sacred art and

poetry; and a continually updated research page and resource list for ACODs (books, articles, podcasts, videos, art, music, and more)

- *Online community and mentorship*: a private, exclusive, moderated online forum for ACODs
- *Additional Products*: items available for purchase to help aid your healing journey such as a companion workbook to go with this book, prayer cards, art, Rosary booklets, et cetera.

More information can be found on our website (*lifegiving wounds.org*). We are continually developing new and enhanced materials, so we encourage you to sign up for our newsletter to receive the latest information (*lifegiving wounds.org/newsletter*). And please join us on social media as well (Facebook: *@lifegivingwounds*, Instagram: *@lifegiving .wounds*, YouTube: *@LifeGivingWounds*).

Catholic Leaders

For leaders who have read this book and are interested in partnering with Life-Giving Wounds to grow local support for the adult children of divorce you serve, please get in touch via email at *dan@lifegivingwounds.org* or *bethany@lifegivingwounds.org*. We offer help establishing new Life-Giving Wounds local chapters, which includes assistance with running a "launch" retreat, finding and training local leaders to carry Life-Giving Wounds programs, and providing a speakers bureau of trained LGW leaders available for talks and presentations to various audiences (young adults, priests and leaders, parish missions, et cetera).

Everyone

If this book has inspired you and sparked a desire to bring God's healing to adult children of divorce, please consider donating to Life-Giving Wounds. As an independent, registered 501(c)3 nonprofit organization, we rely on the generosity of our donors to carry out our ministry and grow it sustainably. Help make a difference in healing people from broken families. All major, monthly, or annual donors are invited to a special LGW Insiders group, which receives behind-the-scenes updates about the ministry and other unique perks. Tax-deductible donations can be made by check or online payment, and all information is found on our website (*lifegivingwounds .org/give*). Thank you!

If this book has been helpful to you and you would like it to reach other people, please consider taking a few minutes to leave a review with Ignatius Press, on Amazon, or elsewhere. Reviews help to make the book more visible on Amazon and other distributors' websites, which helps us reach more people. If you have any feedback on how we can improve this book, especially for future editions, please send suggestions to *info@lifegivingwounds.org*.

Finally, *if you would like to stay in touch with us* and hear about the latest news and developments about Life-Giving Wounds, as we mentioned above, please sign up for our e-newsletter (*lifegivingwounds.org/newsletter*).

APPENDIX II

Resources for Mental Health, Suicide Prevention, Addiction, and Abuse

This appendix is not exhaustive. It is also not an endorsement by Life-Giving Wounds or Ignatius Press of any organization listed here, or of any therapist, counselor, person, or service affiliated with the listed organizations. This is meant to be a reference guide for any readers seeking expertise, specific guidance, and professional help in these areas.

Mental Health Crises and Suicide Prevention

If you are having or have had thoughts of harming yourself or others, or feel like you are experiencing a mental health emergency or a mental health crisis, please do any or all of the following:

1. Call 911 or go to the nearest emergency room
2. Reach the Crisis Text Hotline by texting HOME to 741-741
3. Reach the National Suicide Prevention Lifeline by calling or texting 988
4. Chat with crisis centers around the U.S.: Lifeline Crisis Chat, 988lifeline.org/chat
5. For Catholic counseling, visit the Upper Room Crisis Hotline: catholichotline.org

General Mental Health Resources

Catholic Counseling Resources

- National Catholic therapist databases: Catholic Therapists.com, Catholic Psychotherapy Association (*cpa.ce21.com/directory*), and WellCatholic (*wellcatholic.com*)
- Souls and Hearts Ministry (*soulsandhearts.com*): also offering a podcast, *Interior Integration*, and a free course, "A Catholic's Guide to Choosing a Therapist"
- Catholic Counselors (*catholiccounselors.com*): offers virtual and in-person counseling services
- Made in His Image (*madeinhisimage.org*): for women who struggle with eating disorders, depression, self-harm, and physical or sexual abuse
- CatholicPysch Institute (*catholicpsych.com*): offers a unique mentorship program and digital resources, including the podcast *Being Human*
- Local Catholic Charities: diocesan or archdiocesan counseling services, which may have special funds to help subsidize your therapy or counseling

Websites and Books

- Mental Health First Aid USA (*mentalhealthfirstaid.org*): a secular website with a comprehensive list of national resources related to the most common mental disorders
- The Alpha and Omega Clinic's blog (*aoclinic.org/category/blog/*)
- John Cihak and Aaron Kheriarty, *The Catholic Guide to Depression: How the Saints, the Sacraments, and Psychiatry Can Help You Break Its Grip and Find Happiness Again* (Manchester, N.H.: Sophia Press, 2012)

- Chris Alar, *After Suicide: There's Hope for Them and You* (Stockbridge, Mass.: Marian Press, 2019)

Screening Tools

The following online screening tools from Mental Health America can be good indicators of whether you are experiencing symptoms of a mental health condition, and whether seeing a counselor could be helpful. They do not, however, give a professional diagnosis of mental health conditions.

- Screening for anxiety (*screening.mhanational.org/screening-tools/anxiety/*)
- Screening for depression (*screening.mhanational.org/screening-tools/depression*)
- Screening for other conditions (*screening.mhanational.org/screening-tools/*)

Addiction Resources

Catholic Resources and Addiction Recovery Programs

- Catholic in Recovery (*catholicinrecovery.com*): an integrated Catholic approach to overcoming addictions
- The Calix Society (*calixsociety.org*): an association of recovering Catholic alcoholics and their families and friends

Twelve-Step Addiction Recovery Programs

- Alcoholics Anonymous (*aa.org*)
- Overeaters Anonymous (*oa.org*)
- Narcotics Anonymous (*na.org*)
- Sexaholics Anonymous (*sa.org*)

Groups for Families and Friends of Someone Struggling with Addiction

- Al-Anon (*al-anon.org*)
- Co-Dependents Anonymous (*coda.org*)
- Hope's Garden (*hopesgarden.com*): Catholic group for women impacted by a husband's use of pornography, sex addiction, or other betrayal trauma
- Reconnected (*catholiccounselors.com/services/reconnected*): Catholic group therapy program for people who feel betrayed because of their spouses' porn usage
- Navigate Betrayal (*navigatebetrayal.com*): Catholic group for women

Programs for Pornography Addiction

- Integrity Restored (*integrityrestored.com*)
- Reclaim Sexual Health (*reclaimsexualhealth.com*)
- Covenant Eyes (*covenanteyes.com*)
- Angelic Warfare Confraternity (*angelicwarfareconfraternity.org*)
- Magdala Ministries (*magdalaministries.org*): specifically for women
- Fortify (*joinfortify.com*): secular, with specifically Catholic support groups available.
- Fight Club Catholic (*fightclubcatholic.com*)

Websites and Books

- Fight the New Drug (*fightthenewdrug.org*): a grassroots, youth-oriented, nonreligious nonprofit dedicated to raising awareness about the harmful effects of pornography
- Scott Weeman, *The Twelve Steps and the Sacraments: A Catholic Journey through Recovery* (Notre Dame, Ind.: Ave Maria Press, 2017)

- Matt Fradd, *The Porn Myth* (San Francisco: Ignatius Press, 2017)
- USCCB's *For Your Marriage* (*foryourmarriage.org/help-for-men-and-women-struggling-with-pornography-use-or-addiction*)

Screening Tools

- Partnership to End Addiction (*drugfree.org*): to help you determine if you or someone you know might have a drug use problem
- Alcohol Screening (*alcoholscreening.org*): to help you determine if you or someone you know might have an alcohol use problem

Domestic Abuse Resources

Below are resources to report abuse and help survivors psychologically and spiritually heal. In the case of an emergency or an active situation, call 911 or go to your local police department and ask to speak with someone who specializes in domestic abuse.

Abuse Hotlines and National Groups

- National Domestic Violence Hotline: 1-800-799-SAFE (7233)
- National Domestic Violence Text Hotline: Text START to 88-788
- National Domestic Violence Website (*thehotline.org*): including recommendations for creating safety plans for leaving an abusive situation
- Partnership against Domestic Violence (*padv.org*): also including recommendations for creating safety plans for leaving an abusive situation

- Childhelp USA, National Child Abuse Hotline and Website: 1-800-422-4453 and *childhelp.org*
- National Resource Center on Domestic Violence (*nrcdv.org*)

Catholic Resources for Domestic Violence

- Grief to Grace (*grieftograce.org*)
- Made in His Image (*madeinhisimage.org*)
- Catholics for Family Peace

Websites and Books

- USCCB's "When I Call For Help" pastoral statement (*usccb.org/topics/marriage-and-family-life-ministries/when-i-call-help-pastoral-response-domestic-violence*)
- USCCB's *For Your Marriage* (*foryourmarriage.org/domestic-violence*)
- Pax in Familia (*paxinfamilia.org*)

Sexual Abuse Resources

Below are resources to report abuse and help survivors psychologically and spiritually heal. In the case of an emergency or an active situation, call 911 or go to your local police department or child protective services department to report the abuse and ask to speak with someone who specializes in sexual assault.

Sexual Abuse Hotlines and National Groups

- National Sexual Assault Hotline: 1-800-656-HOPE (4673)
- National Child Abuse Hotline: 1-800-422-4453
- Rape, Abuse, and Incest National Network (*rainn.org*)

- Darkness to Light: for help preventing or recovering from child sex abuse, text LIGHT to 741-741

For Survivors of Clerical Abuse

- The USCCB's "Victim Assistance" page (*usccb.org/issues-and-action/child-and-youth-protection/victim-assistance.cfm*): contains a thorough list of diocesan victim assistance coordinators, as well as other helpful resources
- Pope Francis, Letter to the People of God, August 20, 2018

Reporting Child Abuse and Neglect

- Child Welfare Information Gateway (*childwelfare.gov/reporting*)
- USCCB Child and Youth Protection Victim Assistance (*usccb.org/issues-and-action/child-and-youth-protection/victim-assistance.cfm*)

Websites and Books

- National Federation for Catholic Youth Ministry (*nfcym.org/youthprotection*)
- Made in His Image (*madeinhisimage.org*)
- Diane Langberg, *On the Threshold of Hope: Opening the Door to Healing for Survivors of Sexual Abuse* (Carol Stream, Ill.: Tyndale House Publishers, Inc., 1999)

Healing after an Abortion

- Project Rachel (*hopeafterabortion.com*)
- Entering Canaan Ministry (*enteringcanaan.com*)
- Rachel's Vineyard (*rachelsvineyard.org*)

APPENDIX III

The Wedding Feast at Cana
Scriptural Meditation

We use the following meditation on Life-Giving Wounds retreats for the healing of our approach to dating relationships or marriage that may be affected by the wounds of parental divorce or separation.

Scripture: John 2:1–11

> On the third day there was a marriage at Cana in Galilee, and the mother of Jesus was there; Jesus also was invited to the marriage, with his disciples. When the wine failed, the mother of Jesus said to him, "They have no wine." And Jesus said to her, "O woman, what have you to do with me? My hour has not yet come." His mother said to the servants, "Do whatever he tells you." Now six stone jars were standing there, for the Jewish rites of purification, each holding twenty or thirty gallons. Jesus said to them, "Fill the jars with water." And they filled them up to the brim. He said to them, "Now draw some out, and take it to the steward of the feast." So they took it. When the steward of the feast tasted the water now become wine, and did not know where it came from (though the servants who had drawn the water knew), the steward of the feast called the bridegroom and said to him, "Every man serves the good wine first; and when men

have drunk freely, then the poor wine; but you have kept the good wine until now." This, the first of his signs, Jesus did at Cana in Galilee, and manifested his glory; and his disciples believed in him.

Meditation

Close your eyes and visualize the scene. Pause, breathe in, breathe out, and then open your eyes once you have had a chance to visualize the scene.

What are you seeing as you take the place of the bridegroom, or the bride who is by his side? What are your surroundings? Do you hear laughter and sounds of joy all around you at the feast? Is there music? Are you excited about having entered into holy marriage? What smells are in the air? Do you taste the food or sip the wine that is in front of you? Do you see your beautiful spouse? What is your beloved wearing? *Pause.*

Like the bridegroom, you are anxious about the wine running out. Wine represents the joy of life, the joy of love. Perhaps your "wine" too has run out, because of your parents' divorce or separation. Do you feel dry and empty like the wineskin that held the wine? *Pause.*

Recall now a negative experience related to relationships, one that you feel is somehow connected to your parents' divorce or separation. Perhaps you were afraid of becoming too close to someone. Perhaps you were making the same mistake your parents made. Perhaps, as a result, you now think that love does not last forever. Perhaps it is a deep loneliness. Whatever it is, recall it now. *Pause.*

Are you alone or with someone? If with someone, then what would you say? *Pause.*

Our Mother Mary now comes to your assistance, as she did at the Wedding Feast of Cana. She is moved by your sorrow. She turns to Christ, who is there with her, visibly moved with agony. She asks Christ for a new wine, a new joy for your life. Do you see them with you, gazing lovingly at you, and speaking about a wine for you? *Pause.*

At first, Christ's response seems jarring: "Woman, what have you to do with me? My hour has not yet come." Does Christ not care about you? Does he not care about us? Perhaps there is no new wine for your life. Yet then you hear Mary's last words recorded in Scripture: "Do whatever he tells you." She understands the true meaning of Christ's words. She knows that the question of Christ—"What have you to do with me?"—is not a lack of sympathy but an invitation to faith. Mary responds with a perfect act of faith: "Do whatever he tells you." Can we hear these same words spoken by Mary to us? "Do whatever he tells you." What is your response? Will you believe in Christ's power to act in your life? *Pause.*

At this moment, Christ takes water used for Jewish purification rites for marriage, and he turns it into wine. By this surprising act, Christ indicates that he is bringing a new joy to our life by transforming marriage into something unfathomably beautiful and holy. He is making it *new* (a new "wine"). Married love now carries his presence; because of his presence, that love is capable of enduring. Of course, many marriages still end in divorce due to human sin, but when a couple's love is caught up within divine love—in a sacrament—it can never be broken at the deepest level. It is this wine of Christ's love—ultimately poured out for the Church on the Cross and made sacramentally present in the Eucharist—that he offers to safeguard and to strengthen our human love in the face of the sin and brokenness of humanity. Taste this wine that the headwaiter brings to you on behalf of Christ. What does it taste like? Is it sweet or semi-sweet, or dry? Is it cool or warm? Does it smell flowery? Earthy? Fruity? *Pause.*

You are astonished at the quality of this wine. It is unlike anything you have ever tasted before. You look at your spouse with a smile. There is something new here now. The headwaiter says to you, "Every man serves the good wine first; and when men have drunk freely, then the poor wine; but you have kept the good wine until now." Now with a smile, together you and your spouse drink some more. It is so good, so *pure*. It refreshes your lips and mouth, parched dry from the joylessness that resulted from your parents' divorce or separation. As you take another sip of wine, feel this new indissoluble love of Christ entering into every limb within your body—your veins, your hands, your head, and your heart. *Pause.*

Then, with your spouse beside you, you hold the chalice of this new wine together. You do not need to ask the headwaiter where it came from. You both know. You look to Christ and he looks at you. He raises his hands, lays them upon you, and blesses you. Love now lasts forever not because it has been freed from all mistakes or weaknesses, but because your love is in his hands. You begin to believe in this new love, like the disciples at Cana began to believe in Christ. Christ embraces you. You can hear his heartbeat. With every beat it says, "I love you." "I love you." "I love you." Stay there as long as you want and know that you are God's beloved. *Pause.*

INDEX